Ilya Gerber
DIARY FROM THE KOVNO GHETTO
August 1942–January 1943

This book was published under the auspices of
**The Moshe Mirilashvili Center for Research
on the Holocaust in the Soviet Union,**
generously supported by Michael and Laura Mirilashvili
and the Euro-Asian Jewish Congress

Ilya Gerber

DIARY FROM THE KOVNO GHETTO

August 1942–January 1943

Translated from the Yiddish by Rebecca Wolpe

Edited by Lea Prais

 | THE INTERNATIONAL INSTITUTE
FOR HOLOCAUST RESEARCH

The Moshe Mirilashvili Center for Research on the Holocaust
in the Soviet Union

Ilya Gerber
Diary from the Kovno Ghetto
August 1942–January 1943

*Managing Edito*r: Yasmine Garval
Language and Production Editor: Ita Shapiro Haber

© 2021 All rights reserved to Yad Vashem
P.O.B. 3477, Jerusalem 9103401, Israel
publications.marketing@yadvashem.org.il

The publisher has made every effort to trace the copyright holders and to obtain permission to reproduce copyrighted material included in this book. Any inadvertent errors or omissions will be rectified at the earliest opportunity.

This book may not be reproduced, in whole or in part, in any form, without written permission from the publisher.

Responsibility for the opinions expressed in this publication is solely that of the author.

ISBN 978-965-308-639-5

Typesetting: 2W design
Printed in Israel by Offset Natan Shlomo Press, Jerusalem

CONTENTS

INTRODUCTION 7
By Lea Prais

THE DIARY 47

August 1942 49
September 1942 69
October 1942 133
November 1942 193
December 1942 219
January 1943 239

INDEX 273

Introduction

On April 28, 1945, during a march from the Dachau concentration camp to Wolfsratshausen in Germany, Ilya Gerber was shot and killed.¹ He was not yet twenty-one years old. Gerber's brother-in-law, Shlomo (Shleyme) Kalner,² was apparently with him. Kalner noted on the Page of Testimony that he submitted in memory of his brother-in-law that Ilya was shot in the face.³ While they were incarcerated in the Kovno (Kaunas) Ghetto, Kalner lived with the Gerber family; he was the only family member to survive the Holocaust. He immigrated to Israel in 1948, but never recorded his own testimony. Thus, sadly, further details about Ilya Gerber's life—until his final days in Dachau—remain shrouded in darkness.⁴ This includes the

---

1 On April 26, 1945, a group of 6,887 prisoners, among them 1,524 Jews, were sent from Dachau on a march southward. On the morning of April 28, after marching overnight, the prisoners were brought to a forest not far from Wolfsratshausen, where they set up camp. As a result of the extended break, fighting broke out between groups of prisoners. This was in addition to conflicts between the SS men and soldiers from the Wehrmacht and Air Force, and between the guards and prisoners. During the ensuing struggle, many prisoners were injured by the guards' shots. See Eliezer Shvartz, *Beminharot Ashmedai* (Hebrew) (Jerusalem: Yad Vashem, 2015), p. 281. I would like to thank Prof. Sarah Bender for bringing this information to my attention.

2 On Shlomo (Shleyme) Kalner see the diary entry from August 31, 1942.

3 Bert Hoppe and Hildrun Glass, eds., *Die Verfolgung und Ermordung der europäischen Juden durch das nationalsozialistische Deutschland 1933–1945*, vol. 7, (Munich: Oldenburg Verlag, 2011), p. 643; for sections from Ilya Gerber's diary, see pp. 642–652. The editors noted that Gerber was released from Dachau, and indeed, according to lists preserved in the ITS (International Tracing Service) database, Gerber was released from the camp. The Page of Testimony that Shlomo Kalner submitted to Yad Vashem in his memory in 1956, reveals the date and circumstances of Ilya Gerber's murder. See Ilya Gerber, Page of Testimony, Yad Vashem, The Central Database for Shoah Victims' Names, Hall of Names, Item no. 8692962.

4 Alexandra Zapruder, the first to publish extracts from Ilya Gerber's diary, also emphasized the meager information available about him. She added that, according to Gerber's classmate, Dov Levin, "He was tall, and physically attractive, athletic, and aggressive in team sports. He also remembered that Ilya was not a particularly strong student and that his primary interests were music, drawing, and girls." See Alexandra Zapruder, ed., *Salvaged Pages: Young Writers' Diaries of the Holocaust* (New Haven and London: Yale University Press), p. 465.

absence of more information about his personality, what he wrote, drew, illustrated, and collected, and information about his fate after he finished writing the third notebook of his diary. Yet, between the lines of his diary and the notebook of songs that he collected from the ghetto we discern a portrayal of an intelligent and sensitive young man, with an appetite for life, a passion for reading, and a promising talent for both writing and illustration.

The Uniqueness of Gerber's Diary

Gerber's diary expresses a different voice from that of his contemporaries. It is the voice of a critical thinker who is both deeply immersed in ghetto life and aware of the murderous reality engulfing all, while still clinging fiercely to life.

Gerber was able to describe sincerely, and in minute detail, the atmosphere within the ghetto. This includes the various factors that controlled the lives of the ghetto's inhabitants, the sense of transience and anxiety—but also the tendency toward escapism and denial of the impending catastrophe within their midst. His writing challenges that of the ghetto's official establishment, expressed in then-contemporary diaries and records as well as in early memoirs. These materials are what shaped, in time, the story of the Kovno Ghetto. His portrayals of daily ghetto life illuminate previously unknown facets of Jewish society and how it contended with a reality of extreme oppression and persecution.

Ilya Gerber kept an illustrated diary. We do not know when he started keeping his diary, as, sadly, the only remaining notebook is the third one, brought to readers here for the first time. Nevertheless, it is evident that he wrote in it consistently, and it was an important part of his life. His friends, as the diary reveals, were aware of his love of writing. They described him as a quiet person, who did not talk much but observed and wrote a great deal.[5] He began writing in the notebook that has been found (the third one,

---

5 As depicted, for instance, in one of the verses in the poem by Gerber's friend Bebke appearing in the diary entry from January 14, 1943.
   "One of us is quiet and still
   An onlooker in the set
   People say writing is his skill
   He writes books like Hamlet."

Introduction

according to Gerber), on August 26, 1942, and wrote his final entry in that notebook on January 23, 1943. At times he referred to matters that he had written about earlier, even noting the relevant page number in the original notebooks. For purposes of authenticity, these references have been left in the diary as they appear in the original Yiddish text.

About the Author

Ilya (Lyusik or Lyuske) Gerber was born on July 23, 1924, in Kovno, Lithuania, to an enlightened, Zionist family. He frequently mentions his closest family members in his diary: His mother, Rachel (née Feller); his older sister, Chaya (1921–1945); his brother-in-law, Shlomo (Chaya's husband); and primarily, his father, Boris Gerber (1896–1944). Gerber the father was a singing teacher at the Schwabe Hebrew Gymnasium in Kovno, where his son also studied. Ilya's father, who was disabled in one hand, was a well-known personality in Jewish Kovno. In a description of his school days, the historian Dov Levin, who was born in Kovno and also studied at the Gymnasium, recalled, among other things, the following:

> And now [about] the singing lessons with Mr. Gerber the amputee, whose single hand was very good at striking those who disturbed the lesson (including his son Ilya, who sat with us on the bench). Most of the lessons were devoted to Jewish holidays and national events, but the best part—from all of them arose the fresh fragrance of *Eretz Israel* [Land of Israel]. Those were the days of *Homa U'Migdal* [Stockage and Watchtower] in *Eretz Israel*, and Mr. Gerber already taught us *Shir Ha'Emek* [The Song of the Valley] that had only recently arrived.[6]

Later, evidently, life in the ghetto affected the joy his father found in music and creativity. Ilya wrote in his diary that, although his father was a gifted musician and, in the past, had written many melodies,[7] "Now,

---

6 Dov Levin, "Dyukana Shel Kita," in Israel Yablokovski, ed., *Heihal Sheshaka...: Hahinuh Ha'ivri BeKovna—Mosdot Ve'ishim* (Hebrew) (Tel Aviv: Irgun Bogrei Hagymnasion Ha'ivri BeKovna, 1962), p. 183.

7 The National Library of Israel is in possession of one melody composed by Boris Gerber, adapted for a cantor and choir, *Uvenuhu Yomar*. See the National Library of Israel, JMA, 01094.

in the ghetto, he has not composed any melodies."[8] Yet, for Ilya himself, singing songs, music, and dancing were an essential part of daily life in the ghetto, probably inspired by his father, and they feature extensively in his writings, as recorded below.

Gerber wrote his diary in Yiddish, but it is clear from his writings that he could read Hebrew, Lithuanian, and also German. The Yiddish is written using Soviet orthography.[9] Indeed, following the Soviet occupation of Lithuania in the summer of 1940, the use of Hebrew in educational institutions was outlawed. In its place, Yiddish, based on the Soviet format and orthography, was employed. Gerber, who was sixteen years old when the Soviets occupied Lithuania, a student at the Schwabe Hebrew Gymnasium, went from studying in Hebrew to learning in Yiddish and adopted this orthography. It is also possible that the communist idea—with the new Yiddish orthography one of its manifestations—captured his heart. Evidence of this can be found in the colorful illustrations that he included in his diary, usually as the opening illustration for a day's entry—in addition to sketching maps and decorative elements at the end of entries. On November 7, 1942, on the anniversary of the Bolshevik Revolution, he added a celebratory illustration to mark the event. And, on January 1, 1943, to mark the civil New Year, he drew portraits of Stalin, Lenin, and others. However, apart from expressing his enthusiasm about a book by Nikolai Ognev, *Dnevnik Kosti Riabtseva* (The Diary of Kostya Riabtsev),[10] describing the world of young people in the new Soviet state, he does not reveal in the diary anything about his political inclinations.

The Kovno Ghetto—Sources, a Brief History, and its Image

The Sources
Historians have studied the Kovno Ghetto and described it in detail, using sources written during the ghetto period, the extensive memoir

---

8 See the diary entry from December 4, 1942.
9 The Soviet Yiddish orthography emphasizes phonetics rather than the traditional spelling. Thus, for example, the Soviet system abandoned final letters and wrote Hebrew words, which, according to the rules of Yiddish spelling, are written in the same way as they are in Hebrew spelling—phonetically.
10 For more information about the book see the diary entry from October 14, 1942.

literature, and documents from Lithuanian archives. The primary and most significant Jewish sources written during the ghetto period, which were later published, were composed by people connected to the establishment that managed the ghetto. One example is the diary of Avraham Tory (Golub), the secretary of the Ältestenrat (Council of Elders or Judenrat), who succeeded in taking many documents with him when he fled the ghetto in 1944.[11] An additional document of central importance is the text written by members of the Jewish order police in the Kovno Ghetto, which the ghetto policemen buried deep in the ground together with the archive of the Jewish police. It was discovered in the 1960s and has been published in English and Hebrew editions.[12] In the document, the writers—from the perspective of the police—survey the history of the organization between 1941 and 1943, on the backdrop of life in the ghetto. Additionally, an almanac including Hebrew literary and other texts was also published in recent years.[13] These texts were composed by young men and women, members of the Hama'apilim brigade of the Irgun Brit Zion (ABZ, in Hebrew) youth movement in the Kovno Ghetto and the Kaufering camp in Germany. Another important source is the diary of Tamar Lazarson-Rostovski. The writer recounts the suffering, fears, and loves of a young woman from a liberal, enlightened home in Lithuania trapped in the ghetto (from which she later escaped) and her struggle to establish her Jewish and national identity.[14]

Furthermore, as noted, there is an abundant trove of memoir literature from the Kovno Ghetto. Survivors of the ghetto were among the first to publish early memoirs, immediately following their liberation. They offered

---

11 Avraham Tory, *Surviving the Holocaust: The Kovno Ghetto Diary* (Cambridge: Harvard University Press, 1990). The Hebrew version is: Avraham Tori [Tory], *Geto Yom Yom: Yoman Umismahim Migeto Kovna* (Hebrew) (Tel Aviv: The Bialik Institute and Tel Aviv University, 1988).

12 Samuel Schalkowsky, ed., *The Clandestine History of the Kovno Jewish Ghetto Police* (Bloomington: Indiana University Press in association with the United States Holocaust Memorial Museum, 2014); Dalia Ofer, ed., *Mishteret Hageto Hayehudit BeVilimpole: Mismah Migeto Kovna* (Hebrew) (Jerusalem: Yad Vashem, 2016).

13 Ze'ev Mankowitz, ed., *Hikon Likrat Herut! Reshimot Migeto Kovno Umimahane Kaufring: Almanah Gedud Ma'apilim Vehabita'on Nitzotz* (Hebrew) (Jerusalem: Yad Vashem, 2011).

14 Tamar Lazarson-Rostovski, *Yomana Shel Tamara: Kovna 1942–1946* (Hebrew) (Beit Lohamei Hageta'ot and Hakibbutz Hameuchad, 1975).

an important contribution to the work of the historical committees that were active in the DP camps in Germany. Thus, for example, survivors of the ghetto establishment published their short testimonies from those days in the issues of the Yiddish journal *Fun letstnkhurbn* edited by Yisrael Kaplan,[15] himself from Kovno. They depicted the ghetto's public activities in the social, cultural, and educational fields, and wrote about forced labor, health issues, displays of opposition, and more.[16] Likewise, extremely important monographs about the Kovno Ghetto have been published. The first, published in 1948, was written by Yosef Gar, a reporter and writer who was among the employees of the Ältestenrat.[17] The second monograph, penned by Leib Garfunkel,[18] who served as deputy chairman of the Ältestenrat in the Kovno Ghetto, was published in Israel at the end of the 1950s. Garfunkel replaced the chairman, Dr. Elchanan Elkes,[19] for significant periods due to the latter's ill-health.

The historiographical corpus concerning the Kovno Ghetto draws on these and other sources.[20] In all probability, they determined the outline

---

15 Ten issues of the journal *Fun letstnkhurbn* (*Tsaytshrift far geshikhte fun yidishn lebn beysn Natsi-rezhim* were published by the Central Historical Commission between 1946 and 1948.

16 See Yaakov Goldberg, "Bletlekh fun Kovner eltestenrat (biz nokh der groyser aktsiye)" (Yiddish), *Fun letstnkhurbn*, 7 (May 1948).

17 Yosef Gar, *Umkum fun der yidisher Kovne* (Yiddish) (Munich: Farband fun litvishe yidn in der amerikaner zone in Daytshland, 1948).

18 Leib Garfunkel, *Kovna Hayehudit Behurbana* (Hebrew) (Jerusalem: Yad Vashem, 1959). On Garfunkel see the diary entry from August 31, 1942.

19 On Dr. Elchanan Elkes see the diary entry from August 31, 1942.

20 The most comprehensive study of the Holocaust of Lithuanian Jewry, including the Jews of Kovno, was conducted by Christoph Dieckmann. See Christoph Dieckmann, *Deutsche Besatzungspolitik in Litauen 1941–1944* (Göttingen: WallseinVerlag, 2011), 2 vols. Likewise, on the Kovno Ghetto see the introductions written by Samuel D. Kassow for Schalkowsky, ed., *The Clandestine History of the Kovno Jewish Ghetto Police,* pp. 1–59, and Dalia Ofer in Dalia Ofer, ed., *Mishteret Hageto Hayehudit BeVilimpole* (Hebrew) (Jerusalem: Yad Vashem, 2016), pp. 15–102, of the document composed by the Jewish ghetto police, as well as the book by Yitzhak Arad, *The Holocaust in the Soviet Union* (Jerusalem and Lincoln: Yad Vashem and University of Nebraska Press, 2009), and the collection by Dennis B. Klein, ed., *Hidden History of the Kovno Ghetto* (published on the occasion of the exhibition Hidden History of the Kovno Ghetto, held at the United States Holocaust Memorial Museum, Washington, D.C., November 21, 1997–October 3, 1999) (Boston: Bulfinch Press, 1997).

according to which the primary story of the ghetto and its control was constructed.[21]

A Brief History of the Ghetto

The history of the Jews in Kovno under the Nazi occupation can be divided into three periods.

The first period: June 1941 until November 1941. This period was characterized by murderous attacks on the Jews decimating the ghetto's population. The second period, beginning in November 1941 and lasting until October 1943, was characterized by relative stability. The third and final period lasted from November 1943 until July 1944, when the ghetto was transferred to the control of the SS and became a concentration camp. During this period, the ghetto's area was continuously reduced, until its final liquidation in July 1944.

The first period: the Germans entered Kovno on June 24, 1941. In mid-July, they began preparing to concentrate the Jews in a ghetto located in the suburb of Vilijampolė (also known as Slobodka), beyond the Vilija River, which runs through the city of Kovno. The incarceration of Kovno's Jews in the ghetto was completed on August 15, 1941. Concurrently, a series of severe and violent disasters were inflicted on the Jews of the city. These began immediately upon the entry of the Germans and were carried out by Lithuanian nationalists ("partisans" or "Shaulists"), with the silent approval of the occupying authorities.[22] The "pogroms," as the Jews called them, were so brutal that the Jews of the city accepted with understanding their isolation in the ghetto, at first even regarding it as cold comfort. When the German control of Lithuania stabilized, the new regime began to help local elements realize the Nazi anti-Jewish policy. Subsequently, a campaign began of planned mass murder throughout Lithuania and other

---

21 A comprehensive and annotated bibliography regarding the Kovno Ghetto was published in "Hidden History of the Kovno Ghetto: An Annotated Bibliography," *Holocaust and Genocide Studies*, 12:1 (Spring 1998), pp. 119–138. Additional works have been published since this list was compiled at the end of the 1990s.

22 See Christoph Dieckmann, "Lithuania in Summer 1941: the German Invasion and the Kaunas Pogrom," in Elazar Barkan, Elizabeth A. Cole, and Kai Struve, eds., *Shared History—Divided Memory: Jews and Others in Soviet-occupied Poland, 1939–1941* (Leipzig: Leipziger Universitaetsverlag, 2007), pp. 355–385.

regions of the USSR, occupied by Nazi Germany, including in the city of Kovno, which first targeted Jewish men, and thereafter women and children. Most of the murders in Kovno were executed in the network of forts that encircled the city.

At the beginning of August 1941, just before the incarceration of the Jews in the ghetto, the German rulers forced them to choose an Ältestenrat to manage their lives in the planned ghetto. One of the dignitaries of the Jewish community, Dr. Elchanan Elkes, was asked by the community leaders to become chairman of the Ältestenrat. Elkes agreed to do so, albeit unwillingly. Advocate Leib Garfunkel was appointed as his deputy. Other members of the committee included Yaakov Goldberg,[23] Rabbi Yaakov Moshe Shmukler,[24] Rabbi Shmuel-Abba Snieg,[25] and Dr. Ephraim Rabinovitz.

On August 14, 1941, one day before the ghetto was closed off, the Germans demanded that the Ältestenrat provide them with 500 Jewish men, members of the intelligentsia; ostensibly, they were needed to organize the archives. When only 200 men reported, the Germans and their Lithuanian helpers rounded up 534 Jewish men, subsequently murdering them in the Fourth Fort.[26] The Jews of Kovno referred to this as the *Intelligentsia Aktion*.

The ghetto's population numbered 30,000 inhabitants when it was sealed off. It was divided into two sections: the big ghetto and the small ghetto. On September 16, 1941, Fritz Jordan,[27] the official appointed by the civilian administration as the ghetto's governor, transferred to the Ältestenrat 5,000 certificates (*Scheine*) that the governor of the Kovno district had allocated for craftsmen in the ghetto and their families. The leaders of the Ältestenrat understood the importance of these certificates, which were known as "life certificates." When news of this spread through the ghetto, a great panic ensued: masses assembled at the offices of the

---

23 On Yaakov Goldberg see the diary entry from November 16, 1942.
24 Rabbi Yaakov Moshe Shmukler (1889–1943), served as rabbi in Šančiai and Kovno. He died during Passover 1943, in the Kovno Ghetto.
25 Shmuel-Abba Snieg served as the Chief Military Rabbi of Lithuania in the interwar period. He survived the Holocaust. At the end of the war, he headed the Rabbinical Council of She'erit Hapleita in the American Zone of Occupation in Germany.
26 One of the series of forts that encircled the city.
27 On Fritz Jordan see the diary entry from October 14, 1942.

Ältestenrat, demanding certificates. Eventually, the Ältestenrat decided not to limit the distribution of certificates to craftsmen alone.

From the end of September 1941 onward, numerous decrees were imposed on the ghetto's Jews. They were not allowed to leave the ghetto without a permit, were not allowed to bring newspapers or food into the ghetto from outside, and a curfew was imposed. On October 4, 1941, the Germans liquidated the small ghetto; most of its inhabitants, approximately 1,600 people, were murdered in the Ninth Fort. The Germans burned down the plague hospital that was located in the small ghetto; the patients hospitalized there, together with the medical staff, were burned to death. On October 27, 1941, the Germans ordered all the ghetto inhabitants to report on the following day to Demokratų Square. Following a selection conducted by the Gestapo officer Helmut Rauca, 9,200 Jews were taken to the Ninth Fort, where they were shot. The remainder of the ghetto inhabitants were allowed to return to their homes. The inhabitants of the ghetto called this the Great *Aktion*. Subsequently, approximately 17,400 Jews remained in the ghetto working as forced laborers for the German war effort. Between August 15 and December 31, 1941, 13,421 Jews were murdered in the Kovno Ghetto.

From mid-September 1941, until the liquidation of the ghetto, Jewish men and women were used for forced labor in the suburb of Aleksotas,[28] where the Germans built a large airfield. The work at the airfield was the reason for the ghetto's existence, and thousands of its inhabitants— unlucky and without connections—marched approximately 5 kilometers each way and worked at harsh construction under the open skies on a daily basis.

The second period was one of relative calm. At the end of October 1941, following the liquidation of the small ghetto, and at the pressure of military elements and German civil administration personnel in the Lithuanian Generalkomissariat, the murders ceased, and the inhabitants of the ghetto became slaves to the German war effort. Although the period of mass murders in the ghetto had come to an end, and the situation remained relatively stable, new decrees were published on occasion, and the Germans continued to murder Jews on various pretexts. On February

---

28 On the airfield in Aleksotas see the diary entry from August 31, 1942.

27, 1942, the Jews were required to hand over all books in their possession. A number of people with knowledge of Hebrew examined approximately 100,000 books; the most valuable among them were sent to Germany and the rest were dispatched to factories for paper recycling. On May 7, 1942, an order was published forbidding Jewish women in the ghetto to give birth;[29] transgressing this order was punishable by death. Pregnant women were ordered to terminate their pregnancies, and the ghetto doctors were forced to conduct hundreds of abortions.

On November 18, 1942, Nachum Meck, a young man accused of shooting at one of the German guards whilst trying to escape the ghetto, was hanged in public. This public hanging, which Gerber writes about at length, was intended to terrorize and deter, and indeed it made an indelible impression on the ghetto inhabitants.

Life inside the ghetto was managed by offices and departments of the Ältestenrat, which were responsible for the necessary services. The labor office established by the Ältestenrat provided workers to meet the German demands. The labor office was responsible for the workshops in the ghetto and also ensured the provision of a range of services, such as the operation of a bathhouse, pharmacy, laboratory, cemetery, and more. A special committee of the Ältestenrat was responsible for allocating the minuscule rations that the authorities assigned to the ghetto inhabitants, while another committee was responsible for assigning housing in the crowded ghetto. Other departments under the responsibility of the Judenrat included the firefighters, health, welfare, and statistics, and there was also an education department, which was active until August 26, 1942. On that date, the Germans ordered the closure of all schools in the ghetto, although they later renewed their activities.

Large workshops were established in the ghetto in January 1942, and mainly served the German army. These included tailoring, shoemaking, metalwork, and carpentry workshops. The policy of subjugation and production dictated by the Germans forced the Ältestenrat to also ensure employment for artists. Thus, a graphics' workshop was established, and musicians were recruited to serve in the Jewish police. An orchestra was

---

29 The order was first published on February 5, 1942, in all ghettos in Lithuania. The authorities began to enforce it in the Kovno Ghetto only later.

created, which performed for the ghetto inhabitants and the German commanders.

Jews were also sent to work outside of Kovno. On February 6, 1942, the Germans demanded 500 Jews for forced labor in Riga, Latvia. These Jews later met the same terrible fate as the Jews of Riga. In October 1942, another group of Jews was sent to Riga. Others were dispatched to forced labor camps in Jonava, Palemonas, Kėdainiai, and Kaišiadorys. The threat of deportations to forced labor camps outside the ghetto naturally caused great tension and disquiet, destabilizing the ostensibly calm atmosphere.

The third period: There were around 16,000 Jews in the ghetto in November 1943, just before the Kovno Ghetto was converted into a concentration camp and its inhabitants dispersed to forced labor camps (a process known as *Kasernierung*). *Obersturmbannführer* Wilhelm Göcke[30] was appointed as the ghetto's commander after it fell, under the authority of the SS. At the end of October 1943, around 2,700 Jews were concentrated in the Kovno airfield and a selection was carried out. Anyone deemed unable to work in the airfield was deported to Auschwitz or for work in Estonia. At the end of November and during December 1943, between 5,000 and 6,000 of the ghetto's Jews were transferred to camps on the city's outskirts and elsewhere in the surrounding area. Approximately 7,000 to 8,000 Jews remained in the Kovno Ghetto. Accordingly, the area of the ghetto was reduced, and the suburb of Vilijampolė was no longer included within it. Following the roundups, the inhabitants of the ghetto began to prepare hiding places, mainly bunkers dug under buildings, and stockpiled food and water for a long stay. Sometimes these hiding places included wells and lighting systems.

Despite the SS policy to murder all Jews unable to work, especially children, numerous children lived in the Kovno Ghetto and the labor camps. On March 27, 1944, SIPO officials arrested all the Jewish policemen and took them to the Ninth Fort for interrogation, seeking to discover the hiding places in the ghetto where children were secreted. Moshe Levin, commander of the Jewish order police, was tortured, together with other police officers,

---

30 Wilhelm Göcke (1898–1944), was an *SS-Standartenführer*, *Obersturmbannführer der Reserve der Waffen-SS*, and a commandant of the Kovno Ghetto from November 1943 to July 1944.

but did not divulge the children's hiding places. Following the interrogations, forty Jewish policemen were shot; the few policemen that collaborated were allowed to return to the ghetto. The *Kinder Aktion* (as well as an *Aktion* of the elderly) began on the same day. Vehicles entered the ghetto and, using loudspeakers, the Germans called upon the ghetto inhabitants to hand over the children. Following a brutal hunt, approximately 1,000 children and a few elderly people were removed from the ghetto. The *Aktion* continued on the following day, March 28, and another 300 Jews, mostly children, were discovered in hiding places and removed from the ghetto. The inhabitants of the ghetto succeeded in hiding approximately 200 children. Another 300 children were murdered in similar *Aktionen* that were conducted on the same day in camps around Kovno. After the *Aktionen* of the children and the elderly in March 1944, the Jewish order police was disbanded and replaced by a new Jewish order police. The Ältestenrat was also dispersed and the Germans appointed Dr. Elchanan Elkes as "Elder of the Jews." At this time, attempts were made to smuggle children out of the ghetto, escape from the ghetto, and build hiding places. Between July 8 and 11, 1944, inhabitants of the ghetto and the camps in the surrounding area were deported to Stutthof (all the women and a few men); and to Dachau (the men). One week later, 131 boys were sent from Dachau to Auschwitz. The area of the ghetto and its houses were set on fire. At the end of July 1944, the Red Army entered Kovno. Very few of the ghetto inhabitants had survived in hiding and lived to see their liberation.

The Image

Texts written about the Kovno Ghetto portray a deep-rooted Jewish community that sustained a harsh blow following a series of mass murders, a society living in the shadow of continued threat and terrible uncertainty regarding its fate. However, thanks to a responsible and sensible leadership, and the fact that the remaining inhabitants clung to life, the Jewish community in the ghetto managed to pursue a reasonable and solid routine over the course of three years despite this trauma. This narrative, which has been generally accepted over the years, differs noticeably from the descriptions of other ghettos, for example the Vilna

(Vilnius) Ghetto.[31] Depictions of Vilna portray a ghetto characterized by social tension, internal foment, a refusal to endure the situation, and underground elements challenging the ghetto leadership—the Judenrat and its institutions and the Jewish order police. In the Vilna Ghetto, most criticism was aimed at the Jewish authorities, although the reality is described from a wider perspective and the opinions expressed are not unequivocal and are even polemical. This is not the case regarding Kovno.

The question arises: how and why did the solid and fair image of the Kovno Ghetto and its leadership come into being? Did the fact that the mass volume of documentary sources were, for the most part, written by those connected with the establishment affect this image? Does the lack of more and varied contemporary sources unintentionally drown out other voices that could have examined life in the Kovno Ghetto from different angles and painted a more complex picture than that currently available? Did the public narrative silence the individual voice, pushing aside any expression of criticism? These questions are doubly important following an examination of Ilya Gerber's diary. The many entries in his diary (as well as the songs written in the ghetto that he set down in writing) shed light on other aspects, more subversive and less well known, of life in the Kovno Ghetto, the feelings of its inhabitants, and their reactions.

Information and the Whirlpool of Rumors

The isolation and the separation that the ghettos forced upon Eastern European Jewry during the period of Nazi occupation naturally changed the Jewish population's way of life. The German regime imposed numerous decrees on the Jews in occupied Lithuania: for example, the consumption of news from newspapers, radio receivers,[32] or any

---

31 One of the obvious examples is the comparative discussion by Dina Porat in her article concerning three Jewish councils in central Lithuanian cities. See Dina Porat, "Mo'atzot Hayehudim Begeta'ot Hamerkaziyim BeLita: Hashva'a" (Hebrew) *Masu'a*, 22 (1994), pp. 70–80.

32 On January 27, 1942, Herman Kruk, the chronicler of the Vilna Ghetto, wrote the following: "A series of articles appeared in today's press: people are warned not to listen to the Jewish–Bolshevik lying propaganda, and then comes an extraordinary order about the radio:
1. People are not allowed to listen to foreign broadcasts.
2. Spreading foreign communiqués will be punished by death.
3. The order goes into effect on January 13 [?].
Signed: Commissar of Eastern Lands.

other channel of communication not authorized by the Germans was forbidden. Yet, despite this, information continued to flow into the ghetto. Garfunkel notes in his memoir that, following "the thirst to know what was happening in the world," parts of a radio receiver were smuggled into the ghetto and assembled in secret. The instrument was hidden in the cellar of the pharmacy and only a limited circle of activists received news "broadcast from London, Moscow, and Stockholm...."[33] News also arrived from Jewish refugees who fled from their towns following murder operations: they hid for a certain time, and afterwards slipped into the ghetto. Likewise, messengers and visitors arrived from neighboring ghettos and even from other countries as well as from various underground organizations.[34] Working outside the ghetto's borders and meeting with the local population similarly offered an opportunity to receive more varied information, to read newspapers, and to even listen to the radio. However, lacking any other alternative, many were forced to read the German press or what was published by the local authorities, which were filled with pro-German propaganda and antisemitism.[35] Lacking any other source of information, Gerber perused this press. His knowledge of German enabled him to read the German papers thoroughly and quote the news published there in his diary—mainly about developments on the front— to which he added his own reservations and personal interpretations. Gerber, it seems, was a skillful reader, in possession of a wide and realistic perspective. In September 1942, he analyzed a speech given by Hitler that was published in one of the German papers and which came into his possession. He translated and quoted the "Führer's prophecy," which Hitler had first voiced in January 1939. In this "prophecy," Hitler said: "Today I will once more be a prophet: If the international Jewish

---

Because of the order, all radios were confiscated in the city today." See Herman Kruk, *The Last Days of Jerusalem of Lithuania: Chronicles from the Vilna Ghetto and the Camps, 1939–1944* (New Haven and London: Yale University Press, 2002), p. 185.

33 Garfunkel, *Kovna Hayehudit Behurbana*, p. 117.

34 Ibid.

35 For example, Dr. Lazar Epshtein (Łazar Epsztajn) from the Vilna Ghetto described this in the following manner: "...the normal phenomenon of slaves and paid executioners serving their lords in a way that goes beyond what is asked of them..." Lazar Epshtein, *Nishmat Ha'adam Hamushteket: Yomano Shel Rofe Migeto Vilna 1941–1943* (Hebrew) (Jerusalem: Yad Vashem, 2017), p. 66.

financiers in and outside Europe should succeed in plunging the nations once more into a world war, then the result will not be the Bolshevization of the earth, and thus the victory of Jewry, but the annihilation of the Jewish race in Europe!"[36] Gerber's discussion of this "prophecy" is noteworthy: he apparently understood that behind the somewhat clumsy and vague phrasing stood Hitler's decisive policy of total annihilation of European Jewry. Subsequent academic discussions of Hitler's speeches have devoted special attention to this "prophecy." According to historian David Bankier, between 1941 and 1945, Hitler mentioned his "prophecy" in his speeches ten times. Bankier also noted: "The political function of reminding Hitler's "prophecy" repeatedly is plain. By doing so the Nazis promulgated their intended policy and informed the Germans how far they were expected to go, thus testing their loyalty."[37] Moreover, Gerber noticed that mentioning the Jews in Hitler's speeches became less frequent as time passed. Indeed, in Bankier's words, from mid-1943, when the Jews disappeared from the European space, Hitler ceased talking about them in his speeches and their presence in the public discourse in general became minimal. Indeed, the Final Solution "was already yesterday's news," determined Bankier, and the non-party press even refused to devote any attention to it.[38] Gerber noticed this trend already in the speech that Hitler gave in September 1942, before the Winter Relief operation in Germany:[39]

> Obviously, the Führer did not forget to mention the Jews. The difference is only that previously, in his former speeches, he didn't just mention the Jews. Quite the contrary: his entire speech was focused on the Jews. The Jew, and Jewry—is in every sentence of his, in every word. He started with Jews and ended with Jews. And now—now he doesn't talk so much

---

36 Yitzhak Arad, Israel Gutman, and Abraham Margaliot, eds., *Documents on the Holocaust: Selected Sources on the Destruction of the Jews of Germany and Austria, Poland, and the Soviet Union* (Jerusalem and Lincoln: Yad Vashem and University of Nebraska Press, 1999), pp. 134–135.

37 David Bankier, "Signaling the Final Solution to the German People," in David Bankier and Israel Gutman, eds., *Nazi Europe and the Final Solution* (Jerusalem: Yad Vashem, 2003), pp. 34–35.

38 Ibid., p. 39.

39 On the *Winterhilfswerk des Deutschen Volkes* see the diary entry from October 5, 1942.

about Jews, he doesn't say that the Jews are the misfortune of the German people and the entire world; he blames the Jews less now. Up until now he has blamed us enough for every misfortune and event which happens in the world—now he talks about the elimination of the Jewish people. He talks about mass destruction. He, the Führer, already speaks less about us. He says only a few words: he will destroy.[40]

It is not clear to what extent Gerber internalized the meaning of Hitler's threats, was able to interpret the hidden and overt messages in his words, and to act upon them. However, in marking the civil New Year of 1943, he wrote in his diary the following words, explaining to some extent the Jewish reaction and the escapist attitude that enveloped the ghetto, as well as his own personal feelings:

This one, the nation cursed by *Der Sturmer*, the perpetrator of all crimes, the one responsible for the World War, the betrayer of nations, the enemy of peoples, the parasite which lives at the expense of others, the Bolshevik, capitalist, and exploiter of everyone—this is the Jew, upon whose head all the curses of the world pour out, who is guilty of everything. He! He has survived to enter a new year, the forty-third year!

Therefore, indeed, our little Jews "broke glasses," wished each other *Mazltov*, and had a merry time. For an entire week they didn't stop, they really got into it, they drank a lot, ate well (taking their hand off their hearts), and didn't sleep well. It's superfluous to mention the young people. They want to consume the entire world hastily (an old tendency: *Der Sturmer* also reported that "the Jews want to take over the entire world, enslave everyone, and destroy...") and to act up, cause a great stir, dance and sing like in the good times....[41]

This optimism must also be attributed to the many rumors circulating in the Kovno Ghetto, about which Ilya Gerber wrote extensively in his diary. In fact, he often referred to this phenomenon. An examination of other texts

---

40   See the diary entry from January 1, 1943.
41   Ibid.

and diaries written in Kovno and other ghettos demonstrates that this was a widespread phenomenon in the lives of the Jews.[42] What was the reason for this? And what role did rumors play in the lives of the Jews in the ghettos?

The circumstances of the occupation, the lack of reliable and varied sources of information, and the policy of repression that was forced upon the predominantly literate Jewish society transformed it into a society which increasingly used oral communication, passing on information "from mouth to ear." Additionally, the atmosphere of uncertainty and deceit that the occupying authorities dictated created a mental reality shrouded in suspicion and fear of the uncertain future. Under such conditions, the culture of rumors thrived: intensively, daily, and serving as both a source of information and a source of comfort and escape for the soul. Scholars have only recently begun to discuss this central phenomenon in the daily life of the Jews during the Nazi era. Amos Goldberg, who analyzed the development of the culture of rumors in the Warsaw Ghetto, published one of the most important and illuminating studies on this topic.[43] Goldberg claimed that rumors not only replaced the news—but altered their meaning. The culture of rumors interpreted the developing reality in a way that accords with the pleasure principle, expressing hidden wishes, fears, and fantasies.[44] Even when they contained a kernel of truth, the rumors tell us very little about the reality—but much about hope. Furthermore, he argued, the rumor culture created a popular form of social interaction. It generated an alternative public space controlled orally, preserved the lively public domain, and helped maintain a fragment of social cohesion. The circulation of rumors was a type of "psychosis" that, in Goldberg's opinion, transformed the Jews of Warsaw into a community of prisoners: they were not only prisoners of the Germans, but also prisoners of hope.[45]

---

42 See Schalkowsky, ed., *The Clandestine History of the Kovno Jewish Ghetto Police*, and Lazarson-Rostovski, *Yomana Shel Tamara*, pp. 49, 53, 66.

43 Amos Goldberg, "Rumor Culture among Warsaw Jews under Nazi Occupation: A World of a Catastrophe Reenchanted," *Jewish Social Studies*, 21:3 (Spring/Summer 2016), pp. 92–125.

44 On February 15, 1942, Lazar Epshtein wrote in his diary in the Vilna Ghetto: "Sadly, we do not always receive accurate information about the situation on the front. We must be satisfied with rumors, and they are sometimes highly fictional and colored in bright hues of Polish fantasy and mystery." See Epshtein, *Nishmat Ha'adam Hamushteket*, p. 65.

45 See Goldberg, "Rumor Culture," pp. 112–115.

In his attempt to decode what was happening around him, Gerber's hearing, like that of others in the ghetto, was attuned to the rumors and he documented them frequently in his diary. He devoted lengthy paragraphs to this topic and even tried to trace how rumors developed. On October 19, 1942, he described how a rumor that circulated in the ghetto spread "faster than a telephone conversation." According to his depiction, one woman began a rumor by reporting that hundreds of prisoners from the ghetto prison had escaped and only 130 prisoners remained in captivity. At first, Gerber treated these assertions with derision and scorn. Yet it was soon apparent that the rumor had spread by word of mouth, becoming the talk of the day. Indeed, we must remember that the escape of prisoners in these numbers was likely to have led to the immediate destruction of the ghetto, and, therefore, even if the reliability of the information was doubtful, it triggered great tension and fear.

Gerber, who, already while writing knew that no such escape had taken place, traced the development of this rumor. He situated himself as an onlooker, and, in the spirit of the accepted convention, laid the blame for the rumor on women, following how the number of escapees rose from that given in the first woman's report to the accounts of the second and the third women in the rumor chain. Gerber explained that the women were motivated by their desire to become the center of attention.[46] Indeed, he thus summed up the event:

> The Jewish woman, who wanted to draw everyone's attention to herself, remained standing alone in the corridor and whispered in a flustered manner: "Can it be true?...Can it be...?" Apparently, she herself was persuaded that the news, which she delivered, is true and she believed her own lies, because, with frightened eyes and fast steps, she left the dark corridor. I heard all this from a student who was standing right there in the line.[47]

---

[46] The expression "the women say" was very common in the Kovno Ghetto, attributing the tendency to spreading rumors to women. On this see Schalkowsky, ed., *The Clandestine History of the Kovno Jewish Ghetto Police*, p. 135.

[47] See the diary entry from October 19, 1942.

Gerber related a rumor that had spread (which he himself heard from someone else). However, behind the story itself is the wish—one that eventually came true—that the wild story was the product of chattering women's imaginations, those who tend to invent stories to draw attention. In this case, the invented story accorded with his tendency to offer positive interpretations and create an optimistic atmosphere, a call for calm, claiming that these disturbing rumors were only futile chatter.

Another rumor that Gerber related at length, and that he tended to believe, concerned information that reached the Kovno Ghetto from Vilna about a revolt in the Warsaw Ghetto. On September 15, 1942, toward the end of the great deportation from the Warsaw Ghetto to the Treblinka death camp, Gerber recorded the following in his diary:

> Things are happening in Warsaw! Have you heard? Jews took up resistance! As the Vilna Jews who are now in our ghetto relate, some time ago Jews, who were fleeing from Warsaw, arrived in Vilna. The Warsaw Jews tell the Vilna Jews the following story.[48]

Subsequently, Gerber portrayed in detail the armed organization of the Jews of Warsaw who had obtained weapons from the Poles and defiantly refused to obey the order given by the head of the Judenrat to gather at the assembly point. The Jews of the ghetto shot at the head of the Judenrat and afterwards launched a battle:

> The Jews shot and engaged in deadly combat on the streets of Warsaw. The three battalions defended themselves from Jewish shots! Victims fell like flies. The Jews held the battalions in a cage. And they also destroyed them! They destroyed three battalions of soldiers, but Jews fell too, 12,000 people in total! As the Jews from Vilna related, the Poles joined the fight. With united forces they set fire to the Warsaw barracks and captured a few strategic locations for the time being. The Warsaw authorities had to call in motorized German units to calm the "revolt" of Warsaw's Jews. When these divisions arrived,

---

48 See the diary entry from September 15, 1942.

they gradually "returned the calm" to the city. That very same evening, with the help of the newly arrived Germans, they carried out an *Aktion*. They took 125,000 people in one day! They died and fell like heroes![49]

The rumor about a revolt in the Warsaw Ghetto on September 15, 1942, is extremely interesting, not only because it predicted what would indeed happen in the future—heroic Jewish fighting against the Germans, which inflicted great damage on the occupiers, but which was, eventually, quelled. As was noted, this was written during the deportation of the last Jews to Treblinka in the Great *Aktion*. This resulted in the murder of 265,000 Jews from Warsaw, almost seven months before the outbreak of the great revolt in the Warsaw Ghetto (April 19, 1943), and four months before the small revolt, which erupted on January 18, 1943. At this time, the first significant attempts to organize a Jewish underground fighting organization in the ghetto were underway. The entire story, thus, is a collection of invented fantasy. The only detail of information which is, to any extent, close to historical truth is the death of Adam Czerniaków, the head of the Warsaw Judenrat, at the beginning of the deportation. Czerniaków, however, was not killed by Jews for obeying the Germans, as Gerber writes in his dairy, but put an end to his life because he refused to be involved in rounding up the Jews for deportation.

How can we explain the fictitious rumor about a Jewish revolt at this time and the factors that caused its circulation?

Apparently, rumors about Jewish revolts against the Germans had been circulating for some time in the Warsaw Ghetto. On March 28, 1942, the underground newspaper *Jutrznia*, published by Hashomer Hatza'ir, printed a heroic and pathos-filled description of how 200 Jewish youngsters fought against the Germans in Nowogródek.[50] According to Emanuel Ringelblum's historical report, similar feats were also attributed to the Jews of Kowel. The rumors were inaccurate in both cases.[51]

---

49 See the diary entry from September 15, 1942.
50 *Jutrznia*, (March 28, 1942), in Yosef Kermish, ed., *Itonut Hamahteret Hayehudit BeVarsha*, vol. 5 (Hebrew) (Jerusalem: Yad Vashem, 1979), pp. 419–420.
51 On June 7, 1942, Emanuel Ringelblum wrote in his diary: "All the lies that they are telling about Nowogródek, and recently about Kowel, will not help here. They went

Introduction

Goldberg viewed the rumors about a revolt in Nowogródek as a response to the helplessness and weakness felt by the Jews of Łódź and Lublin at the same time—as they were being deported to the death camps. This was in addition to an attempt by the youth movements in the Warsaw Ghetto to breathe life and hope into the idea of an uprising.[52]

The rumor of a Jewish revolt in the Warsaw Ghetto, as documented by Gerber in his diary in mid-September 1942, must be understood on the backdrop of the murder of hundreds of thousands of Warsaw Jews in a period of three months. This was the peak of an unprecedented disaster, one of enormous proportions, which the Jews found difficult to grasp; a disaster that revealed to them the extent of their weakness and helplessness. Thus, it is no surprise that these despairing circumstances generated a fictional reality of Jewish resistance and brave fighting against the Germans—a story intended to redeem the victim and return to him some of his lost existence and crushed honor. The sources for the creation of this rumor and its circulation were probably Jews with a pro-Polish orientation, who aimed to establish a joint Polish–Jewish front against the Germans, because, according to the information in the rumor, the Poles provided significant aid to the Jewish fighters. However, Gerber related this rumor in his diary after describing two *Aktionen* that were conducted at the same time in Kovno. He clung to this story as a comforting response to the feelings of failure and powerlessness that encompassed the Kovno Ghetto following the deportations to work in Riga and the sight of non-Jewish victims being led to the Ninth Fort on the same day.

Another rumor that spread in the ghetto, about which Gerber wrote in his diary, and which was intended to raise the Jews' spirits, concerned the establishment of a Jewish state in Palestine. The desire was so great that, apart from Gerber, Tory noted it in his diary,[53] as did Tamar Lazarson-Rostovski, who added, "The ghetto is rejoicing."[54] This rumor circulated at the end of December 1942, a period during which the free world became

---

passively to their death, and they did so in order to enable others to live...." See Emanuel Ringelblum, *Yoman Vereshimot Mitkufat Hamilhama: Geto Varsha*, vol. 1 (Hebrew) (Jerusalem: Yad Vashem and Beit Lohamei Hageta'ot, 1993), p. 383.

52 Goldberg, "Rumor Culture," p. 105.
53 See December 22, 1942, entry by Tory, *Surviving the Holocaust*, pp. 162–163.
54 Lazarson-Rostovski, *Yomana Shel Tamara*, pp. 66–67.

aware of the vast extent of the murder of Jews in the territories under Nazi occupation. Masses took to the streets in New York to protest against the extensive slaughter of the Jews in Europe; and three days of mourning were declared in the Jewish *Yishuv* in the Land of Israel. It seems that this inaccurate piece of news regarding the establishment of a Jewish state in Palestine was a response to the atmosphere of despair that enveloped the ghetto Jews following this terrible information.

The phenomenon of rumors in the ghetto was not solely an internal Jewish affair. Evidently, the Germans regarded the spreading of rumors as problematic and dealt with it harshly. From the perspective of the occupier, rumors in the ghetto aroused agitation and disquiet that damaged the useful and productive atmosphere necessary to achieve its aims. How did the Germans find out about the rumors circulating in the ghetto and the damage they caused? To what extent were they themselves involved in this? The answers to this lie in the elements that collaborated with the Germans.

The Ältestenrat and the Strong Man

The institution of the Judenrat (the Ältestenrat, in the Kovno ghetto), and the image of its leaders in particular, are engraved in the historical memory as a problematic element facing a highly problematic task. There were a great number of Jews involved in leading such organizations, some of whom adopted many, varied ways of action. And, although it is clear that they were compelled to fulfill a role which was forced upon them, a tragic and thankless role, some of them are perceived and remembered as highly disputed figures. Several of these people exploited for their own benefit the power they attained by dint of the difficult circumstances while others collaborated with the German occupiers at the expense of the Jewish public.[55] This is not the place to go into detail about the factors involved in shaping this image. However, among the Jewish councils and

---

55 On this topic see: Isaiah Trunk, *Judenrat: The Jewish Councils in Eastern Europe under Nazi Occupation* (New York: Stein & Day, 1972); Aharon Weiss, "Jewish Leadership in Occupied Poland—Postures and Attitudes," *Yad Vashem Studies*, 12 (1977), pp. 335–365; Dan Michman: "On the Historical Interpretation of the Judenräte Issue: Between Intentionalism, Functionalism and the Integrationist Approach of the 1990s," in Moshe Zimmermann, ed., *On Germans and Jews under the Nazi Regime: Essays by Three*

Introduction

their leaders, historiography and collective memory have treated some more kindly and benevolently than others. This is the case regarding the Ältestenrat of the Kovno Ghetto. The historical sources emphasize that the chairman of the Ältestenrat, Dr. Elchanan Elkes, an ophthalmologist with a good reputation, a fair and honorable man, a Zionist activist, and among the respected members of the community, was drawn into this role against his will. Members of the local committee pressured him to accept the position, in particular because he possessed these qualities and they understood that his appointment would benefit the Jews of Kovno.[56] In their writings, members of the ghetto establishment praised Elkes's personality and how he carried out his job. His deputy, Leib Garfunkel, who survived the Holocaust, wrote that Elkes's work during the three years of the ghetto's existence proved that the Jews of Kovno had not erred in their choice.[57] In the introduction to the publication of the last testament of Elkes (in a letter to his son and daughter) Dina Porat characterized his role:

> …And during the ghetto period his true stature was revealed, and he became the Jewish community's revered leader. Some of the Germans desisted from their typical behavior when in his presence. His unique personality set standards of behavior to withstand the ghetto's conditions, and also helped several community leaders to rise above the circumstances and to serve their community.[58]

And indeed, the ghetto Jews greatly esteemed and respected Dr. Elkes despite the life of oppression and humiliation that they endured. However, does Gerber's diary depict him as the strongest Jew in the ghetto? And to what extent did the organization he headed—the Ältestenrat—really affect the lives of the Jews in the ghetto?

Generations of Historians. A Festschrift in Honor of Otto Dov Kulka (Jerusalem: The Hebrew University Magnes Press, 2006), pp. 385–397.

56 On this see Schalkowsky, ed., *The Clandestine History of the Kovno Jewish Ghetto Police*, p. 71, and Garfunkel, *Kovna Hayehudit Behurbana*, pp. 47–48.

57 Garfunkel, *Kovna Hayehudit Behurbana*, p. 48.

58 Tory, *Geto Yom Yom*, p. 603. On this letter by Elkes, see also in Tory, *Surviving the Holocaust,* pp. 503–507.

Gerber mentioned Dr. Elkes twice in the extant diary notebook, referring to him as "the most respected man in the ghetto, who holds the highest post."[59] On the other occasion when mentioned, he expressed his amazement that the operation which Dr. Elkes conducted on one of his patients restored the latter's eyesight. This feeling of respect was also true regarding other members of the Ältestenrat. However, a reading of his diary indicates that the members of the Ältestenrat occupied a rather marginal place in determining the fate of the ghetto's Jews, and that the extent of their involvement in important matters, such as assigning ghetto inhabitants to workplaces and sending them to work outside the ghetto, was marginal. Gerber frequently mentioned the officials of the German civil administration who often visited the ghetto and interfered in internal ghetto affairs. The SA men—Deputy of Kovno *Stadtkommissar* Ernst Kaifler and his co-workers Heinz Köppen[60] and later Fritz Müller[61]—often wandered around the ghetto with their subordinates: they investigated, snooped around, and continuously introduced new decrees, leaving the Ältestenrat little room for maneuver. One German officer who was remembered favorably is *SA-Obersturmführer* Gustav Hörmann,[62] who managed the labor office in the Kovno Ghetto on behalf of the German civil administration. The Jews succeeded in capturing his heart, and he helped them greatly, even allowing them to manage his office.[63] And, because work was a vital element in the ghetto's existence, he wielded great power. Indeed, Gerber wrote about him: "Hörmann…is the real ruler of the ghetto, without his knowledge no Jews can be taken to work, without him no order can be given in the ghetto!"[64]

At the same time, the Gestapo, as was its wont, utilized collaborators among the Jewish community. This system of operating Jewish agents in the ghetto—people who had no official role in the Judenrat, or only a

---

59 See the diary entry from August 31, 1942.
60 On Heinz Köppen see the diary entry from September 29, 1942.
61 On Fritz Müller see the diary entry from September 29, 1942.
62 On Gustav Hörmann see the diary entry from September 27, 1942.
63 Concerning Hörmann's close relations with the Jews of Kovno, see Garfunkel, *Kovna Hayehudit Behurbana*, p. 222.
64 See the diary entry from September 27, 1942.

semi-official one, yet wielded great power and influence over the lives and fates of the Jews—is known from other ghettos. In the Warsaw Ghetto, the "Thirteen" network was active alongside other elements;[65] the same was the case in Łódź.[66] In each ghetto the extent of their influence and power depended on the local occupying authorities, the leadership of the ghetto, and its attitude toward the Jewish population. Ghettos in Lithuania that supplied vital labor for the Germans constituted a bone of contention and a source of fierce competition between the German civil administration and the German police force and the Gestapo, which also demanded their share of the spoils. The head of the civil administration in Kovno was Hans Cramer,[67] who was the *Stadtkommissar*, and he appointed subordinates who were responsible for the de facto management of the ghetto. At the same time, the Gestapo officers Helmut Rauca[68] and Heinrich Schmitz, subordinate to Karl Jäger, commander of the German police force and the SD in Lithuania, were responsible for conducting *Aktionen*, police activities, and controlling the Jewish police in the ghetto. There was tension between the two German authorities and never-ending battles over control and maintenance of ghetto property and its inhabitants; the Jews, caught in the middle, were pulverized.[69]

As noted, characteristically of the Gestapo's methods, and in the context of the internal German struggle, it recruited Jewish collaborators in Kovno. One of these was Josef Caspi-Serebrovitz[70] and another was

---

65 Regarding the "Thirteen" network and its activities in the Warsaw Ghetto see Israel Gutman, *The Jews of Warsaw, 1939–1943: Ghetto, Underground, Revolt* (Bloomington: Indiana University Press, 1982), pp. 90–91.

66 In her study of the Łódź Ghetto, Michal Unger described the undermining of the status of Chaim Mordechai Rumkowski, the head of the Judenrat, and the increasing influence of two Gestapo agents. See Michal Unger, *Lodz—Aharon Hageta'ot bePolin* (Hebrew) (Jerusalem: Yad Vashem, 2005), pp. 512–522.

67 On Hans Cramer see the diary entry from August 26, 1942.

68 On Helmut Rauca see the diary entry from August 26, 1942.

69 Garfunkel, *Kovna Hayehudit Behurbana*, pp. 215–217. See also the comments of Arie Segalson in his memoirs concerning his uncle, Moshe Segalson, who was appointed to manage the large workshops that were established in the ghetto at the initiative of the civil administration. The memoir also recounts the blows he received as a result of the rivalry between the two authorities. See Arie Segalson, *Belev Ha'ofel: Kiliyona Shel Kovna Hayehudit–Mabat Mibifnim* (Hebrew) (Jerusalem: Yad Vashem, 2003).

70 On Josef Caspi-Serebrovitz see the diary entry from September 18, 1942.

Benjamin (Benno) Lipcer.[71] The names of these two and their conduct are prominent in the historiography. However, it seems that although the historical sources did not ignore these figures, they reduced their status and power. Garfunkel, who described the activities of Caspi-Serebrovitz in his memoirs, noted, "This character was both grotesque and repulsive. Even before the war, he was known as a wild-tempered and impetuous person, with his hand against every man, and every man's hand against him."[72] The text, written by members of the Jewish order police, devoted a lengthy section to his personality, describing him, among other things, as "this complex person, this raging volcano, this crazy rebel."[73] This depiction portrays a person full of contradictions, loud, embroiled in disputes, an unstable character who placed himself at the disposal of the German police. Although Caspi-Serebrovitz was allowed to live with his family outside the ghetto, he interfered in affairs inside the ghetto, mainly in the work of the police, and tended to pass on to the Germans information about what was happening inside the ghetto. Gerber also mentions Caspi-Serebrovitz: "What kind of role did he play? People said that his role in the ghetto was to be the recipient and distributor of rumors in the ghetto." Gerber added that Caspi-Serebrovitz served as the representative of the Jewish ghetto vis-à-vis the Gestapo and that some say that "he did a lot of good for the Slobodka Ghetto." Among other things Gerber also mentions Caspi-Serebrovitz's influence at the scenes that took place at the "Jewish gate": "Once, actually, the ghetto was grateful to Caspi. He had reproached the Jewish police standing guard at the ghetto gate…that they should not behave so brutally toward their own brothers, their own Jews (at the gate, the Jewish crowd of workers were beaten. And who did the beating? The Jewish police, of course. Caspi apparently took an interest in this)."[74] This situation ultimately worked against Caspi-Serebrovitz and in July 1942, his German operators moved him to Vilna, where they soon murdered him, his wife, and his two daughters.[75]

---

71   On Benjamin (Benno) Lipcer see the diary entry from August 26, 1942.
72   Garfunkel, *Kovna Hayehudit Behurbana*, p. 243.
73   Schalkowsky, ed., *The Clandestine History of the Kovno Jewish Ghetto Police*, p. 303.
74   See the diary entry from September 18, 1942.
75   For a detailed description of Caspi-Serebrovitz, his involvement in the work of the Jewish order police, and his disappearance, see Schalkowsky, ed, *The Clandestine History of the Kovno Jewish Ghetto Police*, pp. 302–318.

Introduction

Caspi-Serebrovitz was not the only Jewish Gestapo agent active in the Kovno Ghetto. Around the same time and thereafter, another Jew, Benno Lipcer, entered the arena, and his influence and power were much greater than those of Caspi-Serebrovitz. Gerber mentioned him and his activities quite often in his diary; from his descriptions, Lipcer was evidently the most powerful man in the ghetto. Lipcer's position—commander of the Jewish work brigade at the SIPO and SD headquarters of Lithuania in Kovno (Gestapo)—which was a large-sized work brigade[76]—allowed him to determine what in fact happened in the ghetto. Although he was not officially the commander of the Jewish police, he was "invited" to serve as an honorary member in its command and, in reality, controlled it. Garfunkel testified in his memoirs regarding Lipcer's strength, even defining him as "a very strong competitor" for the control of the Ältestenrat: "In fact, Lipcer became the supervisor of the Ältestenrat and a powerful man in the ghetto, they were forced to follow his instructions, even if this caused damage to the ghetto."[77] Arie Segalson, one of the ghetto's survivors, described at length in his memoirs the struggle which his uncle, Moshe Segalson, manager of the large workshops, waged against Lipcer. The background to this battle was the never-ending struggle between the German civil administration and the Gestapo for control of the ghetto, with each man representing a different ruling arm. In Segalson's words:

> Lipcer had great influence in the ghetto, in particular in the Ältestenrat. Everyone knew about his connections with the Gestapo and knew that he had a say in ghetto affairs, and thus the Gestapo people penetrated into the ghetto institutions and Jewish police. Through him the Gestapo passed on instructions and orders to the Ältestenrat, and these were carried out efficiently and to the satisfaction of the Germans.[78]

---

76 Lipcer headed the Gestapo's Jewish work brigade, which historian Christoph Dieckmann described as a large and stable work unit. See Dieckmann, *Deutsche Besatzungspolitik*, vol. 2, pp. 1086–1087.
77 Garfunkel, *Kovna Hayehudit Behurbana*, p. 244.
78 Segalson, *Belev Ha'ofel*, p. 167.

The fact that Lipcer's name and his involvement in the work of the police were almost completely removed from the text written by the Jewish police[79] during the period in which he was most active in this organization—while it provided a lengthy, detailed, and highly uncomplimentary description of Caspi-Serebrovitz—demands investigation. These questions become even more pressing in light of the memoranda and orders that Lipcer issued during that period bearing his signature—today found in Lithuanian archives—and Tory's comments in his diary, which unintentionally highlight the great power and massive involvement of Lipcer in the work of the Ältestenrat and its various offices and departments.[80] It seems that Lipcer, who understood the documentary aims of the record composed by the Jewish police in the Kovno Ghetto, "ensured" with great finesse that his presence was blurred so that his actions and his name would not be remembered in the "History of the Jewish police in Vilijampolė," as the document is entitled.

However, in Gerber's diary, Lipcer is present in full force. He is portrayed as the deciding power in the ghetto, and as a man with great authority. Gerber described him as the *Oberjude*. And in his portrait of the short opportunity given to the inhabitants of the ghetto to bathe in the Vilija River, he wrote:

> Even the *shtetl* nobility come here. On Friday, almost the entire staff of the labor office, Lipcer, and many other important people, too. In that moment, as they stand almost completely naked, exactly like the other simple people at the beach, they could almost be the same. There is a Jew and that one is a Jew. One people!

---

79   The text mentions Lipcer's name once, as one of the speakers at the swearing-in ceremony of the policemen, describing him as the person in charge of labor. See Schalkowsky, ed., *The Clandestine History of the Kovno Jewish Ghetto Police,* p. 359.

80   Thus, for example, Tory described on June 30, 1942, a meeting hosted by Dr. Elkes that was attended by Caspi-Serebrovitz and Lipcer: "Police matters in the ghetto will remain in future under Caspi's supervision. Lipcer will supervise all labor force matters." However, shortly after this, Caspi-Serebrovitz was sent to Vilna and murdered. Regarding Lipcer's involvement in the work of the Judenrat, see also July 10–11, 1942, entries in Tory, *Surviving the Holocaust*, pp. 101, 110. In January 1943, he was appointed as an honorary member of the command of the Jewish police in the ghetto.

Introduction

According to Gerber, Lipcer had the power and authority to release a person from being sent to do the most undesirable work outside the ghetto. Similarly, whoever was fortunate enough to have had close connections to him—that person's life in the ghetto was more secure and comfortable. Thus, Gerber wrote:

> If the family knows Lipcer or other senior Jewish leaders, who have a say in the matter, *protektsie* [patronage] can help a lot. They receive a release note and the prison doors open to let the chosen one go. If they have no *protektsie* there is only one choice: that is, to sit in the prison, cursing the day that he was born and the day "the other guy" was born…and waiting for the day when they will be told to leave.

The memoirs written by members of the establishment in the Kovno Ghetto emphasize the status of the Ältestenrat as a center of Jewish power which ensured moral behavior and public responsibility. Apart from "disturbances" caused by "hostile" elements among the Jewish community, it managed to maintain its authority. By contrast, they reduce the power of Lipcer the collaborator, regarding him as an exception and an outsider. Naturally, Gerber's perspective on what happened in the ghetto differed to elements within the ghetto establishment. His diary offers a different picture, revealing Lipcer's significant involvement and great power. Gerber's words indicate that Lipcer was the man "whispering behind the scenes," that the community turned to him regarding fateful questions, and that he had the power to coordinate matters with the German police and solve problems. It seems that the Jews of Kovno indeed respected Dr. Elkes and the Ältestenrat. However, in their hour of need, they fully understood where the real center of power was—and approached Lipcer and his men. Everyone knew that he served as a tool of the Gestapo, but in their distress, they often turned to him, and he indeed provided help. Yet after the war, and perhaps precisely because of this, he was ignored, dismissed, or even described with disdain and disgust in memoirs and testimonies.[81]

---

81 Thus, for example, Nechama (Nekhama) Santotski-Shneerson—whose father was close to Lipcer and worked under him in the Jewish labor brigade of the Gestapo and received quite a number of privileges for his family—did not mention anything about this matter

From this perspective, Gerber's diary focuses the readers' attention on the atmosphere in the Kovno Ghetto from the beginning of the fall of 1942 until the beginning of the winter of 1943, presenting Lipcer and his group from the contemporary perspective of the ghetto's Jews. This reflects a complex picture: The public status of the semi-official alternative and highly dubious leadership of the Kovno Ghetto—the emissaries of the Gestapo—who were "contaminated" yet at the same time were accepted and highly involved in the lives of the ghetto inhabitants. Juxtaposed with them was the weakness, and in certain cases marginality, of the official leadership—the fair and respected Ältestenrat—which later historiography awarded them many accolades.

Ghetto Solidarity and Protektsie[82]

Gerber's diary sheds light on the social atmosphere in the Kovno Ghetto. Despite deeply mourning the murder of thousands of their co-religionists, including among them were their friends and relatives, and living in fear of what the future held, the surviving remnant of the Jews in Kovno clung to life with all its might. They worked for the Germans because this promised, or so they thought, their survival, and work was what colored their daily routine and existence. What work did this entail? And where did it take place? Would they join a good work brigade? Would they have to march a long way, especially on days of heavy snow and freezing temperatures, to reach their workplace? And where would they labor? Under cover of a roof or outdoors, under the open skies? How much food would they receive? How would the "masters" behave? Would it be possible to make "deals" with the locals? And the main thing—for which they were all hoping in vain—was to not be sent for harsh labor at the airfield at Aleksotas. However, the work at the airfield was the foundation of the ghetto's existence, everyone knew this, and therefore, every day,

---

in her testimony. See Nechama (Nekhama) Santotski-Shneerson testimony, Yad Vashem Archives, 0.93/8842.

82 *Protektsie*, otherwise known as "Vitamin P" among the Jews, was the term used for mobilization of personal ties—having the right connections at the right time and the right place

thousands of workers, both male and female, went from the ghetto to work there. These workers were called the *aerodromshtshikes*,[83] and, even though they carried the ghetto's continued existence on their shoulders, their harsh labor was considered the lowest of work placements.

Indeed, the question of allocating a workplace opened deep fissures in the ghetto's social fabric. Gerber described in his diary that he was assigned to work in the airfield—and how his father successfully intervened to lift this decree by using his connections with several senior people in the ghetto. So, too, his sister, Chaya, after prolonged struggles, tremendous efforts, and a great deal of frustration, succeeded in entering the large workshops as a simple "laundress." Ilya wrote:

> ...and how much *protektsie* did one need for this, that she should work behind the firmly closed and locked doors?! How much of her health did it cost her until she was nonetheless allowed to work in the workshops for the important people of the ghetto? And for who do they work here? For the Germans, for our torturers![84]

In contrast, his friend Dov (Beke) Kot, who lost all his family, was sent to work in forced labor in the Palemonas camp. According to Ilya, "Since people living alone (without families) were, for the most part, sent to Palemonas, he was dragged from his bed in the middle of the night and sent there,"[85] and he added later in the diary:

> Whoever has no "P" (short for *protektsie*) and wants to get out of prison, that is, he doesn't want to go to Riga, must apply the best and strongest protection money. One gives a bribe to a Jewish official, the latter takes it, puts it in his pocket—

---

83   Yisrael Kaplan explained it in the following manner: "These were men of their own separate social caste, the lowest and most oppressed. They would pound on the door of the labor deployment office and beg the Jews who worked there to change their workplace. An ear was seldom lent to their anguished complaints." Yisrael Kaplan, *The Jewish Voice in the Ghettos and Concentration Camps: Verbal Expression under Nazi Oppression* (Jerusalem: Yad Vashem, 2018), p. 63.

84   See the diary entry from October 14, 1942.

85   See the diary entry from September 18, 1942.

and makes change by giving a release note... So, who remains in prison? The one who has no *protektsie* and no dough [money].... Who is the most unfortunate? Mostly the airfield worker, who, from the very beginning, has been going to the airfield, suffering all day long in the cold wind and rain, and has the good fortune to be called by Lurie, the Jewish airfield inspector, names like: murderer, sloppy, underworld, and other similar choice words he uses for the airfield worker.[86]

Gerber also described how Jewish work brigades returning to the ghetto had to bribe the Jewish policemen at the gatehouse. Workers carrying goods that they had purchased outside the ghetto and who wanted to smuggle them in, had to pay both the Lithuanian policemen and the Jewish policemen. Thus, he wrote:

"Oh! Less than eighty marks—and you won't be going through the gate!" comes the ultimatum from the Jewish ghetto police. With these words they stop the flow at the gate. Having no other choice—they paid eighty marks.... The Jews "tore away" thirty marks from their own brothers—also Jews. And so it is with every brigade.

Recently, they are "flaying the skin from us," the people in the brigades: the Jewish ghetto police are already demanding up to 150 marks for ten people to go through the gate! And what will be later?! Even worse!![87]

Giving bribes and exploiting personal connections with those in important positions, people with status and power, to improve an individual's situation—known in popular slang as *protektsie*—was very common in the ghetto. *Protektsie* became more important than ever in this period of distress and radical oppression. Connections with members of the ruling authorities could change the lives of the individual and his family from one extreme to another, even saving them from death. And yet, even

---

86 See the diary entry from October 23, 1942.
87 See the diary entry from November 27, 1942.

though this was a common phenomenon which occurred everywhere, and during all periods, the population—mainly those without connections and links—found it difficult to accept. It usually caused social tensions, great frustration, and discontent. These feelings were expressed primarily in the small and medium-sized ghettos, in which the *protektsie* was evident, and aroused significant anger. Gerber was very curious about and interested in what happened around him, noting on more than one occasion the phenomena of *protektsie* and bribery that were common in the Kovno Ghetto and that it radicalized its class structure. Despite the fact that, to a certain extent, he could have been considered one of the more privileged, due to his father's connections with key figures in the ghetto, his words represent the general population. The social disparities were expressed in the creation of a special language—slang—that took root among the inhabitants of the Kovno Ghetto. Apart from the well-known term *protektsie*, the term *yale (veyovo)*[88] also came into being and was first used by the *aerodromshtshikes* at the airfield. These expressions, which later became an inseparable part of the vernacular used by the inhabitants of the Kovno Ghetto represented the widespread feeling that double standards existed: one rule for the privileged, another for those who were less fortunate. Such sentiments were documented also in songs written by the ghetto inhabitants, some of them collected by Gerber. Some songs express the frustration among those in the lowest positions, who felt that their voice went unheard, and they were the first to be sent to harsh labor.[89]

Ghetto Songs and Music

Ilya Gerber devoted a great deal of time and attention to collecting songs written in the Kovno Ghetto. Although he did not note this explicitly, in addition to keeping a diary which testifies to a strong tendency for personal expression, his decision to collect these songs was apparently motivated by a desire to document and preserve an artistic genre that

---

88   An explanation of this term and its usage appears in the diary entry from August 26, 1942.
89   See, for example, the song *Vitamin P* by G. Shenker in Garfunkel, *Kovna Hayehudit Behurbana*, pp. 292–295.

was, it seems, very widespread in the ghetto,[90] and which expressed the mood and yearnings of the general population. At the end of the war, a notebook of songs that Ilya collected (the second notebook) was found and subsequently served as one of the sources for a collection of "Songs from the ghettos and the camps" collated by Shmerke Kaczerginski,[91] who even noted this in the introduction to his book.[92]

In his diary, Gerber discussed the songs that he collected, provided a few examples, and even tried to typify them:

> The ghetto creates many songs but sadly very few melodies: better put, almost none. Despite the fact that my father is a musician of the best kind and once composed a lot, now, in the ghetto, he has not composed any melodies. The music for the words is taken from Soviet melodies, and a few tangos, but no Jewish ones! The people create gradually, recording and expressing the pain of Jewish life in songs. In this way, they relate, recite, and sing about the life of the Jewish ghetto inhabitant at work. Every song is a fragment of life, embracing a unique epoch in our times. A ghetto song generally starts with the pain and misfortune of the Jewish people and ends with the hope for a better, lighter, and more fortunate future.[93]

The young Gerber's statements are verified by studies conducted after the war concerning ghetto songs. Most songs were written in the form of contrafact—adapting new words to an existing melody. The musicologist Gila Flam claims that playing a familiar melody evokes feelings of calm and

---

90 Lerke Rozenblum from Kovno Ghetto wrote a song about this, entitled "The Rhyme Industry in the Ghetto:" "Everyone writes songs in the ghetto / From early until very late / everyone thinks he is a poet." See ibid., pp. 300–301.

91 Shmerke Kaczerginski (1908–1954), was a poet, journalist, and Yiddish writer. He spent part of the duration of World War II in the Vilna Ghetto before becoming a partisan.

92 Kaczerginski wrote in the book's Introduction: "I will honor the memory of the martyr Lyusik Gerber (who was sent from the Kovno Ghetto to Dachau, where he perished). His notebook containing songs that were sung in the Kovno Ghetto was found among the ruins after the war. I included the songs in this collection." See Shmerke Katsherginski [Kaczerginski], *Lider fun di getos un lagern* (Yiddish) (New York: Tsikobikherfarlag, 1948), p. xxv.

93 See the diary entry from December 4, 1942.

comfort, yet the contrafact arouses pain: attaching a familiar melody to new words intensifies the power of the song and endows it with greater meaning. The old melody recalls the good days of yore, while the new words return the ghetto inhabitant to the terrible reality of the here and now.[94]

Moreover, most of the songs written in the ghettos in those days expressed feelings of pain, fear, and affront, as well as introspection and criticism. Many conclude with an aspiration for change and hope for better days in the future. The musician Moshe Hoch, who studied the topic, distinguished a wide variety of types of songs that the Jews wrote during the war. "Naturally, the role of the depressing and mournful motifs in the songs stands out, but many of them also contain motifs of encouragement and hope," he wrote.[95]

In addition to the collection of songs, Gerber provided insight into musical activities in the ghetto. The story of the police orchestra in the ghetto, which Gerber discusses, was documented in pictures by the photographer Zvi Kadushin.[96] It is mentioned briefly in the text written by the Jewish police, and is described at length in Tory's diary, as well as in other sources. Garfunkel noted that the orchestra was established to raise the spirits of those imprisoned in the ghetto, to encourage them, and to also provide work for the professional Jewish musicians and others with a good reputation incarcerated there. After the police succeeded, with great effort, in obtaining the Germans' consent for the orchestra and prepared a hall in which to hold the concerts (the building of the former yeshiva), they encountered strong opposition from a number of public figures who claimed that this could desecrate the memory of the recently murdered martyrs; some even threatened to protest against the concerts and disrupt the performances. However, in Garfunkel's words, with time, the opposition dissipated and the orchestra "developed very well and became a cultural and artistic factor of

---

94 Gila Flam, "The Meaning of Contrafact in Yiddish Songs of the Holocaust," *World Congress of Jewish Studies*, 11D:2 (1993), p. 270.

95 Moshe Hoch, *Kolot Mitoh Hahosheh: Hamusika Bageta'ot Ubamahanot BePolin* (Hebrew) (Jerusalem: Yad Vashem, 2002), p. 263.

96 Zvi Kadushin (George Kadish) (1910–1997), was an amateur Lithuanian Jewish photographer who independently and secretly took thousands of photographs of daily life in the Kovno Ghetto from 1941 until the summer of 1944, when he was forced to go underground.

the first order in the life of the ghetto."[97] Such was the opinion of Garfunkel and Tory, who viewed the activities of the orchestra in the ghetto as welcome and useful. Yet in contrast, the songs that were written in the ghetto created a different tune. "Why the concerts, if the mourning is so great / and the hunger is raging and the suffering is immense?"[98] wrote Abraham Akselrod, one of the ghetto's poets. The teacher Abba Diskant, among the most prolific writers in the Kovno Ghetto, wrote a harsh song expressing his anger at the conversion of the yeshiva into a concert hall: "You have transformed the yeshiva, where God's presence fills the realm/ and where the *bahurim* [yeshiva students] spend their days and nights/ into a desecrated concert hall!"[99]

This bitter disagreement[100] and angry tone are also echoed in Gerber's diary. He found it difficult to accept the musical activities that the official ghetto establishment produced. Indeed, upon hearing that his father had been appointed as conductor of the police choir that was to perform with the orchestra at the swearing-in ceremony for the police officers, he wrote:

> My father has a new job in the ghetto, one that has never been heard of and one that was not hoped for. He has become the conductor of the policemen's choir which is now being established. As the newly appointed conductor, my father must now assemble a four-voice choir made up of 100 ghetto policemen. It sounds like a dream: Jews in the ghetto, people sentenced to death, not so much people but rather shadows of people, living corpses, future "bagel-bakers," [unknown]— they are to form a choir in the ghetto? For whom? To entertain the embittered public? For whom? For the Germans? Hebrew songs, *Khazonish* [cantorial] laments, *Yomkiper*-style songs— all for the Germans?! For whom are they making this choir? For the labor office? For Margolis, for Lurie? For the people

---

97 See Garfunkel, *Kovna Hayehudit Behurbana*, pp. 250–252.
98 From the poem *Emor Li Yehudi Me'HaGhetto* ("Tell Me, a Jew from the Ghetto"), cited in ibid., pp. 290–291.
99 From the poem *Be'veit Ha'yeshiva* ("In the Building of the Yeshiva"), by Abba Diskant, cited in ibid., pp. 296–297. The words in the original song, in Hebrew, rhyme.
100 A similar disagreement existed in the Vilna Ghetto regarding the moral legitimacy of cultural events. See Kruk, *The Last Days of Jerusalem of Lithuania*, pp. 174, 176.

whose friends, brothers, sisters, and relatives have been taken to the Fort?! For whom?...[101]

Later he recorded the response of the Jewish policemen who were required to participate in this choir. They too, according to his report, were unwilling to take part in this initiative:

> Many of the policemen have little desire for the entire matter and come to our house, one by one, seeking to get out of singing by using their *protektsie*. This one can't, and this one doesn't want to—his heart won't let him. "When the entire world is fasting because of our destruction shall we go and sing?! The Pope too has been fasting and we should enjoy ourselves?! No! My father listens to such arguments but is compelled to answer them all with one word: No! He cannot excuse anyone. He is being forced—and so he must force others.[102]

Did Ilya Gerber change his opinion over the course of time, as concerts became a weekly, routine event in the ghetto? It is impossible to know, since the last entry in the diary's only surviving notebook is dated late January 1943. However, the feeling of revulsion that he displayed toward the orchestra and the choir established in the ghetto did not contradict his love of music, mainly popular music and even jazz, which he shared mainly with his friends.

The Springtime of Youth

Ilya Gerber did not isolate himself in his suffering or capitulate to the fear of death that characterized life in the ghetto. Typically for an eighteen-year-old young male, his social connections were intense, he continued to meet with his friends on a daily basis, and they sang, danced, and enjoyed themselves whenever the opportunity presented itself, mainly at the birthday parties they organized for themselves. The dulling of the senses, the feeling of "living for the moment," and taking their minds off the great catastrophe hovering over the ghetto was even stated explicitly:

---

101 See the diary entry from November 10, 1942.
102 Citation and comments, see the diary entry from December 31, 1942.

> Each one bewails his own tragedy and isn't interested in the misfortune of others. Should I take it to heart that this Yoske or that Mishke was taken away? Who will worry about me, who will sympathize with me, if they, God forbid, will take me away?...
>
> These are the feelings of not one or two Jews in the ghetto—all the Jews in the ghetto think this way. "As long as the misfortune doesn't know me—I don't know him [the victim]. And if I do sympathize with him, how does that help him? Will it make things easier for him? No! Not at all! On the contrary—it can also harm me! I won't lament for anyone else and I don't want anyone to lament for me and I just want to be left alone." This is what every Jew in the ghetto thinks and as one can see—each one lives a selfish life, a life for himself. And so one lives...[103]

The egocentric and escapist impulse to deny the terrible reality or become accustomed to it, to concentrate on the here and now, and to cling to a seemingly normal life characterized the lives of some ghetto inhabitants, mainly the youth. Gerber's diary provides a faithful reflection of the world of youngsters aged between sixteen and twenty-one, trying in their own way to live a normal life in circumstances that were far from ordinary. Most of them entered the ghetto while still school students or just after completing their studies. They worked in various work brigades, even at the airfield, and the danger of being rounded up for work outside the ghetto, which was perceived as a death sentence, hovered over their heads daily. Yet all this did not suppress their appetite for life, their desire for social connections, friendship, love, and other small pleasures. They created close-knit social groups that included several young men and women, they met on a daily basis in their homes (they lived with their parents), next to the ghetto gate, or on the street. The birthday parties they organized were the crowning jewel of their social calendar: they served food, sometimes brought along a record player—which one of them who had connections managed to obtain from his workplace—and played music, sang, and danced. Gerber, who was, in his own words, an expert dancer, explained it this way:

---

103 See the diary entry from October 17, 1942.

> That evening, I wanted to be happy. I had to be happy, because I wanted to forget.
>
> The red light and the simple cheerfulness had a good effect on me; as did the dancing and I danced with everyone. I had to…
>
> The night was beautiful and full of stars. I remembered Heni again—she should have been there today, I thought to myself, but then again, to tell the truth, I wouldn't want her to join the group. Why? I don't know (maybe because she herself doesn't want to).[104]

Heni Shpitz[105] was, for some time, Ilya's great love. The diary records this short-lived and unfulfilled love story, from its beginning until it dwindled. Heni is one of the dozens of young ghetto inhabitants, males and females, that Gerber mentioned in his diary, some of them his good friends, others work colleagues or mere acquaintances. Are they mentioned in the diary as an aside—or did Gerber want their names to be remembered as part of ghetto life, similarly to the names of the more prominent figures in the ghetto? Great effort was invested during the academic editing of this diary in tracing the dozens of characters that appear in the diary, their stories, and their fates, many of them young men and women in the prime of their youth.[106]

The Story of the Diary

Immediately following the war, the survivors of the ghettos in Lithuania—led primarily by survivors from the Vilna Ghetto, the partisans Avraham Sutzkever, Abba Kovner, and Shmerke Kaczerginski—embarked on the task of redeeming the spiritual assets of the Jews and collecting the materials left behind in Lithuania by the Holocaust victims. Naturally, they were occupied mainly with materials about the Vilna Ghetto and the Jews of Vilna, with the intention of establishing in the city a Jewish

---

104 See the diary entry from September 3, 1942.
105 On Heni Shpitz see the diary entry from September 3, 1942.
106 Thanks to the great expertise and help of Hani Gat, who works at the Yad Vashem library in Heichal Yahaduth Wolyn (in Givatayim), it was possible to identify most of them. However, sadly, a significant number, including the diarist himself, were murdered during the Holocaust.

museum to exhibit the Jewish cultural treasures that had survived.[107] Additionally, the Jewish Historical Commission that was established at the time in Vilna contacted people from outside the city, among them Meir Yelin and Dmitriy Galperin, the partisans and writers from Kovno, who passed on to them materials found in the ruins of the Kovno Ghetto.[108] Among the extensive documentation they received were the two surviving notebooks written by Ilya Gerber. As noted, the song notebook came into the hands of Kaczerginski, who included songs from it in the collection he created. However, the third notebook, containing the personal diary, remained shelved in the national archive in Lithuania, and later in the Vilna Gaon Museum of Jewish History. Pages from the diary were first exhibited in the West at the end of the 1990s, following an exhibition on the Kovno Ghetto at the United States Holocaust Memorial Museum in Washington, D.C. Certain pages have been published in English and German,[109] however, this is the diary's first comprehensive edition. Ilya Gerber ends with a wish:

> My last worry while writing these lines is: where I can get a new notebook, a new diary. Ha! Tell me, maybe you know where I can get one? I will be very grateful for this…[110]

Lea Prais

---

107 Concerning the activities conducted immediately after the war ended to save and collect the Jewish cultural assets in Vilna, and about the documentation work, see David E. Fishman, *The Book Smugglers: Partisans, Poets, and the Race to Save Jewish Treasures from the Nazis* (Lebanon: ForeEdge, University Press of New England, 2017). See also Dina Porat, *Me'ever Lagashmi—Parashat Hayav Shel Abba Kovner* (Hebrew) (Tel Aviv and Jerusalem: Am Oved and Yad Vashem, 2000), pp. 198–205.

108 Elizabeth Kessin Berman, "From the Depths: Recovering Original Documentation from the Kovno Ghetto," *Holocaust and Genocide Studies*, 12:1 (1998), pp. 104–106.

109 See Klein, ed., *Hidden History of the Kovno Ghetto*; Zapruder, *Salvaged Pages*; Hoppe and Glass, eds., *Die Verfolgung und Ermordung der europäischen Juden durch das nationalsozialistische Deutschland 1933–1945*, vol. 7, pp. 642–649.

110 See the diary entry from January 23, 1943.

THE DIARY

This is the original illustration as it appears on the front cover of the diary's third notebook.

Ilya Gerber

So It Must Be

The words which I write to you
I write without ink, with tears alone...
The best years are coming to an end,
Nothing came of this love once sown.
Something destroyed is hard to fix,
Our love is hard to unite,
What a pity [are] your words, I swear,
Yet the blame is not mine to bear.
Because so it must be...
So it must be...
We must part, the two of us...
So it must be...
The end of love is in pain.
Do you remember when I met you on the way,
Then fate spoke, declaring,
From me, you must walk away,
On the path to happiness I will not disturb you,
Even though I remain alone...
Because so it must be...
After receiving the letter, I burned it—
Our friendship vanished
Not long our acquaintance, just a bit,
Already our friendship banished...
Something destroyed is hard to fix,
Our love is hard to unite,
What a pity [are] your tears, I swear,
Yet the blame is not mine to bear.
Because so it must be...
So it must be...

Written by Dora*

---

* Dora (Dvora) Rabinovitsh, the sister of Ilik Rabinovitsh, was murdered in the Holocaust; there are no extant details about her. Ilya Gerber included this poem in the opening pages of his diary notebook.

AUGUST 1942

August 26, 1942

A new journal—new Jewish troubles.

Today is already the seventeenth day since I have neglected my writing. Seventeen days! Seventeen days of fear, unrest, panic, and craziness have passed.

As can be seen in my second journal, (on p. 282)[1] the mood in the ghetto was not particularly good. People muttered and spread rumors, saying that soon, in another day, or in another hour, all that will remain of the ghetto will be a mountain of ash. Jews (so it seemed at that moment) were simply in despair regarding how the Kovno Ghetto will be destroyed! Every minute there was a new rumor,[2] a new crisis, a new plague.

---

1 The author, Ilya Gerber, wrote his diary in several notebooks. Unfortunately, the only remaining one is the third notebook presented here. In the original text, Gerber refers to this and other notebooks, as well as page numbers from his writings and illustrations. These references were kept alongside the text of the diary as is for authenticity, although they may not always be accessible. A footnote was added to mark references to the lost notebooks.

2 Gerber often mentioned the phenomenon of rumors, which was widespread in the ghetto. Due to the unique circumstances in which the ghetto inhabitants lived, the culture of rumors was prevalent throughout all the Eastern European ghettos, as Amos Goldberg has discussed at length. Although Goldberg's research focuses on the Warsaw Ghetto, the background and the psychological explanation for the creation of the rumors and the role that they played in the lives of individuals and the general public in a period of radical oppression and enforced isolation are also relevant to this diary. Goldberg, "Rumor Culture among Warsaw Jews under Nazi Occupation," pp. 92–125.

The more people talk, the more they get caught up in the stories. The peasants from the town told the Jews who work there that the camps are already prepared for us, that they had even received documents from their Butai-Skirais[3] [?] entitling them to our ghetto homes. This was one reason for the ghetto brimming with rumors. The second reason for the rumors: The ghetto was full of high-ranking Germans. One after another, the taxis drove around the ghetto and disappeared in a cloud of dust. The Lithuanian general and representative of the Lithuanian people to the Germans, Kubiliūnas,[4] demanded none other than a complete destruction of Lithuanian Jewry. To this end, several high-ranking officials came to the ghetto, such as Cramer,[5] the commandant of Kovno, Rauca,[6] the *Standartenführer* of the Baltic states (renowned for the Great *Aktion*), Lentzen,[7] General Wisocki,[8]

---

3   Lithuanian: the housing department.
4   Petras Kubiliūnas (1894–1946), chief of general staff in Lithuania, led a coup against the Lithuanian prime minister Antanas Smetona in 1934. He was subsequently sentenced to death but was released from prison in 1937. Under Soviet rule he was arrested again and released with the German occupation in June 1941. The Germans appointed him as a senior advisor to the *Reichskommissar* and granted him extensive authority. He remained in this position until 1944. He fled to Germany when the Red Army entered Lithuania. However, he was caught by Soviet agents who extradited him to Moscow, where he was tried and sentenced to death.
5   Hans Cramer (1904–1945), who worked in a printing house, joined the Nazi party in 1928. He reached the rank of *SA-Brigadeführer*, served as mayor of the town of Dachau, and was appointed mayor of Leslau (Włocławek) with the occupation of Poland and its partition. From 1941, he served as head of the civil administration in Kovno and as the city's governor.
6   Helmut Rauca (1908–1983), was an official in a trade house and later a policeman in the Saxonian police force. He became a member of the Nazi Party in 1931. In 1936, he joined the SS and served in the Gestapo in Plauen. From 1941, he was assigned to *Einsatzkommando* 3, under the command of Joachim Hamann. In Kovno, he directed the department for Jewish Affairs at the Gestapo and supervised the selection during the Great *Aktion* that took place in the Kovno Ghetto on October 28, 1941. At the end of the war, he fled to Canada and managed a hotel there. Following the discovery of his identity, he was extradited to Germany but died while the investigation was still underway.
7   Arnold Lentzen (1902–1956), a baker, became a member of the Nazi Party in 1923, and later served in the SA. He was governor of the Kovno district (Kauenland) from August 1942 until the summer of 1944.
8   Lucian Demianus Wisocki (1899–1964), was commander of the police and head of the SSPF (SS und Polizeiführer) in Lithuania.

August 1942

as well as many other journalists.⁹ They comprised the committee which had to consider the Jewish situation in the ghetto and whether it is possible to divide the Jews of Kovno. In short, more taxis [taxes], more committees, and, obviously, also more rumors. The Jewish police continue to run around¹⁰ and shout that people must disperse, they must not stand on the streets, and small children should stay at home.¹¹

The ghetto was a dead city for an entire week. Here and there a person would run by quickly but with time this ceased, too. The ghetto was completely silent. The mood among the ghetto Jews was exceptionally bad. People were simply waiting, impatiently, for our day of judgment. And that day arrived. The German committee went around the entire ghetto, visited the workshops and departments, looked at the gardens and the prettier places. Then the committee left. The next day, they announced that they would only allow goods to be brought into the ghetto until the twenty-sixth of the month. From then on people won't be allowed to bring into the ghetto even 1 gram of produce (this had been talked about for almost an entire month, but now it was confirmed). The way people are talking in the ghetto, it seems like they have already published an order that the Kovno Jews should leave the ghetto within two hours! The situation was that tense. They already established three camps: 1) Behind

---

9   The original word in the Yiddish text means journalists but, in this context, and with the preceding word "other," may imply soldiers.

10 Concerning the Jewish order police that operated in the Kovno Ghetto see the journal written by members of the Jewish police force in the years 1942–1943, which was published in English and in Hebrew. See the Introduction for more information.

11 The journal composed by the Jewish police documents the visit of this German–Lithuanian committee in August 1942, which was headed by General Wisocki and included high-ranking figures. The description indicates that the arrival of the committee aroused great anxiety among the Jews who did not know the aim of the inspection and feared the destruction of the ghetto. The police ordered the ghetto inhabitants to avoid going outside and to congregate in the workplaces, in order to impress the committee and show that the ghetto was efficient and productive. The result of the inspection was a strict prohibition on bringing food and goods from the city into the ghetto, which affected the inhabitants' economic condition. See Schalkowsky, ed., *The Clandestine History of the Kovno Jewish Ghetto Police*, pp. 300–301.

Petrasun,[12] 2) behind Maistas[13] on the hill, and 3) in Versheves.[14] However, until today, the committee discussing "ejecting" the Jews from here has not confirmed anything: at its order, a statement was placed opposite the committee (the labor office) declaring that all rumors regarding the evacuation of the Jewish population from Vilijampolė[15] are false and are not confirmed. The rumormongers must be handed over to the police.[16] The note calmed the ghetto spirits a little. The mood then became lighter and freer.

Three days ago (or perhaps four days ago) a few high-ranking Germans came to the labor office (*Arbeitsamt*) and asked to be shown the cash chest. They found 37,000 marks in the box!

"Why do you need so much money in the ghetto?" they asked.

---

12   Petrasun (Petrašiūnai) is a suburb of Kovno. A forced labor camp was established there, close to military bases. Avraham Tory (Golub) (1909–2002), secretary of the Ältestenrat in the Kovno Ghetto, wrote in his diary on July 30, 1942, "Unfortunately, rumors spread again last week about harsh edicts lying in store for the ghetto after a long period of respite. The rumors say that all the Jews are to be transferred from the ghetto to Petrasun, and that huts are being built there for that purpose." Tory, *Surviving the Holocaust*, p. 116.

13   Maistas, meaning food in Lithuanian, was the name of a large slaughterhouse and factory for the production of preserved meat which belonged to a large Lithuanian company. The factory was located in a suburb of the city of Kovno; women from the ghetto were employed there as forced laborers. A. Tzipkin wrote the Yiddish song *Lid* about the work brigade in Maistas. See Leib Garfunkel, *Kovno Hayehudit Behurbana*, pp. 277–278.

14   Also known as Versheves in Yiddish, and Lampėdžiai in Lithuanian. This was a summer vacation spot close to Kovno, where dozens of Jewish families lived.

15   The Vilijampolė (Slobodka) neighborhood of Kovno, where the ghetto was established, is located beyond the Vilija River. In 1940, its population numbered around 18,000 residents.

16   According to Tory's diary, in the last week of July 1942, rumors spread that the inhabitants of the ghetto should expect harsh decrees, concerning particularly the expulsion of the Jews from Kovno. This news aroused great concern and anxiety, as well as a steep rise in the price of goods. The SD claimed that the rumors were baseless and that they were apparently spread by Lithuanians. "The persons responsible for spreading those rumors will be punished." See July 30, 1942 entry in Tory, *Surviving the Holocaust*, pp. 115–117.

August 1942

Following a brief conversation, the Germans took with them 32,000 marks and left behind 5,000 Reichsmarks for the moment. Yesterday, the twenty-fifth, they also took those 5,000 marks.[17]

It is difficult to describe what happened over the last few days in the ghetto. People were quarrelling and jostling at the ghetto gates. Each one wanted to grab a place in a better brigade[18] to smuggle in goods and to not go hungry, to provide for later, in a more difficult time. People quarrel at the gate, jostle and curse each other (a usual thing in the ghetto). In short, it's crazy...the police tried to restore order. Lipcer,[19] the Jewish Elder of the ghetto (*Oberjude*), *Gestapobrigadier*, and beloved of the SD, also tried to establish order, but even he gets lost in such a crowd. The gate guards, the NSKK[20] men, brandished their whips, slapped backs, and punched "snouts" but the people pay no attention. One falls out of the line, bloody from the German whip—and another takes his place right away. People jostle, people hit—as long as the pulse still throbs, as long as the "I"

---

17   On August 20, 1942, Tory noted in his diary: "At 3 P.M., Köppen and Kaifler came to the Council and confiscated money from the cashbox (31,000 marks). They left only 5,000 marks." Leib Garfunkel later recalled that the sum of 35,000 marks was confiscated but that the council managed to save 25,000 marks and continued managing a cashbox in secret. See Tory, *Surviving the Holocaust*, p. 126.

18   Work brigade.

19   Benjamin (Benno) Lipcer (1896–1944), was born in Grodno. Before the war, Lipcer lived in Kovno and worked as a salesman for a company that manufactured radio sets in Kovno. During the first days of the occupation, he was arrested by the Lithuanians; while imprisoned, even before the establishment of the ghetto, he gathered together a group of craftsmen: tailors, shoemakers, mechanics, and carpenters, and offered their services to the Gestapo. With the German's knowledge and their authorization, he signed documents as the "authorized representative of the SIPO and the SD." At the instruction of the Gestapo and in return for the help he offered, Lipcer was made responsible for the ghetto's labor office. Following the deportation and the murder of another Jewish collaborator, Josef Caspi-Serebrovitz, Lipcer was appointed in charge of the Jewish police. On August 17, 1943, after many months of serving as the de facto head of the police, Lipcer suddenly announced his resignation, although he continued to serve in this role. During the liquidation of the ghetto, in July 1944, he went into hiding together with his family. The Germans discovered his hiding place and shot him. His wife and son survived the Holocaust.

20   Nazionalsozialistischen Kraftfahrkorps (NSKK), the transport unit of the Nazi Party, founded in 1931. During the war, the unit became a paramilitary unit of the German order police (ORPO), and its members were sent to serve in the occupied territories. A unit from Hamburg was stationed in Kovno. The unit arrived in January 1942, and was tasked with guarding the ghetto.

will live. And the people don't care about anything: bread, flour, a bit of vegetables!! I want to live! And I, too, want to live, and I, and I, and I! This call cries out from the despairing eyes, from the movements of the sweaty bodies which jostle and climb over each other unwillingly. I, I will live!

This is how the last few days passed by the gate on Ariogalos Street. So it was, and yesterday was even worse.

The jostling became dangerous. The square, the assembly point for workers, was packed and everyone fought and pushed. The last day! The twenty-fifth! People will no longer be allowed to bring any products into the ghetto! And that day, the last day of being allowed to bring something home for one's family, turned everyone into beasts. Nothing more than the "I" existed. "My children, my wife, they're hungry, they're begging for food: I must bring something for them today!" This was the day's slogan. On the twenty-fifth, a small mission left for the airfield. People (I mean Jews) broke into the brigades, new brigades were created for collecting "rations" (one pays a partisan[21] and goes with him to who knows where, to get hold of something. The ghetto guards viewed it as something necessary and did not prevent it). It was interesting at the airfield—more than half the airfield workers were not at their workstations. Where were they? They paid a partisan, gave him something in his hand, as the saying goes, and he left with small groups of twenty to forty men "to forage." The work gradually stopped. At noon, as usual, the group leader arrived to distribute the 200 grams of bread which they give out in the kitchen for the workers. How great, however, was the latter's wonder, when there was no one to take the bread. Everyone had gone either individually or in groups to villages, through fields or forests, to bring home whatever they could. There is a brigade in Vitshun[22] that includes about ten women. On the twenty-fifth, the last day that one could bring anything into the ghetto, an "army" of 300 women marched off! Seven men from the airfield lined up and went off until they got in back of Marve![23] There,

---

21 Nationalist Lithuanian auxiliary serving the Germans.
22 A suburb of the city of Kovno, on the left bank of the Neman River, home to approximately 300 residents. Known by the Jews as Vichu, and Vičiūnai in Lithuanian.
23 A manor house near Kovno. During the occupation, Jewish laborers from the ghetto were sent there for agricultural work. Among these was Tamar Lazarson-Rostovski. See her diary, Lazarson-Rostovski, *Yomana Shel Tamara*, pp. 41–42.

August 1942

four men rented a farmer's wagon and travelled directly to the ghetto gate with full rucksacks. At the gate, a man from the labor office snuck into the wagon, took hold of the reins with the whip and—voilà! With a crash and a commotion, they entered the ghetto! The other three men were busy in the village for as long as possible and arrived at the ghetto gate exactly at 11:30 P.M.![24] (This is the truth! One of the seven men told me so!)

One could write a whole novel about the 300 women from Vitshun. Twice, a *parokhod* (Russian, for steamer) had to cross from Kovno to Vitshun to take some of the women. When it got late and no steamer wanted to make the crossing, the women remaining in Vitshun raised an "alarm" and their guards, having no other choice, were forced to call for an extra motorboat, to bring the feisty women back to Kovno... These are just a few facts about the events which took place on the twenty-fifth.

Every brigade arrived at the gate with 50 kilograms of flour, potatoes, and "the rest of the vegetables." Whatever was difficult to carry into the ghetto, they hired a wagon from a farmer and, voilà—just like in the good times, and even better. A large military car was positioned at the Varnių gate on August 25. The car's manager [owner] was a friend of Lewerenz[25] (a German, the commander of the ghetto gates). The car stood at the Jews' disposal! Jews paid 1,000 new rubles (100 marks) for it and the car was in the hands of the Jews, they could go and travel in it all the way to America. They drove to the village, packed it to the hilt, returned to the ghetto gate, unloaded the provisions, leaving it waiting for new customers... Since there were always more customers, the fortunate manager called for another six such cars. In short, seven cars drove back and forth on the twenty-fifth.

There was the usual inspection at the gate through which the workers returning from the city must pass. On the last day, however, the "inspectors" began "to not see" the large packs which the Jewish people carried and dragged. However, when a bag was so big that they could not ignore it, they ordered the Jew to remove something. It even happened that they ordered someone to pour out a bit of flour into a sack which was

---

24   A curfew was enforced in the ghetto and Jews were not allowed to be outside after this time.

25   Lewerenz was one of the commanders of the NSKK unit responsible for guarding the ghetto gates.

prepared especially for this purpose. This one pours out, that one pours out, and the general sack becomes full. When the sack is full they take it away with a wagon to the ghetto guardhouse on Stulginskio Street. In short, they ordered a certain young man to pour out some [flour]. The latter turned here and there and tried to run through the gate without taking out any flour. However, they grabbed him. First, they beat him and afterwards they also took his bag from him. This happened more than once. In a similar case, which happened to a friend of mine, they took 30 kilos of corn from him!

Truthfully, people brought a lot into the ghetto, but a great deal was also confiscated. Everything that I described here took place day and night.

The committee has a lot of power concerning trade. First, the "very heartfelt" acquaintance between the NSKK posts and the committee has helped and, second—there is an old rule in the world—when one applies grease,[26] it runs. The committee members have so much money that it really helped them. One wagon after another travelled through the Varnių gate packed full with flour, potatoes, and other produce. Carts, cars, wagons.... As night fell, wagons began to pour out, squeaking and not squeaking; cars with lamps and without lamps—in short, it seemed to me that on the main street of Kovno at that moment there were not enough droshkies [carriages] and "four-legged animals," that is, cars.

Two, three nights in a row, they took provisions to the committee members: Having already prepared for themselves food for who knows how long, they started to bring wood for themselves. And not only them, but anyone who had *smekalka*[27]....In general, he who has money also has brains, and could thus provide for himself. In one word—the ghetto became a city, full of trade and traffic. One person drags flour, another one drags that or the other, all dragging, all carrying, all sweating.... This is how things go: everyone sees the one who dragged [a sack], but the one who didn't drag anything, who had nothing to drag, he always remains in the shadows and darkness and no one sees him, or better put—no one

---

26   Bribe money.

27   The Russian *smekalka* is a colloquial term for the ability to quickly grasp issues, wrap one's head around them, get one's bearings.

August 1942

wants to see him! This is the nature of people today! Almost every home in the ghetto was ready to "usher in" the twenty-sixth! When people had something at home, they were more or less sure that they would not die of hunger. The same was true in Shavli[28] and in Vilna.[29] This is how people live there and, as they say—they have a better life than us.

Everything which I wrote above until now—all this happened until August 26. Now to what happened after that:

From the night between August 25 and 26, the traffic increased even more. At the very last minute before the prohibition, a delivery of flour went through the gate.

On the same night (at about 9 P.M.), the Jewish police went from home to home and again warned the ghetto inhabitants that, from the following day, (August 26) nothing must be brought in, not even in people's pockets. Apart from that, one must not wear any jewelry on their hands, not to mention having money, of course.

August 26, 8 A.M.: Taxis still drive around the *yale veyove*,[30] an old word which exists among us in the ghetto since the airfield became operational. This is a wink to the senior officials who come to inspect the

---

28 On August 25, and mainly on August 29, 1942, entourages of high-ranking officers from the German command of the city of Shavli (Šiauliai) arrived in the local ghetto and conducted close inspections of its environs. They then decided to reduce the ghetto area and demanded that Jewish smugglers be punished with the death sentence. Concerning this episode, see Eliezer Yerushalmi, *Pinkas Shavli: Yoman Migeto Lita'i (1941–1944)* (Hebrew) (Jerusalem: Mosad Bialik and Yad Vashem, 1958), pp. 102–107.

29 At the beginning of September 1942, the Germans raided the gates of the Vilna Ghetto and began a campaign against smugglers returning from work outside the ghetto. See Grigori Shor, *Reshimot Migeto Vilna* (Hebrew) (Tel Aviv: Igud Yotzei Vilna Vehaseviva Be'Israel, 2002), pp. 71–72.

30 Meaning the big shots or overseers. This expression, which was common in the Kovno Ghetto, was coined by Jewish workers at the airfield. The writings of the Jewish police depict it in the following manner: "At work one had to look out so as to rest a little during the few minutes when the bad master turned away. But one had to be careful, or else one could be struck from behind with a shovel; one would pass the word to the others that he was approaching. Since the Germans understood our language [Yiddish], we used Hebrew words. Someone would utter the words *Yale veyavo* [May it ascend and come–the first words of a Jewish prayer] meaning that the master, who walked back and forth around the place, was coming and that one must work. The word *veyavo* was later omitted. The airfield expression also took root in the ghetto: gradually, every senior Jewish official in the ghetto was designated with the word *Yale...*". See Schalkowsky, ed., *The Clandestine History of the Kovno Ghetto Police*, p. 167.

work. When one says *yale veyove* it refers to them and then one immerses oneself [in his work] a little. The *yale veyove* inspect the entire ghetto. So the mood has not yet improved.

I went to the labor office in the morning. A group of people was already standing around a few large signs. I wanted to push in, but I was met with great resistance and had to move back a bit. At that moment a (Jewish) policeman began pushing the group of people which was pressed together, shouting that important people were coming. It was like a bomb had fallen on the group of Jews, because in a second no one was standing there. There was silence. The place opposite the sign became free for me.

The words printed on the sign, in brief, were as follows:

– From the twenty-sixth of the eighth month of this year, the authorities warn that no one may bring any products through the ghetto gates. There must be no trade. Should even the smallest measure of products be found on a person—he risks his life and along with him anyone else coming to the gate will be punished.[31]

– All exchanges of money in the ghetto must cease. Products will be obtained without money, and services, such as using the public bath, will be without charge. In short, using money in the ghetto must officially cease.[32]

– The labor office is strongly prohibited from collecting taxes from the ghetto inhabitants. Thus, from today onward, trade with money is forbidden. The authorities have taken the remaining 5,000 rubles, what was left from the 37,000 rubles (this was also written on the sign...).

As I was reading the sign a droshky went by carrying a few uniformed men and a policeman pushed me away from the sign. I walked a few steps, and then turned around: a taxi (which had just gone by) stopped outside the committee headquarters on Varnių Street. A man in civilian clothes

---

[31] Beginning on August 25, 1942, the Gestapo imposed a strict prohibition on bringing goods into the ghetto. See Tory, *Surviving the Holocaust*, p. 128.

[32] On August 25, 1942, two SA officers who were responsible for the ghetto on behalf of the civilian administration, Köppen and Kaifler, announced that the use of money in the ghetto was henceforth banned and the Ältestenrat was forbidden to deal in it. The order caused difficulties, both for individuals and in the running of the ghetto. See the section "An Economy without Money," in chapter 10 of Schalkowsky, ed., *The Clandestine History of the Kovno Ghetto Police*, pp. 319–321.

August 1942

was the first to exit the vehicle, followed by a few important people with many "toys" on their chests, all wearing the same hats.[33] The last of those exiting the taxi was a Jew. In his hand he held a folder with a wide ribbon around it. They slowly marched into the committee (the labor office). I left. When I came home, my mother[34] told me that Germans from the Gestapo, with a few Lithuanian policemen, are searching homes. The simple people are not afraid: the searches are only conducted among prominent Jewish figures and this is also done according to a list. For example: Lurie,[35] Rappaport,[36] Zakharin,[37] Margolis,[38] and many other members at the labor office. During their search of Rappaport's home (he did not hide things well, the fool...) they found a large quantity of bacon, butter, a lot of sugar and, most of all, flour. They took it away from him. At the homes of the others they only wrote down what they found and sealed up the homes. (There are rumors in the ghetto, which might also be believable, that Margolis has 2,700 weights of flour. In Lurie's home they found approximately 600 weights of flour, but apart from that they did not find anything else. Later they probably restored it, because the seal was removed.) The searches continued not only on August 26 but also on the twenty-seventh and during the twenty-eighth. They were superficial searches.

---

33 On August 25/26, 1942, *Oberscharführer* Ernst Stütz, the Gestapo officer responsible for ghetto affairs, visited the ghetto. See Tory, *Surviving the Holocaust*, p. 129.

34 Rachel Gerber, the diarist's mother, was deported from the Kovno Ghetto to Stutthof in 1944, where she was murdered.

35 Wolf Lurie was an attorney and a manager at the airfield. On July 7, 1944, on the eve of the final liquidation of the ghetto, he refused to leave for Germany and, together with his wife and son, attempted suicide by ingesting poison. His son died a few days later, but the couple remained alive and were shot by the Germans for refusing to leave their home.

36 Rappaport was a member of the nutrition department in the Kovno Ghetto's Ältestenrat.

37 Dr. Benjamin Zakharin served initially as manager of the surgical department in the ghetto hospital and later was appointed as director of the health department in the Kovno Ghetto.

38 Pavel Margolis was responsible for recruitment of workers in the labor office. Known for his harsh character, he stood at the ghetto gate and inspected the workers. After the war, he was tried by the Soviets and sentenced to twenty-five years in prison.

Now something about the rations.

We are not allowed to bring in anything from the city; so what are we supposed to live on, the people of the ghetto asked one another.

"Oh," someone says, "that's no problem. I heard that the ghetto will give every individual a good ration and those that work will receive something from time to time. People say that they will give us the same products which they give to the peasants, which today they give only to the workers—according to the count they will feed us more and better than the Lithuanians. Not bad. We won't die of hunger in the ghetto. You'll see."

This is how people talked between themselves in the ghetto.

An announcement regarding the rations was posted on the fence outside the committee:

The committee (its employees) will receive the following once a week:
> Flour: 112.5 grams
> Meat: 120 grams
> Bread: 700 grams
> Shortening and margarine: 75 grams
> Salt: 50 grams

The ghetto inhabitants who do not work in the city will receive the following rations once a week:
> Flour: 112.5 grams
> Meat: 120 grams
> Bread: 700 grams
> Fat: 20 grams

The airfield workers are given a daily ration of 200 grams of bread. The brigades which work in the city itself make their own collective— that is, they buy products in the city and cook them there. Around forty Jews work in the Metalas factory.[39] They also took four women to work there, as cooks. This is gradually happening in other brigades, too. The

---

39 This, apparently, was a munitions factory in Kovno.

August 1942

situation is good in the children brigades:[40] because they work in the village their ration is 300 grams of bread and a half liter of milk every day! It's unbelievable, but it's a fact!

Yet people maintain that the rations which we receive in the ghetto will improve after August 28.

People waited impatiently by the ghetto gate for the arrival of the working people from the city. Everyone wanted to see whether they would obey the warnings to the working masses and how the NSKK would behave at the gate. The NSKK carried out searches on August 26. They checked everyone's pockets and they found things![41] They found an intestine sausage on one man! He is simply risking his life! The signs warned not to carry anything, threatening the death penalty, and later they also announced this verbally. Eventually people listened in fear! And that little Jew—he risked his life on the very first day! Two guards stood at the gate. One of them was the famous "murderer" and thug Hemfler.[42] He began hitting him with his whip. The second guard, a man who apparently has a heart, took the beaten man from Hemfler's hand, punched him, and shoved him into the ghetto. On the same day, a second person tried to smuggle 2 kilos of butter through the inspections. He succeeded in doing this. When the Jews saw that even though people were caught smuggling they were not killed—the crowd started to feel a bit more confident and people carried things in their pockets. Just now, an order was issued that if someone is caught smuggling in products he will be punished with confiscation of the forbidden things which he was carrying, and, in addition, will spend "three days misfortune in the Jewish prison." But the people aren't afraid. When one doesn't take a risk, one has nothing, so they say, and people hold with this rule.

---

40 On June 14, 1942, 200 young men aged between fourteen and fifteen years old were rounded up to work in agriculture at Marvianka. See Tory, *Surviving the Holocaust*, p. 96.
41 A play on words in Yiddish: *Azoy tapendik hot men oykh dertapt!*
42 Hemfler was an officer in the NSKK.

August 31, 1942

And now, a bit about personal matters.

Exactly three weeks ago I began working in the ghetto as a carpenter in the Vocational School.[43] Before that, I was a loyal airfield worker.[44] I went to work every day, while my former gang had arranged things for themselves: one in the city in a good brigade, another in the ghetto itself, and so on. My papa[45] couldn't bear to watch as I got up at four in the morning, without getting enough sleep and hurrying to work. He tried to employ means to arrange things for me.

---

43   The Vocational School in the Kovno Ghetto was established in March 1942 (over Purim). The founders had previously been employed in Kovno's ORT educational network, under the direction of Jacob Oleisky (for more information on Oleisky see the relevant footnote in the Introduction). The school was initially intended for young men and women aged thirteen and above. In 1942, the school had 150 students. However, by 1944, the number had increased to 440 and the minimum age had been reduced to ten years of age. The school offered instruction in metalwork, carpentry, and sewing.

44   The airfield was located in Aleksotas, a suburb of the city of Kovno, approximately 5 kilometers from the ghetto. The Germans attributed great importance to construction work at the airfield, expanding and renovating it, and this was a significant factor in the continued existence of the ghetto. On September 11, 1941, the first group of 500 Jews left for work at the airfield, and after a few days the number was increased to 1,000 workers per day. In October 1941, 4,500 Jewish laborers were working at the airfield. Due to the dearth of laborers, women and young people were added to the workforce. At first, the workers were transported to the airfield by trucks, but after a few weeks they were required to walk. The work, conducted in shifts (at first three and later two shifts per day), was very exhausting, without any consideration for the weather. As a result of the harsh conditions many sought to escape from this work placement. See Garfunkel, *Kovno Hayehudit Behurbana*, pp. 86–89.

45   The diarist's father was Boris Gerber (1892–1945). Before the war he worked as a singing teacher at the Schwabe Hebrew Gymnasium in Kovno. In the summer of 1944, he was deported from the Kovno Ghetto to the Landesberg Camp, where he died of hunger and exhaustion.

August 1942

On a few occasions my papa submitted requests to the labor office asking them to give me a place in a city brigade or at least arrange some other place for me. But the requests apparently got lost there, since we did not receive an answer to any of them. Then, my papa used the following tactic.

My papa is a singing teacher in the ghetto. That means he works as a teacher here in the two schools which were opened some time ago. Since he gets nothing for the teaching—that is, he derives no benefit from it—he refused to teach singing in the schools. Teachers would come and ask my father to return, but Papa would not be moved. Dr. Shapiro[46] himself came to our house and asked my father to explain why he will not return to teaching (Dr. Shapiro is director of the education department: all the schools are under his authority). My papa had already prepared his excuse: My entire family (by this he meant my brother-in-law Shleyme[47] and me) go to the airfield to work and not one of us goes into the city, while in other ghetto families as many as two men from each family go to the city. I want them to arrange for my son to work either in the city or to be employed here in the ghetto itself. Until this matter is resolved, I refuse to teach, on principle.

Dr. Shapiro took an interest in this matter and he promised my father that he will arrange work for me in the ghetto. A teacher came to our house and submitted a request in my name to the Vocational School asking them to accept me as a carpenter. A short time later I received an order to report to the committee.

I reported to the committee. They called me in, and I entered a beautiful room. Ten men sat around a round table. I recognized Dr.

---

46 Chaim Nachman Shapiro (1895–1943), a Zionist activist, was an educator, an expert on Hebrew literature and philosophy, lecturer at Kovno University, and director of the department of education and culture in the Kovno Ghetto. His father, Rabbi Avraham Duber Shapiro, served as the chief rabbi of Kovno. On December 3, 1943, Chaim Nachman Shapiro was murdered, together with his family, at the Ninth Fort.

47 Shlomo (Shleyme) Kalner (1915–2000), the diarist's brother-in-law, was married to his older sister, Chaya, who was murdered in the Holocaust. Kalner was deported from the Kovno Ghetto to the Dachau concentration camp, together with Ilya Gerber. On the Page of Testimony that Kalner submitted to Yad Vashem, he reported the murder of his young brother-in-law Ilya Gerber on April 28, 1945, close to Wolfsratshausen, near the Förenwald camp.

Shapiro, Oleisky[48] (also a big shot in the Vocational School), and there were many other familiar and unfamiliar faces. From a corner, quite set off on the side, sat a little man with a bald spot which was adorned with a big bump in the middle of his head.

"What is your family name?" I heard a voice from the corner.

"Gerber, Ilya Gerber," I answered, enduring the sharp and unpleasant gaze from the one with the bump.

"Your age?"

"Seventeen," was my answer, although I was a year older.

"Where did you work until now?"

"At the airfield." While answering I produced both my work cards and passed them to him. He considered the expired card and looked at the second, which then, three and a half weeks earlier, already had eight weeks stamped on it.

"Yes, this is the best love letter," he smiles. "And do you have any clue about carpentry?"

"Yes, I more or less understand the trade. I learned once with a certain Segalovitsh."

"Can you make a bench, a stool, a chair on your own?"

"Yes!" was my answer, and at that moment my heart gave a leap from the fat lies I was telling. I, who learned my entire "young life" in school and at the Gymnasium, how could I have learned a trade, especially carpentry?

The man with the bump sitting in the corner asked some questions about work tools. I answered with "half a mouth" as they say, briefly, managing to endure his scrutiny until I heard the words "You can go!"

I had no doubt that I was accepted. I had the best advocate at the table. First: Dr. Shapiro, the director of the education department. And

---

48   Jacob Oleisky (1901–1981), agronomist and chemist, was director of the ORT network in Kovno before the war. He established the Vocational School in the Kovno Ghetto. In 1944, he was deported from the ghetto to Stutthof and subsequently to Dachau. He was liberated in 1945, immigrated to Israel in 1949, and served as director of the network of ORT schools in Israel and as head of the Association of Lithuanian Jews in Israel.

August 1942

second: Attorney Garfunkel![49] The right-hand man to Dr. Elkes,[50] the most respected man in the ghetto, who holds the highest post. Could there be a better application than mine with signatures of the above-mentioned?!
I started acquiring work tools. I bought a frame saw for twenty marks from the master carpenter at the trade school (it looks like this)

and later I purchased a scrubbing plane also for twenty marks, a smoothing plane for thirty marks, and two chisels for fifteen marks. When I came to the trade school, I discovered that the man with the bump is Engineer Freinkel[51] and that he is the director of the Vocational School. The masters and the instructors at the trade school are our acquaintances and this can be helpful. For example, Instructor Peres (a brother of the one who came back from Dvinsk, see the second half of p. 235 under the red line)[52], instructor Tarshish[53], Master Segalovitsh (I used to know his brother, who was also a carpenter, very well), and others.

---

49   Leib Garfunkel (1896–1976), was a lawyer and public activist on behalf of the Jews of Lithuania. A member of the city council of Kovno, representative of the Jews in the Lithuanian Sejm, he was also among the founders of the newspaper *Di yidishe shtime* and was its first editor. Garfunkel was an active member of the Zionist movement. In 1940, under the Soviet regime, he was arrested for Zionist activities and was released upon the German invasion of Lithuania. He served as deputy chairman of the Ältestenrat in the Kovno Ghetto. He was deported to Dachau, but survived the Holocaust. Following liberation, he immigrated to Israel and served as the Cooperative Association Registrar in the State of Israel.

50   Dr. Elchanan Elkes (1879–1944), born in the town of Kalvarija in Lithuania, was a well-known ophthalmologist and a central activist in the Lithuanian Zionist movement. A respected figure in the city's public life, he was chosen by the local Jewish committee, against his will, to serve as chairman of the Ältestenrat in Kovno. In 1944, he was deported from the Kovno Ghetto to Dachau, where he was murdered.

51   This apparently refers to Lazar Freinkel (1900–1945), an engineer, who was deported from the Kovno Ghetto to Dachau, where he was murdered.

52   This refers to a lost notebook.

53   Chaim Tarshish (1910–?), was a professional carpenter and inhabitant of the Kovno Ghetto. He perished during the Holocaust.

I worked there for approximately two weeks. One could really learn something here, but everything comes to an end. Until the twenty-sixth, we, the young, newly enrolled students, made progress in carpentry but, all of a sudden, on the night between August 25 to 26, announcements were published by the committee, stating:

"Following the order of the authorities, all schools without exception (including the Vocational School) will be closed."[54]

This was a blow for us. Should we now stop work midway and go off to the airfield?

I, however, remembered the pieces of paper that the labor office had given us, as certificates confirming that we work at the Vocational School. The first certificate is from the Vocational School. The second is from the police. The latter states that I am not obliged to work six days a week (that means in the city or in the airfield), I am only obligated to work once a week—only on *Shabes* [Shabbat]. The certificate is valid until September 15. This is really not bad, I think to myself. The fifteenth is a long way off and perhaps they will open the trade school again during this time. Everything is possible...

At 8 A.M. on August 26, I went to the Vocational School. The instructors were already there. They explained to us the school's situation and expressed their hope that the school would be quickly reopened.

A few days passed. The school is still closed. They think that tomorrow, September 1, (Thursday), the school will begin to function again, even more extensively. They say that the Germans will check the work that the school produces. The inspector will be a German.

---

54 On August 25, 1942, Köppen and Kaifler ordered the closure of all schools in the ghetto. The second part of this order stated that all existing schools in the ghetto were to close immediately and all those employed in them were to be transferred directly to forced labor deployment (*Arbeitseinsatz*). See Tory, *Surviving the Holocaust*, pp. 128–129.

August 1942

A Tale about a Beach

A beach in the ghetto?[55] We were talking about this in the *shtetl* when the ice still decorated the banks of the Vilija. It was unbelievable. Jews also need a beach? Are we also considered humans? This, indeed, was interesting. This year [the weather] was not normal but perfectly suited to the bizarre, sick times. At times cold, then warm, and vice versa. People shrugged their shoulders, turned their eyes to the heavens, and did not understand whether it is winter or spring, or whether it is summer or fall!

I remember wintertime, in the morning, there was a terrible scathing wind with snow, peoples' noses, cheeks, and ears were frozen, but by 12 or 1 o'clock people had to slowly take off their coats. When summer came, I remember, people went to work with high fur collars. In the morning they shivered as if with fever and within a few hours—a heat wave, a steam bath.... But recently, God above has finally put the weather in order—the beach season has opened. People didn't hold a ceremony, no glasses were raised; rather, it was a very quiet opening. People came, undressed, bathed, got dressed, and left looking exactly how they did when they arrived.

The best thing about it is that when one comes to the beach one forgets the situation in which we find ourselves, one is happy, one frolics about, one does a bit of sport... It is fine weather, so the beach is full of Jews— you can't find room to fit in a pin. Little kids, adults, and also old Jewish men and women, they all come. They swim, they splash around—as one should.

The "bath" is ideal for the airfield workers. One returns from work dusty and exhausted; a bit of cold water, a beach, refreshes the working man. Young people find in this pleasure and a way to pass the time (they do not go to school, after all). The grown-ups have dates on the beach (also a pleasure) and old Jews come to refresh themselves sometimes— that too is no sin. People remember the good times of their past, their youth, and try to recapture their former vitality. The beach is a pleasure and provides enjoyment for everyone.

---

55   For more details about the beach see Schalkowsky, ed., *The Clandestine History of the Kovno Ghetto Police*, p. 299. See also September 6, 1942 entry in Tory, ed., *Surviving the Holocaust*, p. 132.

Ilya Gerber

The time for bathing is from 5 o'clock in the evening until 8 o'clock. But the youth don't pay attention to this. They come and go as they please.

Recently, people in the ghetto are saying that from September 1, bathing in the Vilija will be prohibited. First, as a result of the darkness. As the days are already much shorter and the nights are the opposite, they stretch out in their length and breadth, and the authorities fear that under the cover of darkness people will be able to escape via the water to the other side of the Vilija. Do you think that this has not happened yet? A few Jewish policemen swam (they really only waded—since this year the Vilija is very shallow) across the water. They conducted a lengthy conversation with peasants on the other side and then returned.

People also swim over to our side, the ghetto side, to visit. A while ago a man swam across the Vilija dragging along a little suitcase in his hand. The police noticed him and handed him over to the ghetto guard, the NSKK. People say that the swimmer is a Russian fighter, a paratrooper.

On another occasion, pranksters came to visit the ghetto beach. The Jewish police also took them to the NSKK. A Jew arrested the superior, the Lithuanian. Is that not funny?

I am also a regular, daily visitor and beach devotee. I find here freedom, the vivacity of youth, and respite from the ghetto sounds. The ghetto sounds do not reach the beach. Here one bathes, "a carefree youth," and knows nothing of bad things. One grabs what one can, when one can.

Even the *shtetl* nobility come here. On Friday, almost the entire staff of the labor office, Lipcer, and many other important people, too. In that moment, as they stand almost completely naked, exactly like the other simple people at the beach, they could almost be the same. This is a Jew and that one is a Jew. One people! One armband covers both the simple airfield worker and the *shtetl* elite. And yet so separated, so divided! Why is it thus? Can the Almighty not make this people, His people condemned to death, equal? Why can the beach accomplish this? It makes everyone equal for a moment: all are half naked, here. One sees no patches [armbands], no privilege [distinction]! Everyone is in one "bath"— everyone is in the same water! Here one seems to see a naked people without differences—one nation.

SEPTEMBER 1942

September 1, 1942

1942. IX. 1 —

I got up early today and went to the Vocational School. Some of the younger guys were already there. Some of my friends also arrived later. We talked about the reopening of our school. One of these days it will certainly reopen, Master Peres said to us. Nu, we can only hope.

Now, a bit of world news.

According to German reports, the Russians are launching big assaults on the Eastern Front, in particular at Rzhev[56] (200 kilometers from Moscow), and in Kuban. The Russians, the newspaper notes further, have no regard for people or material [needs]. Their assault stretches from the Caucasus to Leningrad. Every week there are rumors in the ghetto that the Russians have broken through the front in Leningrad. In Rzhev, the Russians are said to have taken 45,000 SS men as prisoners.

In the past week, Russian airplanes have become frequent guests "among us in Kovno."[57] They are here almost every night. They have

---

56 During World War II, Rzhev was occupied by German troops from October 14, 1941, until March 3, 1943. During this occupation, the general area of Rzhev was the site of a series of major military conflicts between the Red Army and German military forces.

57 This was part of the Siniavino Offensive, an operation planned by the Soviet Union in the summer of 1942, that was intended to break through the Siege of Leningrad. The main Soviet offensive was on the Volkhov Front. This offensive lasted from the morning of August 27 until September 9, 1942.

not done any damage here or near Kovno. It seems that they are not interested in bombing here. They fly to Memel, Königsberg.[58] They have also reached Great Berlin and have bombed the suburbs.

It is very quiet at 9 and 10. The siren, sounding the alarm, is also late again. I recall that standing near the committee, suddenly at 10 P.M., I heard the noise of a plane high up in the sky. I lifted my head, but nothing was visible. A few minutes later the alarm sounded. The siren whistled and grated. I ran home with all my strength even though the evening was quite pleasant for me.

Western Front! Eastern Front! Northern Front! Southern Front! From all four directions a battle is now underway against National Socialism, against the Führer, driving the German people to defeat, to eternal darkness. Down with him—so long as you have where to retreat![59] Throw off the bloodshedder and then there will be happiness in the world. If not—a complete destruction of the Third Reich! There will be no feelings of mercy! Your fate lies in your hands. Make your decision: a content, peaceful life, but one without mass murder, or a complete destruction of the Führer together with the people! The battle continues and intensifies! The moment of the Führer's defeat is drawing closer! The German people will say their word. The final one!

Such proclamations were dropped on Kovno by the Russian airplanes on Friday.

Battles are underway in Yugoslavia[60] between the "local thugs"[61] and the Germany military. According to German reports, they have taken

---

58 On August 27, 1942, Soviet bombers attacked Königsberg, East Prussia, Germany. From August 7 to September 5, 1941, Soviet bombers that arrived from the Island of Saaremaa, which is situated not far from Tallinn, repeatedly attacked Berlin and its outskirts. See Miroslav Morozov, *Torpedonostsy Velikoi Otechestvennoi: Ikh zvali "smertnikami"* (Moscow: Kollektsiia Iauza, Eksmo, 2011), pp. 63–65.

59 This possibly means that the German people should dispose of Hitler while they still have their country, to which they can retreat.

60 On April 6, 1941, the German army invaded Yugoslavia. The invasion commenced with heavy bombing of Belgrade, which lasted for several days. German, Italian, Hungarian, and Bulgarian forces occupied Yugoslavia and divided the country between them. After the battles between the regular armies concluded, local forces embarked on large-scale partisan warfare against the occupiers that lasted until 1945.

61 Presumably partisans.

September 1942

prisoner 2,000 "robbers" who tried to disturb the peace of the land and terrorized the poor population...

Since the war with the Soviet Union began, people have started talking about a second front. People have been discussing it quite a lot. They also gesticulate with their hands, obviously, everyone proclaiming their opinion about it until people determined that a second front can be useful. Again and again—the English, with the help of the Americans, Canadians, and some other "savage nation" have united all together and tried to come ashore on the French coast at Dieppe.[62] The Germans report that the attack was very well prepared and that the first blow more or less succeeded. In five places along the coast at Dieppe the English soldiers tried to come ashore but succeeded in only two places. The Canadian leadership made a good show, although sixty officers fell prisoner into the hands of the Germans. Already from the outset the German sea batteries saw from afar an entire convoy of cargo ships, cruisers, armored ships, and other "sea animals" that were supported by hundreds of planes. The Germans shot down over 100 iron birds. While far-reaching English cannons shot from the sea at the German land fortifications and the first "Tommy" airplanes (English) shot at the coast from up high, the quick and light little English military ships packed with English soldiers attempted to reach the French coast. In several places the English were able to penetrate deep into the land while the tanks and armored vehicles that had disembarked on the coast tried to clear a way through for them. And so the English and Canadian soldiers penetrated 25 kilometers deep into the dry land, to the city of Dieppe.

The Germans received reinforcements and launched a counter-offensive. One cannon, which was positioned at a good strategic point, without any help, destroyed forty-eight tanks and armored vehicles, the newspaper reports. The German soldier stood at his post and even in the tragic minutes did not abandon his position—he fought for the security of the French people, he fought for the victory of the Führer and the German people, the newspaper concludes. The battle for the French coast lasted for

---

62   A port on the English Channel, at the mouth of the Arques River. It was the site of a terrible battle for the Allies during World War II. On August 19, 1942, Allied soldiers landed at Dieppe in the hope of occupying the town for a short time, gathering intelligence, and drawing the Luftwaffe into open battle. The Allies suffered more than 1,400 deaths; additionally, 907 Canadian soldiers were killed, and 1,946 Canadian soldiers were captured.

nine hours. Such and such number of prisoners were taken, the newspaper states in an additional report, and now not one enemy foot remains on our land! The attempt to open a second front was a complete failure!

Rumors were recently spread in the ghetto that the English have lost two further landings, in France and in Norway. I don't know to what extent this is true. I haven't read any newspapers recently. Although it seems to me that this doesn't fit with reality.

Today, September 1, the fourth company of the NSKK, our guards in the ghetto, left the Jewish *shtetl*, where they had it really good, and departed for the front.[63]

It happened at 2 o'clock. Our former NSKK guards stopped at the ghetto gate. They were accompanied by two young, blonde, Jewish women. There they had to bid farewell. They were brought something—probably a present from the labor office. Lewerenz, the gate commander, lifted

---

63 Tory recorded in his diary that the NSKK unit left the ghetto on August 30, 1942, see Tory, *Surviving the Holocaust*, p. 130. Following its departure, responsibility for guarding the ghetto was assigned to Lithuanian policemen under the command of Viennese Schupo officers. The text composed by the Jewish police in the Kovno Ghetto notes that the unit left at the end of September 1942. See Schalkowsky, ed., *The Clandestine History of the Kovno Ghetto Police*, pp. 278–279.

September 1942

up one young woman off her feet in front of everyone and, disregarding the Lithuanians, who were standing around and watching, began to kiss her. A second German kissed the other young woman. A third, watching how his friends—Germans—have no regard for the severe law about racial humiliation,[64] apparently his heart was saddened and he ran off... Looking now at these Germans, who are sentenced to death, who must travel to the front, it was hard to tell that for a year and half they had had the power to whip and kill a Jew for wanting to bring home a bit of bread. They, who beat people with their whips—they now weep, they now kiss Jewish young women, having no shame to publicly transgress and pay no attention to the Führer's laws.

The Lithuanian police now remain as the ghetto guards. People say that this will be only temporary. And after them, the Vienna Protective Police (*Schutzpolizei*) will come.

* * *

In the last few days, people have nevertheless brought some things into the ghetto, usually in their pockets (if someone has a lot of things, he hides them on his back, on his stomach, or elsewhere).

On September 1, at 2:30 P.M., a brigade arrives at the gate. About ten steps from the gate the Jewish workers arrange themselves, one behind the other in rows, and approach the inspection. Two Lithuanian policemen stand at the gate. The first in line stopped right by the Lithuanian policeman. At that moment he took out a pack of cigarettes and turned to him. "Do you smoke?" The Lithuanian took the present with a smile and the brigade went into the ghetto undisturbed.

The clock on the gate has changed. It shows 4:05 P.M. A brigade of ten men arrived. It stopped at the gate.

"Who has cigarettes?" asks the policeman

Silence, no one answers.

"No one has any?" he asks again.

Silence. Not a word.

The inspection began. He double-checked the flares of the trousers.

---

64 On the decree concerning racial shame, see Marion A. Kaplan, *Between Dignity and Despair: Jewish Life in Nazi Germany* (New York and Oxford: Oxford University Press, 1998), pp. 45–46.

September 3, 1942

Yesterday was Ida Santotski's[65] birthday. Our group had already been preparing for some time. What does it mean preparing? We didn't prepare anything substantial, but we had been talking about it a lot...
Since we are already talking about birthdays, I will write a bit about this. Our group is made up of seven people. I will list the group again: The women are Ida Santotski, Dora Rabinovitsh, Lyusya Maniewitz,[66] and the guys are Avremke Tiktin,[67] Izke Kagan,[68] Ilik Rabinovitsh,[69] and myself. Occasionally we also include Abrashke Levin.

---

65 Ida Santotski/Santocki (1927–1944), was burned to death in her hiding place during the liquidation of the Kovno Ghetto. A Page of Testimony in her memory was submitted by her sister, Zlata Santotski-Siderer, who is also mentioned in the diary. See Ida Santotski/Santocki, Page of Testimony, Yad Vashem, The Central Database of Shoah Victims' Names, Hall of Names, Item no. 611854.

66 This apparently refers to Shulamit Maniewitz, born 1924, who lived in the Kovno Ghetto during the war. In 1944, she was deported to the Vaivara camp in Austria, where she was murdered. Her mother, Esther Maniewitz, submitted a Page of Testimony in her memory: Shulamit Maniewitz, Page of Testimony, Yad Vashem, The Central Database of Shoah Victims' Names, Hall of Names, Item no. 364783.

67 Avraham Tiktin, born 1924, was murdered in the Holocaust. See the Page of Testimony submitted by his uncle: Avraham Tiktin, Page of Testimony, Yad Vashem, The Central Database for Shoah Victims' Names, Hall of Names, Item no. 8879149.

68 Israel (Izke) Kagan attempted to escape from the ghetto in 1944. In his memoir, Arie Segalson wrote the following about him: "He studied at the Hebrew Gymnasium in Kovno and was a member of the underground Irgun Brit Zion (ABZ, in Hebrew). The home of the Kagan family was next to the fence that surrounded the ghetto. One day, without telling his parents and sister, he left home and started going through the fence to the other side. Unfortunately, a passing German guard noticed and shot him a few times. He was wounded while half of his body was already over the fence. His father was at home and heard the shots. When he went out to see what had happened, his son was already dead. His funeral was quiet and restrained..." See Segalson, *Belev Ha'ofel*, p. 401

69 Ilik Rabinovitsh and his sister Dora Rabinovitsh were both murdered in the Holocaust.

September 1942

It started with me. My birthday was on July 23 (see volume II, p[?])⁷⁰. That entry shows that they regard me as a good friend, and they showed their friendship on that day.

The second birthday, chronologically, was that of Ilik Rabinovich (on August 19. Ilik, who is a year older than me, turned 19). They celebrated that birthday at home. I gave him a greetings' letter on behalf of our group. There was cake with cream, pastry, biscuits, sweets, beer, schnapps, cigarettes, gooseberries, not to mention coffee. There were also LP records (Russian, English, and German). Lights of any color you could want. You want red lights? We had it. Blue? We had blue… In short, it was really cheerful. I smoked a lot. On the evening of my birthday celebration, which the girls had arranged in my honor, there was no record player, but that did not stop them: they stomped their feet, clapped their hands, clicked their tongues, and smacked their lips. In short, there was a good beat and the group also danced. At Ilik's party there was lots of dance music (it seems that he brought the records from the Gestapo)⁷¹, but no one danced. Why? Because Abba Rabinovitsh left with the first 530 men for work.⁷² Ilik swore not to dance. And no one felt like dancing.

The third birthday was Ida's. At about 8 P.M., Izke and I came to her home. The light in the house was red (apparently because Ilik had brought the red lamp). The mood was good. The group included Ida's parents,⁷³ of course ("underworld youths"⁷⁴), and her sister, Zlata, who is older than

---

70 This refers to a notebook that is lost.
71 Ilik Rabinovich worked in a Gestapo workshop in Kovno.
72 "A demand came to the Elder Council on August 15, [1941], to provide by seven o'clock on the morning of August 18, 500 young men of good appearance. […] Many volunteers signed up, because their conscience dictated that when Jews were required to provide workers, they should not stand on the sidelines […] On the morning of August 18, Germans and Lithuanian partisans came to take away the people. It turned out however, that the quota was not fulfilled; […] Their exact fate has not become known to us, much as with all the other gruesome acts against us that still remain unknown to us." See Schalkowsky, ed., *The Clandestine History of the Kovno Ghetto Police*, pp. 83–84.
73 Yankel Santotski, Ida's father, born 1903, was murdered in Dachau. Eta Santotski (née Zivov), Ida's mother, born 1905, was murdered in Stutthof.
74 *Blateyungen* in Yiddish (influenced by the Russian language). Probably means acting like young people, go-getters, who are in the know. My thanks to Vicky Shifris.

her. Nekhomele[75] and Genya,[76] also sisters, and Lyusya Maniewitz, Dora Rabinovitsh, another young woman or girl, eighteen years old (we knew each other but I don't remember her family name, it has slipped my mind, never mind), Asya, a young woman aged nineteen or twenty, of ample figure and short in stature (like most Jewish women), who sings beautifully and can dance well. More women arrived later: a certain Riva, a very proud woman, with a haughty face, like a white ruler, sitting stiffly, as though to say: Don't touch me (so it seemed, although I think it was the opposite...). There was also a female neighbor, likewise a short young woman but more cheerful. From our group were present: the most important pal (from Ida's side)—Avremke Tiktin (he gave her a beautiful bag with a red heart in the middle, quite romantic), Izke Kagan, Ilik Rabinovitsh, Danke Liberman[77] (Zlata's date, a cheerful fellow, who knows the art of tap dance and is a good partner). There was another young man, twenty years old, a handsome guy, with a dark complexion, and he was the one who brought the records that evening (he brought twenty-four records).

The pink or red lights kindled a good mood amongst us all (possibly because the lamp was indeed red and not another color...) [There was] coffee with pastry and cake (or babke—it's all the same) and while the physical space was tight, the mood was good and the snacks were happily consumed.

"Are you on form today?" Ida asked me.

"Yes, today yes!"

I danced the first tango with Lyusya. To be honest, I feel a sympathy toward her. The sympathy of a friend, the feeling of a male friend toward a female friend. I know about her life in the ghetto until today: her sorrows, too. And, therefore, I sympathize with her more than with her

---

75 Nechama (Nekhama) Santotski-Shneerson, born 1929, was deported from the Kovno Ghetto to Stutthof in 1944, but survived the Holocaust. See her testimony, Yad Vashem Archives (YVA), O.93/8842.

76 Genya Santotski, born 1933, was murdered during the Holocaust. See ibid., and the testimony submitted by her oldest sister, Zlata Santotski-Siderer. Genya Santotski, Page of Testimony, Yad Vashem, The Central Database of Shoah Victims' Names, Hall of Names, Item no. 1999217.

77 According to the testimony of Nechama (Nekhama) Santotski-Shneerson, her oldest sister, Zlata, married in the ghetto. It is reasonable to presume that she married Daniel (Danke) Liberman. See Nechama Santotski-Shneerson testimony, YVA, O.93/8842.

September 1942

other friends: not because I consider them inferior but rather because I empathize with her. She has suffered and perhaps still suffers, and I know her sorrows—because I also suffered once...

I was really on form. I danced dance after dance, I wanted to be happy. Why? I wanted to forget an unforgettable thing: her...(more about "her" another time). Ida requested a quick foxtrot. The dance was successful. Asya (see p. 328, 11th line) also asked me to dance. I tried to "celebrate"...

Lyusya, who for a long time has been distant from Abrashke Levin, and who that night made up with him, didn't dance too badly. Ida danced beautifully, as did Dora. That evening, Ilik tried to dance for the first time in the entire period that we have been in the ghetto. Izke danced a bit like a drunk; Avremke danced and wanted everyone else to dance but did not manage every time; mostly, he unwillingly pushed someone, trying to bend someone over, but it doesn't matter, it was cheerful. There was a sense of friendship. The guy who brought the records (see [p.] 320, 2nd line) also danced well and easily. He is a very sympathetic guy and young women like him.

At around 9:30, Abrashke Levin decided to go to the police department and persuade some of the policemen to come to Ida's later and accompany us home,[78] because some of the guys thought they would go home later. Abrashke and I left at 10. I went in the direction of our block, to inform them at home that I would be coming back later than usual. Going past the fire station (at 22 Vytenio Street) I noticed two familiar faces: Heni[79] and Misha Yatkunski[80] (they live together in the same apartment). I stopped opposite them.

"Why so fast? Did you fight with them?" asks Heni.

---

78   According to the German order published on January 26, 1942, inhabitants of the ghetto were forbidden to be outside after 9 P.M. See Tory, *Surviving the Holocaust*, p. 67. According to the text written by the police, the prohibition began at 8 P.M. In June 1942, many broke the curfew order, and the police was forced to arrest those walking around the streets after 10 P.M., and to punish them. This is apparently the reason that the young people sought the protection of the police in this case. See Schalkowsky, ed., *The Clandestine History of the Kovno Ghetto Police*, pp. 353.

79   Heni Shpitz (Yofe), was born in 1925, in Klaipėda (Memel), Lithuania. After the annexation of Klaipėda by Nazi Germany, in March 1939, she fled to Kovno with her father. She was deported from Kovno to the Stutthof concentration camp in 1944. She survived the Holocaust. See the letter she wrote to the ITS (International Tracing Service database, TID 124582).

80   Misha Yatkunski, born 1923, was murdered in the Holocaust.

"No! I am going home to tell them that I will only be coming back later." She looked a bit angry to me.

At home I told them that I would be back an hour later. I did not see Heni again on my way back. It annoyed me a bit. I wanted to talk to her about something.

That evening, I wanted to be happy. I had to be happy, because I wanted to forget.

The red light and the simple cheerfulness had a good effect on me, as did the dancing and I danced with everyone. I had to...

I danced a tango with Ida.

"How do you like me tonight?" (At the time I misunderstood, it seemed that she had said: "How do you like it here today...") she asked.

"Very well."

"That can't be!" I hear her voice close to me.

"Very well," I said again

"That can't be!" I hear her voice close to me. "That can't be!" she repeats a few times. The tango came to an end.

"How do you like the tall, handsome young man?" I ask her, indicating to the guy who brought the records.

"I don't like him so much—only enough for dancing," was her answer.

Our friends made merry until around 10:30 P.M. No police came. Lyusya, Dora, her brother Ilik, and Izke bade everyone farewell. They all left together, wishing Ida and her parents all the best.

Avremke, Abrashke (the guy who brought the records), and Danke Liberman remained. I waited for them, because we all go to the blocks in the same direction. We were still making merry. The record player (Mrs. Zelder's[81]) was still playing. Around 11 P.M. someone knocked on the door, but so politely that it was nothing like the Jewish policemen. The place went silent. Everyone looked around, scared. Avremke, who was sitting near the door cast a frightened look at Abrashke and asked him to go and open the door (we thought at that moment that Germans were behind the door and Abrashke can speak German well). No one moved. Mrs. Santotski took a step toward the door. I followed her. She opened it. At that moment two Jewish policemen entered!

---

81 No extant information was found about her.

September 1942

"Work cards ready!" they said. "See how cheerful it is here," one said to the other.

We were around twelve people in the room and everyone's documents were in order. They left. The hidden records were taken out again and the record player started spinning again. Among all the Yiddish records we liked the *Lebedik Yankel*[82] album the best. At 11:45 P.M. I danced the last dance with Ida, a quick foxtrot. Abrashke Levin sang a beautiful Yiddish medley of folk songs for ten minutes. We all bid farewell in a friendly manner and parted ways. Danke and the guy who brought the records went to the right and Abrashke, Avremke, and I went straight in the direction of the blocks.[83]

The night was beautiful and full of stars. I remembered Heni again—she should have been there today, I thought to myself, but then again, to tell the truth, I wouldn't want her to join the group. Why? I don't know (maybe because she herself doesn't want to).

After we had gone a little way from Ida's, we heard voices in Yiddish.

"Who goes there?!" The three of us heard a voice. In the brightness of the night we made out the armbands of the Jewish police.

"Police," answered Avremke. We walked a few steps. Abrashke made a few jokes in German.

"Come and let us see who is there!" we heard from behind us the same, familiar voice.

We stopped. The three policemen approached us with papers in their hands.

"Ah! Alyoshke! It's you?" I called out, recognizing Alyoshke Levin, the policeman.[84]

---

82 *Lebedik Yankel* was a popular song in Warsaw in the 1930s. The melody for the song is a folk tune, better known from the song *Hanukah hoy Hanukah*, or, in its popular form, *Yemei HaHanukah*.

83 The blocks in Slobodka were first built by the Lithuanian government and later by the Soviet authorities as workers' quarters. The large blocks were three-story brick buildings consisting of twenty-four dwellings, equipped with modern conveniences. The more affluent echelons of the Jewish population lived there. There were apartment blocks, that, once inhabited, consisted of mixed populations. See Schalkowsky, ed., *The Clandestine History of the Kovno Ghetto Police*, p. 103.

84 This appears to refer to the policemen Lazar (Alois) Levin, born 1922 (or 1921). He was deported from the Kovno Ghetto to Stutthof and from there to Dachau. He survived the Holocaust.

"Go home 'children,'" he said to us, "a Lithuanian patrol might come by any minute."

So off we went. The three of us parted next to the blocks. I went into the stifling room where we, five people from our family, sleep.[85] Outside it remained a beautiful, starry night...

September 5, 1942

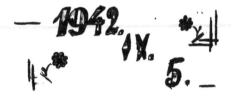

Yesterday, September 4, for the first time in a week, or should I say, for the first time since August 26, I worked at the Vocational School. Master Peres had us (Shike Bernstein and me) make an extra [word unclear ...] for the directors. We immediately set to work. I have a bit of trouble with Shike: he wants to make things but he can't. I need to constantly watch his work. I had to redo his work on more than one occasion. He is unable to calculate by himself. Mostly, however, we do get by. What if I were in his place and I was not able to do anything well? I put myself in his position and watch over him. Sometimes he gets irritated when I show him the mistakes in his work and teach him how it should be done properly. But it's nothing. He needs us and I don't push him aside. We both work at the same table. I cannot bear the gnarled school director. He wanders around, too much like an "evil dragon"...

At lunchtime (we have from 12 noon to 1 P.M.) I went home (this was all yesterday). I ate quickly, then went to Heni's home. Lubetski was already there. He gave a reading of his own poems in German, Lithuanian, and Yiddish. His *Ghetto Freylekhs* [cheerful tunes] sound very beautiful.

---

85   Gerber in his diary takes a look at the living conditions of a Jewish family in the Kovno Ghetto.

September 1942

He left. Heni stayed with me in the room. We planned to go out for a walk at 8 P.M. (We meet very often, to be more exact, every day).

That day I went to the beach at 6 P.M. Heni was also there. She told me that she would probably be busy that evening, she had to go somewhere. That evening we were all together (I mean the seven of us, old friends). I felt very bad.

Around 8:30 P.M., while having a good time in the little garden at Lyusya's, we heard the hum of planes: the noise of the motors announced that these were Russian bombers. "Where have the sirens gotten to today?" we asked each other....

From the side of the airfield we notice red rockets. Have they made a mistake at the airfield thinking that these are their own German planes? It's hard to understand. We said goodbye to one another. Izke with Dora and Ilik turned to the right, past the ghetto guards. Avremke, Ida, and I went to Vytenio Street. As we made our way there the sirens suddenly whistled and screeched from all three sides. Police ran around screaming, ordering people to put out their lights. Avremke went off with Ida. I went home on my own (not running, God forbid).

When I came home, I found my papa had just finished covering one window and my brother-in-law was at the other window, which was now covered.

"Put on the light," my father turns to me.

The place filled with light. My sister went outside to see whether the light was showing outside.

"Cover a bit underneath," we heard my sister's voice saying to my brother-in-law. "That's good. Now it's good. No. A bit more to the side, a bit more," she instructs from outside and Shleyme, inside, does as she says. A step away from the window and one could not see any light; but standing right by the window one could indeed see something. At that moment a policeman went past. He quickly ran to our entrance.

"Put out the light!" cried my sister from outside. "A policeman! A policeman is coming."

Our home became dark. In the corridor we could hear fast and firm footfalls. The door gave a crash.

"Put on the light!" we heard a nervous voice.

"Put it on, you hear!" the voice came again, when the order was not carried out punctually.

Shleyme, who was standing barefoot on the sofa, put on the lamp (in the darkness he had jumped onto the sofa from the window. The sofa stood right up against the wall, opposite the door).

"What is your family [name]!" the blond (perhaps even yellow) policeman shouted at Papa.

"Gerber," answers Papa. "Why?"

"Tomorrow you will go to the police station to get the lamp!" And at that moment two things happened: First, the door opened, and my sister Chaya came into the room. And second, at that moment, the policeman turned off the lamp.

"What's the number on your hat?" We heard my sister's voice in the darkness.

"None of your business!"

"No, first tell us your number," my brother-in-law added.

The policeman grabbed the door handle and tried to open it.

I came from the side and barricaded the door with one foot.

"First tell us your number! Then you can go."

"It's none of your business what my number is! Are you starting a rebellion?!" The policeman thundered and at the same time stormed the door. But the door did not give way. My brother-in-law from the sofa together with me held the door against the policeman.

Suddenly the clattering at the door stopped. A match was struck in the darkness of the room. Shleyme was holding a match in his hand and looking at the policeman's number, which was on his hat. The policeman bent down to the ground and looked for his hat.

"113," called out my brother-in-law. "Take it, here's your hat." He turned to the policeman. The latter angrily grabbed the hat from my brother-in-law's hand and ran out of the door. No one disturbed him. We knew the number—113!

"You haven't heard the last of me!" we heard from afar the voice of the angry policeman…

Our home was silent for a moment. "You think that because you wear a patch you are so privileged?" my sister screamed after him.

We didn't hear an answer.

September 8, 1942

I saw her in the city. She was mostly in another group, always happy (so it seemed to me, looking from the side) and cheerful. I found out her name and surname and looked at her as one does at a beautiful girl. But to say that I liked her a lot already then, that I can't say, because I didn't know her well. Passing by her, I looked at her, just like my friends back then (some of them do now, too). One look, one little moment of admiration, a strong beat of my heart, and that's it, like it never happened. But nevertheless...

HS is the acronym for Heni Shpitz.

September 10, 1942

On September 6, I received notification at home that I must report to work at the airfield on September 7 through September 12.

When I arrived at the assembly point, Lurie, the supervisor in charge of the airfield, put me in the brigade of youngsters who received similar notes. We were the last to leave the place. We were accompanied by Hirsh, the shift manager. He took us to the Schultz Dobrick[86] company for light work. Our work brigade is comprised of sixty young guys (ranging in age from nine to twenty), mostly students from the Vocational School. The mood was good, with lots of joking around. The work was light—carrying rails! But that day we were allowed to go home at four in the afternoon (because on the seventh they didn't give out any bread at the airfield). On September 8, we again went to work at Schultz Dobrick. The work, again, was light—leveling a hill. We left work at half past five, arriving in the ghetto around 7 o'clock.

Yesterday, on the ninth, we again worked at the same firm. The group was a happy one, and comprised of Zerubavel,[87] Zshezshmorski, Shleyme

---

86   Each section of the airfield was assigned to a particular German firm. One of these was Schultz Dobrick. According to the Jewish police, the work there was not very hard. See Schalkowsky, ed., *The Clandestine History of the Kovno Jewish Police*, p. 166

87   This refers to Zerubavel Rosenzweig (1926–2000). He was a member of the Irgun Brit Zion movement in the Kovno Ghetto, and was transported from the ghetto to Dachau. After he was liberated from Dachau he immigrated to Israel. I would like to thank his late sister, Mrs. Rachel Levin, for this information.

Finkelstein,[88] and me, and we made a cheerful group. The work again is light and we lay around in the grass most of the time. On the way back to the ghetto after work (at around 6:30) I started to feel unwell: my legs became weak and started to give way, my head hurt, and I was dizzy. Arriving in the ghetto, meaning at home, I ate and took my temperature. It was 37.7 Celsius. The clock showed that it was after 7:30. The doctor at the office [labor office?] receives patients until 8 P.M. I went to him, but he wouldn't see me. They weren't accepting any more patients. From the doctor's office I went straight across the street and wanted to go to Heni, to see whether she had gone to work in the city. She had still not returned from work. I went back home, took off the airfield clothes, changed, and went straight to the gate. The clock read 7:45. I stood by the gate and waited. My head was hurting badly, my legs were starting to give way and heat emanated from me. I waited. She didn't notice me. On Linkuvos Street I caught up with her. She was walking with quick steps alongside another girl. While walking we met Larik and Riva. Heni and I stopped. The girls carried on. The two of us went home together. She told me how her day had passed.

"Tomorrow I will go into the city again," she told me.

"And I probably won't be able to go to work," I answered.

"Why?"

"I don't feel well. I have a bit of a fever, too."

"What's your temperature?"

"A little high, not too much. Anyway, it doesn't matter."

"No, tell me what it is?"

"Oh, it's nothing, 37.7."

"What's with you? Are you crazy?! You're sick. That's almost 38 and that is a fever! Why did you come wait for me?!" she reprimanded me.

As we were parting I asked her: "So, when will you have time for me?"

"Tomorrow we won't see each other, I will probably be lying in bed. And the day after?"

"The day after I am busy: I have to see to my card."

With a heavy heart I went home. They were angry with me at home for walking around with a fever. I ate supper—a glass of tea with a little roll

---

88   Shlomo (Shleyme) Finkelstein, born 1924, was murdered in Dachau.

which my mother baked, and I asked for a warm blanket to cover myself. I was shivering. I could not sleep during the night between September 9 and 10 and felt nauseous. I had to spend time that night in the bathroom or in other words, "I travelled to Riga"...

On the morning of the tenth (that is today) I again "travelled to Riga." My fever was already over 38. My head felt very heavy. My mother called the doctor. The doctor [Einstadt] came. I took my temperature in his presence. It was 37.4! My fever had dropped. He prescribed three days furlough for me. Ten minutes after the doctor had left our house, I measured it again. The thermometer registered 38.4!

The clock just struck 6:30. I am lying in bed, writing. My sister is annoyed about the situation, as I am not the only sick one now. My father lies to my left. His temperature is 37.5. He has a stomach bug. My sister lies opposite me. Her temperature is 37.6. Also with a stomach complaint. In short—it's a sickbay here... Papa had no patience to lie in bed. He got dressed earlier and went out onto the street. He is home now, lying next to me again.

The ghetto is buzzing with the latest news: According to an order from the Kovno Ghetto commander, the place where the small ghetto[89] once stood will now be settled by all the Poles and Russians[90] who have arrived in Kovno since 1939. The order was carried out and the abovementioned Poles and Russians have taken a few streets here. The Gestapo arrived during the night between September 9 and 10 (around 2, 2:30 A.M.), accompanied by Lithuanians and, as people relate, they separated the Poles and the Lithuanians, to the right and to the left. Others say that they put the

---

89   The Kovno Ghetto was divided into two parts. One part was known as the small ghetto and the other as the big ghetto. A wooden bridge above Panerių Street connected the two sections. Due to the high quality of the apartments in the small ghetto most of the inhabitants there were members of the ghetto elite. On October 29, 1941, following the Great *Aktion*, the small ghetto was liquidated and most of the inhabitants were murdered in the Ninth Fort.

90   Tory noted in his diary on September 10, 1942: "An *Aktion* in the area of the former small ghetto, recently populated by Russian, Polish, and other women. Jewish workers were mobilized to help in the transfer." This incident is known as one of the most degrading and complex events that took place in the ghetto, in which Jewish workers were forced to assist in moving non-Jews who had been living there. By forcing the Jews to participate, the Germans thus gave the local Lithuanians yet another reason to hate the Jews. See Tory, *Surviving the Holocaust*, p. 133.

elderly and the children onto cargo trucks which drove in the direction of the Ninth Fort.[91] The younger ones were taken by foot. Others yet say they were actually separated, put on trucks, and taken away to the beach where steamers were waiting for them and they travelled to Sapizshishok.[92] They also took with them small bags. One added that they took along ten Jews from the ghetto, to help the Poles and the Russians get settled. We will discover the truth later. This is significant news for the ghetto.

My Relationship with Heni

As you can see from p. 341 onwards, it's very obvious that while we lived in the city, we did not know each other personally. I knew her from afar and, she told me that she had not know me then. I saw her a few times, also from a distance. She was in Edith Getz's[93] group. On more than one occasion I considered her from afar and I thought about her, more than once.

One morning (this was a long time ago, I don't remember exactly when...), while going to work on Kriščiukaičio Street, I heard a voice from behind me.

"What is the time?"

---

91 The Ninth Fort was a site of mass murder of Jews. Located near the city of Kovno, it was the largest of the murder sites of Jews in Kovno. Over 50,000 people were killed there during the German occupation, from June 1941 to the summer of 1944. Many were Jews from Kovno or Jews who had been deported from Germany.

92 Sapizshishok or Zapyškis (Lithuanian), is a small town in the Kovno district on the right bank of the Neman River. A forced labor camp, in which Soviet POWs worked, was set up near the town. This place name appears again later with other spellings.

93 Edith Getz was born in Klaipėda. She was deported from the Kovno Ghetto to Stutthof in the summer of 1944. She survived the Holocaust.

I turned around. Heni was talking next to a woman and she had asked her the question.

"I don't know," answered the other woman.

"5:45!" I said to Heni.

We both compared watches. Both of us needed to go to our respective workplaces. We talked about this and that, not any important news, and about airfield life. We parted. My heart was pounding.

Spring passed. Summer arrived. The beach season began. I saw her there again. After not seeing her for a long time, I might have gradually forgotten her (I liked her, but just as a pretty girl), but now, when I saw her on the beach, feelings of restlessness and longing filled my heart. I was drawn to her. A few times our eyes met between the water and the sand on the beach…but I did not greet her. She recognized me and I knew her and wanted to get to know her, but I couldn't greet her. It seemed a bit comical to me, my lack of boldness with her, but this is part of my character. I wanted to greet her, but I could not do so! Greeting her would lead to talking, and I was scared of this. If I would speak to her even just a few times, I would totally fall apart, I would fall in love! I felt this and therefore I wanted to avoid it. I already know what love is. I know what suffering is (don't laugh!) because I have experienced it once…I wanted to avoid this, I did not want any problems, no heartache…I didn't want it and at the same time I did want it! It drew me like a magnet. I felt that I must give in! I cannot battle against love! I knew that the time of love is a time of jealousy and suffering and arguments. I foresaw it all, I knew everything, and I had to bow my head…for whom? For Heni! For her! Because I loved her silently in my heart, because she had conquered me!

(I have just interrupted my writing, five minutes ago, because Izke Kagan came to pay a sick call. A few words and he was already on the other side of the door.)

"Call the girls to come for a visit," my sister called out after him.

"Yes, most of all the new star, his new hit," he answered…

September 11, 1942

I finished writing in my diary yesterday at 9 P.M. (night must have fallen outside already) and today I began writing with the last chime of 9 o'clock.

During the night I perspired a lot. My temperature today at 8 A.M. was 35.9. My father had the same temperature. I feel very weak. (I am writing this while lying in bed). Yesterday there were three sick people and today there are already four of us sick in the room. My mother has joined our group. She is nauseous (she suffers from gallstones and this causes nausea) and can barely stand on her feet. She, too, is lying down now. My sister has already left the bed a little (she, too, has no fever) and will make breakfast or lunch. Papa has also become a hare. He is busy in the shed.[94] I, too, am thinking about getting up.

Yesterday, Izke told me that he has furlough today. I would like him to come visit me. For one thing, it would be a bit merrier here, but I also want to talk to him.

Yesterday at 9:30, my sister read through the short chapter about my relationship with Heni.

"People need to be a bit bolder," she said to me, "and especially a young man. A man must always be bold."

"If so, you don't know anything about life," I answered her. "Before marriage, while the man in love is courting his beloved, she controls him. Then she can carry out all her caprices and whims and he, poor thing, must keep quiet and agree, because he doesn't want to lose her. After the wedding, in married life, it's almost always the exact opposite: As he did before, protecting her will and yielding to her whims, so now (most of the time) she

---

94   Presumably, referring to the toilet.

ensures his well-being, and endures his caprices. He becomes more tense and touchy, and she—she becomes more yielding. She is already weak."

"Yes, ok," I heard her answer, "before the wedding," she adds, "I was also one of those proud ones. I never told anyone that I was in love and after the wedding one changes a little…yes, one changes roles…right…"

And now the continuation (see p. 351):

In short, I met her a few times at the beach. Our eyes met a few times, but we remained like strangers, two separate people.

However, I felt that this couldn't go on for long. I had to approach her. I waited for the moment. She was leaving the beach after bathing with Rivke Keidan.[95] I watched from afar. Giving an excuse that I had to go home earlier that day, I left my group of guys and girls and went off alone in the direction in which Heni had gone. At the edge of the beach the two girls had stopped. I went over to them.

"I think," I turned to Heni, "that we have met somewhere, right?"

"Yes!"

"I think it was on the way to work, right?"

We looked at one another. She smiled and I smiled back (we understood the ploy I had used as my excuse for approaching her…)

Thus, our acquaintance began. My mood improved. I accompanied the girls home (they live near to one another) and then "danced" myself happily home.

A person in love always talks or writes (it should be more romantic) about how he slept the first night after a long awaited meeting with the other person and he will always say that the first night was a night without sleep, a night of thinking, a night of happiness…Therefore I will not write here how I slept that night, because it's obvious—I didn't sleep.

In this manner I accompanied Heni home from the beach for a few days. At the beach, when we met, we greeted one another and then separated. We were close while going home.

"Do you have time this evening, Heni?" I asked her once before we parted.

---

95 It has not been possible to find any information about her.

September 1942

She looked at me.

"Yes, today I have time."

"What time?"

"9 P.M. Here," said Heni.

I shake her hand. We part until 9 P.M. I am already at the appointed place before 9. Heni arrives shortly after I do. We walk around a bit. She was looking to get hold of a rucksack. She had obtained a travel certificate for Vilkomir[96] (this was for September 26), and did not have the bag that Jews always carry. I agreed to come along.

This went on for several days. Short conversations, not of much importance, during the short time that we walked together.

We got to know each other better. Time did not stand still. We walked on Varnių Street, past the trees, trying to look at the stars and the moon. These were beautiful, pleasant moments—moments when I felt happy and joyful. I led her to understand, as though in passing, that things are not so simple for me, that two is always stronger, two is always better. I hinted that I am not indifferent to her (I didn't yet say it openly) and to tell the truth, I did not meet any great resistance to my words in her answers and this made me very happy. How many times did the siren bother us? I don't remember. Very often, the siren would catch us while we were walking together, and then it would separate us. She would go to her home, I to mine. During the days when the Vocational School was closed, and I was walking around unimpeded on the streets like a dandy, smoking cigarettes, I would always be at her house at around 12. In the evening—at 9 P.M. So I saw her twice a day. I felt a closeness to her, and she felt it, too. We more or less understood each other. Not only did we understand this—but our friends understood this, too. Lyusya asked me how things are going, Dora and Ida congratulated me. Avremke asks me how things are going on that front.

"The offensive is still underway," I answer. "But we are progressing gradually, moving forward step by step, and the first troops are already inside, it seems, in the suburbs. The rest of the commentary about the situation I will share in a separate report..."

---

96 Vilkomir (Ukmergė), a town in Lithuania, located 76 kilometers northwest of Vilna.

"How are things between you and Heni?" Izke asks me.
"In the meantime, not bad."
"I am really pleased," he says to me, shaking my hand.
A few evenings I walked with her arm in arm. I felt so happy. She became closer to me. And she meant more to me.

How many times, when she would stop by a tree and lean on it, she would be so beautiful, so attractive, that I had to stop myself before I grabbed her and kissed her limbs. Heni! I loved her! And I love her!

The clock is showing 11:45 A.M.

My mother, although she feels bad, is baking rolls. She has been lying with a hot-water bottle on her stomach for the last fifteen minutes. She has also already taken a Cibalgin to calm the pain. Her gallbladder is troubling her.

Izke has furlough today but he hasn't come to see me. The girls will certainly not come, because they won't want to come on their own; they would certainly come together with Izke. At any rate, I won't say anything about Heni—the day is still young.

I tried to read a book earlier, and took out a book in Hebrew, I opened it in the middle (the book is titled *Yehefefiya*, p. 171), and this is what I read [it rhymes in the original Hebrew]:[97]

No fire, no coals	אֵין אֵשׁ אֵין גַּחֶלֶת
Burn in this way	כָּכָה אוֹכֶלֶת,
Like hidden love	כְּאַהֲבָה נִסְתֶּרֶת,
Burning in one's heart.	בַּלֵּב בּוֹעֶרֶת

---

97   *Yehefefiya* (יְחֶפְהפִיָּה) is the Hebrew translation of *Barfüssele* first published in German in 1856 by Berthold Auerbach (1812–1882), a well-known German–Jewish writer and poet, who created a new and highly successful genre in German literature, known as Black Forest Village Stories: sentimental folk tales about village life. *Barfüssele* is a more modern version of Cinderella, telling the story of two poor village orphaned siblings, the self-pitying brother immigrating to America and the cheerful and hardworking sister who

It doesn't rhyme in Yiddish, but the meaning is right, fitting perfectly!

Only now, at 5 P.M., (I write with "variables"[98]), I discovered that this evening is *Rosheshone* [Rosh Hashana]. I am now reading the book *Seedtime* (*Przedwiośnie*) by Stefan Żeromski.[99] This is the first book with such content that I have read. It is written in a very anti-revolutionary manner. But when there is nothing to do, one reads.[100]

It is boring to lie in bed, but I wouldn't have the energy to dance.

September 13, 1942

1942. IX.13

Rosheshone

Friday, *Shabes*, Sunday

On Friday, September 11, I lay in bed until exactly 7 P.M. I had no more patience to lie like a salmon and be the worst patient in bed, so I got up, got dressed, and went out. First, I went to Heni. I was told that she had just left, just five minutes earlier. I wandered over to Lyusya's house. I spent

---

meets a rich landowner and marries him. The book became a contemporary bestseller and was translated into many languages, including three translations into Hebrew. Gerber was in possession of the first Hebrew translation by Y. Schaf, published in 1922. In the diary he lists the name of the story in Hebrew, which is a play on words of barefoot and beautiful.

98 Written in Yiddish as *peremenyes*, it corresponds to the Russian word *peremennye*. Gerber probably meant that he writes at various times of day, intermittently.

99 Stefan Żeromski (1864–1925), a Polish novelist and dramatist.

100 An order by the Germans that books in the possession of Jews in the ghetto would be confiscated, published on February 7, 1942 (the Book *Aktion*), did not prevent young people in the ghetto from owning books. They continued to read books in various languages, exchanging them regularly and without fear. For more information see Rami Neudorfer, "The Book *Aktion* in the Kovno Ghetto," *Legacy*, 9 (2016), pp. 22–33.

a few minutes with her and noticed, from afar, Dora, Ilik, Avremke, and Izke. Avremke was a bit upset and went off with Ilik. We said hello to each other from a distance. Dora, together with Izke, came up to Lyusya and me and the other two friends wandered in the street. Izke called me aside.

"Do you know, Lyuske, that they are snatching people at the gate!"

"Really? Seriously?!"

"Word of honor! Apparently, they are saying that they are separating the people who are not wearing material or a sewed-on patch."

"It seems to me that something about this business is not right!" I say.

"You know, Avremke's Batske is among those taken."[101]

"Him too?!" I cry out, "It's hard to believe. One would have to be really good to be able to catch him...."

"So listen, don't interrupt me," he whispers in my ear, "Yoske Melamed[102] is there, too!"

"Yoske?!"

"Yes! Him, too! Do you think that maybe we should go and tell Mrs. Melamed? Because if it's a serious matter, she has friends. She knows Lipcer well, and he will help her."

"Come!"

"What are you talking about over there?" Dora and Lyusya were upon us from all sides. Dora did not yet know about all of this. Izke told them.

"And where have the guys gone?" I ask Izke, indicating to the side of the street.

"To Lipcer."

All four of us went to Mrs. Melamed. Izke went inside. He didn't find her at home. Just then Ida came up to us. We formed a circle in the middle of the street.

"Guys, go home quickly, do you hear! They are snatching people off the streets!"

We turned around. A few Jews were standing behind us and repeated their words.

---

101 Meaning father. On the basis of Ukrainian and Belorussian, it must refer to Avremke's father.

102 It is likely that this refers to Yosef Melamed, born 1925, who was incarcerated in the Kovno Ghetto. He survived the Holocaust and later served as the chairman of the Association of Lithuanian Jews in Israel.

September 1942

We slowly moved away from where we were standing.

"Bye, Lyusya and Dora, I am running to Heni!" I said to them quietly.

"Bye, Lusik."

With quick steps I went to her. If trouble was brewing, I wanted to warn her to be careful.

She is still not home. Larik Lubetski[103] showed up while I was standing near the window of Heni's house and asking after her.

"Heni is not home," I told him, and informed him and Misha Yatkunski about the situation in the ghetto. They didn't believe me.

I went off with Larik to the old city. The closer we got to Kriščiukaičio Street, the greater the hubbub and bustle became.

"Oy, woe is me and my children," suddenly we heard across from us the wail of a woman who was holding her head and sobbing with bitter tears…

We exchanged silent looks.

"It seems to me that it really happened," Larik says to me.

I didn't answer him.

I saw my father approaching us. We stopped. At that moment Heni's father also approached us. Each of the four of us asked for news. No one knew the truth. People were saying that those separated because of the patches would be sent to the forest and from there they would provide the ghetto with wood…still others said that those caught would be sent to Yaneve.[104] Most people believed that this **was** an unofficial *Aktion*.

How many people have they seized? People are saying more than 200 men.

I went back to the area where the committee is located, hoping to see Heni. In the middle of everything I remembered that Ida was in possession of the notebook of ghetto songs[105] (I have a special one in which I collect all the songs created in the ghetto. Heni first had the notebook, then Ida

---

103 Leib (Larik) Lubetzki, born in 1922, was murdered in the Holocaust.

104 The author describes the anxiety that more Jews would be sent away from the ghetto after approximately fifty Jews were sent to work in the forest near Jonava (Yaneve) in July 1942. Jonava was a large town in the Kovno district. All the town's Jewish inhabitants were murdered in the summer of 1941.

105 In his second notebook, Ilya Gerber collected songs that were sung in the ghetto. On the left side is the heading in Yiddish "Second notebook – Ghetto songs," and on the right page appear the words "Notebook II—property of L.G. [Lyusik Gerber].

had it). So I went to Ida and retrieved it. I left her straight away and went home. Papa came home later.

"I spoke with Dr. Brandz and with the policeman Genz.[106] They both say that those who were seized will be taken to Palemonas[107] to dig peat." (This would be the second group of Jews to be sent there since the creation of the ghetto until now, see notebook II, p. 176 and following entries).[108]

"How many will be sent away?"

"People are saying 150, but 200 have been seized!"

All this occurred since 7 P.M. on Friday, September 11.

On *Shabes*, September 12, in the morning, someone told us—through our window—that a house search had taken place that night. People were dragged from their beds, everything was done according to lists. People are saying that they are taking people who were among the first Jews at Palemonas,[109] who already have experience in working there. I want to find out what is happening with the Tiktins. I later found out that with much pain and effort they had dragged the father out of the ghetto prison (whoever was under arrest in the ghetto prison was taken by car, first thing in the morning, to Palemonas...)

But I also discovered another piece of news: They also wanted to take my friend Avremke away at night, according to the list. Both he and his father were spared, thankfully. The Santotski family (Ida and her parents)[110] and most of all—Senke Lipcer[111] (the son). Yosef Melamed

---

106 Hirsh Genz, born 1891, an accountant by profession, served as a policeman in the ghetto.

107 A forced labor camp was established in Palemonas, approximately 10 kilometers from Kovno, where Jews worked in peat quarries. The conditions in the camp were extremely harsh and many perished there.

108 This refers to a notebook that is lost.

109 On September 9, 1942, Tory noted in his diary that the authorities demanded 250 Jews to dig peat in Palemonas. On the night of September 11, he notes that 150 Jewish workers were recruited to work there, and on September 12, he writes that 105 Jews were sent to dig peat in Palemonas. See Tory, *Surviving the Holocaust*, pp. 132–133.

110 Yankel Santotski, the head of the family, was a butcher before the war. While living in the ghetto he was close to Benno Lipcer, who assigned him to work in the Gestapo kitchen in Kovno. The Tiktin family used this connection to secure the release of their father and son, as the two families knew each other.

111 Shimon (Senia or Senke) Lipcer, born 1926, was the only son of the Gestapo agent Benno (Benjamin) Lipcer. On July 9, 1944, during the liquidation of the ghetto, the Germans discovered the family's hiding place and his father was shot to death. His mother, Maria (Malka), was taken to Stutthof but survived the Holocaust. Shimon was

September 1942

was also taken. One hundred and four men were taken to Palemonas on *Shabes*. The rest were released.

This afternoon I went to Lyusya. At 6:30 P.M. I went home, promising that I will return in twenty minutes.

"I will wait for you!" she says to me, "and then we will all go to Dora or to Ida. Senke and Bebke will be there, too."

Having come home and eaten latkes,[112] I look at the clock and see it is 7:25.

It is too late to go to Lyusya, I think to myself, I will go to the gate, to wait for Heni and her brigade, Ostland, which does agricultural work in the village.[113] I waited and finally saw her. Heni saw me, too. The two of us went home. She was angry that others had been able to bring in big heads of cabbage and other types of produce. At the gate, they let everything pass.

I tried to talk to her about "not having time." She became visibly upset. I didn't talk about it anymore. We parted. I went home.

Today, Sunday, the second day of *Rosheshone*, my sister was "born."[114] Today she turned exactly twenty-one. I wanted to give her a smack, but it's not appropriate: she's already "big" and "married."

I got up feeling some resentment. Heni told me yesterday, that today, September 13, she is going to work at 8:30. I thought that I would get up today around 8 and accompany her to the gate. Why? Because I want to talk to her seriously. I want to get an answer from her: "yes" or "no." I want to play with open cards—there can be no secrets here!

I get up very early. Everyone is still busy drawing as much air as possible into both nostrils, which will go into the depths of the lungs, with a whistling and squeaking, with singing, and also with a groan.

I think that it is still very early. I look at the clock with sleepy eyes. It's hard to see. I close one eye, exert the other, but that doesn't help. I sit and fix both eyes on the clock: It's five minutes before half past eight! I

---

deported to Dachau and he, too, survived the Holocaust. See Shimon Lipcer testimony, YVA, O.93/13499. Regarding Shimon Lipcer's involvement in his father's activities to save Jews from being sent away from the ghetto, see Segalson, *Belev Ha'ofel*, p. 172.

112 Potato pancakes.

113 A unit of children and young people that worked in the village of Marwianka.

114 Chaya Gerber-Kalner, the diarist's sister, was born on October 3, 1921; the Hebrew date was Tishrei 1, 5682.

fall back on the sofa, with a strange feeling in my heart. I understood that now I can continue sleeping, at least until broad daylight.

I venture outside at around eleven o'clock to get some fresh air. I think that I need to go to the Vocational School. I change direction to go there. From afar I hear the banging of the hammers and grating of the saws. I go inside. A few students were hanging around together with the master.

"Come up to me," Shleyme Finkelstein says to me.

I go up to the second floor, in the hall where the workstations (carpentry tables) stand. He alone is working here today. It's empty all around.

"I think you have an idea about music, huh? So listen, we are forming a 'new kind of orchestra'...."

With those words he grabs his wooden measuring stick and twists it in two, making a kind of fork. In his other hand he grabbed a piece of veneer, and the beat of a foxtrot resounded in the empty room. His hair was tousled, and sounds flew from his mouth, so strange, shrieking and grating, that a musical ear would in no way be able to bear it. His feet shaking on the ground, setting the beat of the strange foxtrot. Every one of Shleyme's limbs was alive and called others, too, to life, to happiness. I also entered the ecstasy. I helped him to grate, cry, tap with my feet, banging the table—in short, the empty hall with the empty space of the room were filled with "negro" music: the modern, new, and popular music—jazz!

"Louder! That's good, that's how I like it!" Shleyme Finkelstein pressed my hands into his. "We can accept you into our band. You know, Lyuske, I mean it seriously, if you come upstairs to us on the second floor from the first floor, it will be merry...."

I went home. However, I cannot sit still at home. I am drawn outside. Next to the fire station I met Heni. I express my wonder at seeing her in the ghetto. She was too lazy to get up to go to work. I told her my good intentions to accompany her earlier today to work. She was silent. A sharp look in the eyes and we parted. I went directly to Lyusya. Dora was also there. Lyusya scolded me in a light tone for not coming to her at the appointed time. I tried to defend myself. All three of us went to Ida where Ida's mother entertained us along with another woman I did not know. We were reminiscing about the good old times...

We parted quickly, and I accompanied Lyusya to her home, then went off.

September 1942

Straight after lunch I went to Heni. I "coincidentally" found her at home. (I say "coincidentally," because most of the time when I come to her house she is not home).

Among the things we talked about, I also asked for a picture of her.

"I don't have any pictures of myself," she answered. This I knew already from earlier, because I had looked through her two albums and did not find any pictures of her there. As I watch her, she takes out another album and shows me a few large-size pictures of young people. In the beginning she holds the photographs on her knees, but the album is turned with the good side to me. She explains to me who is in the photographs. In the middle of explaining she turns the album to herself. To see the pictures, I must stand up and stand near her and look at the album. I bent over. Her hair touched mine; it tickled me... I became nervous. I felt like my hand, which was resting on her chair, was shaking nervously. This is the first time that this has happened to me. With a light and quiet voice she continued explaining. I didn't hear her words. It was like I was not myself. I restrained myself. Then, with one quick step I was again, as before, on the couch opposite her. My breath was hot and I still felt the touch of her beautiful hair. She had control over me, but I also controlled myself.

"Heni," I say to her, "when will you have time for me? I want to consult with you about something."

"Can't you say it now?"

"No, not now, it has to do with a girl..."

"Lyusinke, if this has to do with gossip about a girl, then it's better you don't, because I hate such things."

"No, that has never happened to me!" I cry out. "Have I ever gossiped about a girl behind her back? I don't think I ever have... I am referring to something else entirely. I hate gossip and it is not in my nature!"

"When you have time," I draw out my words, "tell me and I will consult with you!"

My heart was beating agitatedly while I was talking. I want to put it to the test—on her! The girl that I want to talk to her about— is her! I will tell her that I have fallen very deeply in love with a girl, and I am in love to this day to the depths of my heart. I want to tell her that I have happy evenings with the girl, even though I have never declared my love for her. I have stifled the love within myself; I wanted to turn away from the girl, I didn't want any pain, but no, I can't do it, or better put—I couldn't do it. I stifled the love inside me and it choked me. It overcame me. I want to tell her and ask her advice, that she should show me the right way: Should I suffer further and try perhaps even to forget the girl, who has not revealed her feelings to me—neither good, nor bad—or should I tell her that I love her, that I adore her more than others? I really want to know the answer. It is important to me.

I left her and went to Lyusya. She didn't look well: her face not blue not grey, her eyes running with tears, her lips grim. She took her temperature in my presence—37.2 degrees. I stayed a bit and then left. Next, I went to the committee, where I met Avremke Tiktin and Zlata Santotski (Ida's sister). Just then Jozef Volpert[115] approached me.

"Lyuske, come with us to Ida's, the entire gang is there!" Zlata says to me with Avremke. We are also coming right away."

But I just ran home. To tell the truth, I wanted to get rid of Jozef, because I know that the girls can't bear him, including Heni.

"Lyuske," Jozef says to me, "are you going to Ida's?"

Apparently, he had waited for me near the committee.

"Come!"

"Do I have a choice?" I say jokingly.

We went to Ida's. This is a list of everyone who was there: Her parents, Zlata, Danke Liberman (her suitor), Ida, Avremke (Ida's suitor), Dora, Izke (Dora's suitor), another two girls, Jozef, and myself. It was joyful. People whistled, sang, enjoyed themselves, laughed, and joked. "Young" people smoked. Me too. The clock moves, it doesn't stay in one place. The crowd moves too, it also can't stay in one place—better put, it can't sit still. People want to go. The two girls whom I don't know leave.

"Jozef," I say to Volpert, "come, us old guys don't have what to do among young people. Come, it's time for bed...." Come, I say to him in the quiet, we must not disturb anyone. Only the couples remained there alone.

---

115 Jozef Volpert, born 1925, was shot dead in the Kovno Ghetto in 1944.

September 1942

"You know what, let's go to the Vocational School. There's dancing there every evening. There's a piano with instruments and lots of couples dancing. Come!"

We went. Passing by the block where we both live (he is my neighbor), he ran home to bring a coat.

"Are you cold, Jozef?" I ask him. So young and already cold, I joke. "Look, look at me," I say, and show him my unbuttoned jacked and my light clothing.

"You know, Lyuske, I have a strange custom: when it's cold, I put on a coat...." I look at him; where does he find such words?

We arrived at the school (No. 1). The piano playing could be heard from outside.[116] We went down a long corridor, and from there we entered a dark room. Someone was sitting at a piano and playing somber music, beautifully. A girl was sitting with a guy in a corner. My heart gave a thud and I felt that all my blood had rushed to my face. I thought that the girl sitting there in the darkness was Heni. However, I caught my mistake. We listened to the beautiful piano playing for five minutes and then we left quietly, the same way we had come. We returned home. The Sunday evening blew a chilly wind at us and I rushed home, leaving him outside. On the night between Sunday and Monday a siren was sounded. Russian "steel birds" appeared in the sky over the Führer's territories.

A few short reports before going to sleep:

Newspapers from Tilsit[117] and Memel report that thirty Russian planes were shot down over Kovno! The newspaper fell into the hands of a German soldier in Kovno. They had to evacuate him with emergency services. The German doctor diagnosed a laughter attack. This has been a good night. Sunday, 11 P.M. The Russian planes are still humming in the sky. Be successful! That is my wish!

---

116 From the memoirs of Jacob Oleisky, founder of the Vocational School and its director, it is evident that, in addition to professional training, the institution was concerned with enriching the students' education and furthering their social life, "That they should have opportunities for recreation for a few hours, that they would dream about a better and more beautiful world." See Yankev Oleyski [Jacob Oleisky], "Di fakhshul in Kovner geto," *Fun letstnkhurbn*, (2), p. 26.

117 A city in Eastern Prussia, on the banks of the Neman River.

September 15, 1942

An *Aktion!* (against non-Jews).

On the night between September 9 and 10 (see pp. 350 and 351), they removed the Poles and the Russians from the (former) "Small Ghetto." The abovementioned had emigrated to Lithuania starting in 1939. They are, in reality, enemies of National Socialism. People said that some of them were taken to the Ninth Fort. That's correct. People say, or rather people said, that others were taken by ferry to Sapizshishok. Ten Jews accompanied them. The returning Jews reported that they were taken all the way to Sapizshishok.[118] There, they ordered the Russians and Poles to disembark. The ten Jews returned, not knowing why they had been taken along. The Russians and the Poles felt happy during the journey. They were singing and their mood was good. They were not anxious about where they were being taken. The Russians sang three new songs which they had composed while sitting and watching the suffering of the Jews in the ghetto. The songs are: "The Song about the Great Aktion Against the Jews;" "Why Did Our Husbands Bring Us to the Baltics"; and a third song, [untitled] also about the Jews.

This morning, our neighbor from apartment one, (Mrs. Alkanovitsh),[119] shared with us quietly that the Poles and Russians from Sapizshishok met their brothers and sisters, who had already been sent to the Ninth Fort, in the next world. And we can very well believe what she says. She doesn't talk for no reason. She doesn't pull stuff out of the air.

---

118 Gerber wrote several other names for this place: Zapisok and Zapizshok.

119 Apparently referring to Rissa Alkanovitsh, born 1903. She was murdered during the Holocaust.

September 1942

The second *Aktion* this week:
Sunday morning, beginning at 5 A.M., little peasant wagons appeared, packed with villagers, on the way leading to the Ninth Fort! Women, children, men, all without exception, travelling on the wagons, not knowing where they were being taken. On Panerių Street, where the hill begins and where one of the sides of the ghetto is located, a policeman spoke with one of the travelers. All the carts with the people, escorted by partisans,[120] are Russian village workers, burly fellows from Shaki[121] and from Suwałki[122] (most of all from that region, that area). They will be "resettled" somewhere else. The way to that place goes over the hill... From five in the morning until around noon the unfortunate ones travelled to the well-known and popular Ninth Fort, not knowing what awaited them. Thus, all the Russian field workers residing in the Suvalk [Suwałki] district found their demise at the Ninth Fort. All without exception (according to the information from the Lithuanians) fell victim at the fort. The horses, wagons, and remaining inventory were confiscated by the authorities.

The third *Aktion* this week:
They attacked the poor village of barge haulers near Yaneve and carried out the *Aktion* in that very spot, near Yaneve. Apparently *Aktionen* are not only perpetrated against Jews, but also Lithuanians, Russians, and Poles. And in other lands? Yes. Wherever the hands of Hitlerism—the word which symbolizes barbarity—reach, is where they shoot people, there people weep, their groans are heard...

Aktionen of Jews

This week, on Friday, they once again selected people for Palemonas. People were chosen during Friday evening and that night. By *Shabes* morning they had already sent the people to work in Palemonas. People thought it would be to work in the peat fields, but a note at the labor office

---

120 Lithuanian auxiliaries.
121 Šakiai, a district capital in southwest Lithuania.
122 Between 1919 and 1939 Suvalk (Suwałki) became an autonomous town within the Białystok Voivodeship. After the outbreak of World War II, the town was briefly captured by the Red Army. However, on October 12, 1939, the Soviets withdrew and transferred the area to the Germans, in accordance with the Nazi-Soviet Pact.

announced that those sent away are working on the highway construction near Palemonas. The note states that anyone who has a relative among those sent away can send a package with linen, pillows, and so forth. They have not sent them to the Fort "for the moment," (tfu, tfu, tfu, we shouldn't talk about it...). But for now, it is enough for their relatives that they are not here now: they are missed at home, they are missing from the community. They have been taken out of the ghetto, they are not at home, who knows when they will return... This can be considered half an *Aktion*. They are alive—but they are not here! However, Jews are not panicking. People have become hares! Whoever had the chance—went into "hiding." Four people have already disappeared from the ghetto prison. The vehicles (cargo trucks) that took those "caught" to Palemonas were heavily guarded as they travelled. Sitting together with the Jews were the labor office representatives with their red patches. At the front, ahead of the cargo trucks, was a taxi and at the back, a second taxi. "Front and back—a guard of honor!" So heavily they guarded the little Jews. The next day, Sunday, fifteen Jews arrived from Palemonas—hares! And how many ran away on the way?! Just like there, near Palemonas, "they are lacking workers," and so, during the night between September 14 and 15, they again snatched people from their beds. That morning a cargo truck full of Jews (people say sixty men) departed. People say it went to Palemonas.

Aktionen abroad

As the Lithuanian newspaper *I Laisve*[123] reports, news has arrived from Lublin[124] that the city is now clean of Jews.

---

123 *I Laisve* (Freedom), was a Lithuanian daily newspaper. It was published in Kovno from June 24, 1941, until December 31, 1942, by Lithuanian nationalists who supported Lithuanian independence.

124 The ghetto in the city of Lublin, in occupied Poland, was liquidated in the spring of 1942. Most of the inhabitants were deported to the Bełżec death camp and the remainder to the ghetto of Majdan Tatarski and the Majdanek concentration camp.

This, sadly, is not the first such information that the newspaper reports. The article about the Bessarabian Jews was even longer:[125] "Bessarabia is free of Jews" cried out the headline (see notebook II, p. 286).[126]

Aktionen were conducted in three French cities. In Boulogne and in two other bigger cities. They removed 10,000 Jews from one city.

In another French city they carried out an *Aktion* among small children. One thousand infants were taken that day from their mothers' breasts.

Things are happening in Warsaw! Have you heard? Jews took up resistance! As the Vilna Jews who are now in our ghetto relate, some time ago Jews, who were fleeing from Warsaw, arrived in Vilna. The Warsaw Jews tell the Vilna Jews the following story:

One fine day, the head of the Warsaw Judenrat ordered all the Jews to assemble in an appointed place. The Warsaw Jews, however, had been warned by the Poles that the Germans were intending on carrying out an *Aktion* among Warsaw Jewry. The Jews in Warsaw wanted things to continue as before, with not even one single *Aktion* to harm them. A group of guys had gathered and gotten hold of weapons from the Poles. Even more daring, they asked the head of the Judenrat to withdraw the order concerning a gathering of all the Warsaw Jews in one place. The latter refused to withdraw the command he had given. They shot him. He fell, himself a Jew, at the hands of Jews using a Polish bullet... The Jewish community of Warsaw armed itself. They awaited those who were going to carry out the *Aktion*. At an appointed time, three battalions of three different peoples appeared in the Jewish quarter: one Lithuanian, one Latvian, and one Rumanian battalion. They were to carry out the *Aktion*. The Jews defended themselves. The Jews shot and engaged in deadly combat on the streets of Warsaw. The three battalions defended themselves from Jewish shots! Victims fell like flies. The Jews held the

---

125 On September 15, 1941, the Romanian ruler Ion Antonescu expelled all the Jews of Bessarabia to Transnistria, the Romanian-occupied area of Ukraine, beyond the Dniester River. Around 25,000 Jews were murdered on the way to Transnistria, and tens of thousands were thrown into an improvised mass grave in the forest of Cosăuți in central Bessarabia, through which the convoy passed. Tens of thousands more drowned in the Dniester River while crossing to Transnistria. In 1942, at the height of the war, a census conducted in the territory of Bessarabia found only 227 Jews. Indeed, Bessarabia was, in accordance with plans, "free" of Jews.

126 This refers to a notebook that was lost.

battalions in a cage. And they also destroyed them! They destroyed three battalions of soldiers, but Jews fell too, 12,000 people in total! As the Jews from Vilna related, the Poles joined the fight. With united forces they set fire to the Warsaw barracks and captured a few strategic locations for the time being. The Warsaw authorities had to call in motorized German units to calm the "revolt" of Warsaw's Jews. When these divisions arrived, they gradually "returned the calm" to the city. That very same evening, with the help of the newly arrived Germans, they carried out an *Aktion*. They took 125,000 people in one day! They died and fell like heroes![127]

In the Lithuanian newspaper, quite some time ago, a small report appeared:

"One hundred Poles were shot in Warsaw for being in contact with Jews and for disturbing the peace of the city."[128]

* * *

Yesterday, September 11, the kitchen at the airfield began to function. There is one kitchen on the side of the construction site management, and a second kitchen on the other side of the airfield. They distributed last year's sauerkraut and today's fresh water with 100 grams of bread. My friend, Izke Kagan, reports:

Lysuke, you probably saw the pot which I dragged out of my home, right? It holds 5 liters of water. I took that pot and went with Bebke Vidutshinski[129] (they always work together in delousing at the airfield) to

---

127 This rumor has no connection to actual events at the time in the Warsaw Ghetto, during the summer of 1942. Between July and the end of September 1942, around 265,000 Jews were deported from the ghetto to the Treblinka death camp; thousands more were killed during the roundups. The armed resistance was not yet organized. In his article discussing the culture of rumors, Amos Goldberg mentions that a similar rumor spread among youth groups in the Warsaw Ghetto concerning a Jewish revolt in Nowogródek. This rumor circulated in March 1942, at the time of the first deportations from Lublin to the death camp and the news of the murders in Chełmno. In his opinion, this was a response to the feelings of helplessness and weakness expressed by the Jews of Łódź and Lublin. It seems that in Kovno, too, the rumor about an ostensible revolt in Warsaw was a response to the great catastrophe which beset the Jews of the Warsaw Ghetto (and the Jews in general) and their feelings of failure and helplessness. See Goldberg, "Rumor Culture among Warsaw Jews under Nazi Occupation," pp. 104–105.

128 This was another unfounded rumor.

129 Benjamin Vidutshinski, born 1921, lived in the Kovno Ghetto. He survived the Holocaust.

September 1942

the kitchen and asked for a *Yushnik*[130] for two people. We have so much *protektsie*[131] (in short, Vitamin P) that they poured out a full pot of fat soup for us. We went happily back to the delousing area and, grabbing the spoons, began to guzzle it.

"Gross, what is this that they have given us?" I ask my neighbor, whose face is contorted. But he couldn't get a word out, as if something was stuck in his throat.

After deliberating at length on what to do with the *Yushnik*, or more accurately with the bullion, we decided to throw in our four last portions of saccharine. We threw it in and tasted it. It's neither here nor there. Salt is also a commodity we have. We pour in salt and had ourselves a vinaigrette…in short, I won't keep you long, we had to give away the 5 liters of vinaigrette to people who have no taste buds. This is a lesson for later. *Protektsie* doesn't always help.

---

130 This term, widely used among Lithuanian Jews, referred to a pot of soup. It is probably derived from the Slavic word *Iushka*, which has two meanings: 1) soup, usually made from fish; and 2) a colloquial term for blood. Thus, the word *Yushnik* combines the two meanings—both as "soup" and as a sarcastic Jewish term for "vile slop" (in Russian, *Iushnik* has the direct meaning of a soup made with pig or goose blood). See also Kaplan, *The Jewish Voice in the Ghettos and Concentration Camps*, p. 51.

131 *Protektsie*—mobilization of personal ties. For a more detailed explanation and discussion see the Introduction.

September 18, 1942

It's been a month (and maybe even more) since the rumor began circulating in the ghetto that Caspi-Serebrovitz[132] had been shot in Vilna. A few words about him. During the Lithuanian period, Caspi was a Shaulist [member of the Lithuanian Riflemen's Union, or the LRU—*Lietuvosšauliųsąjunga*] and was more Lithuanian than Jewish. He would insinuate himself with the Lithuanians (among the highest levels, obviously) and often inform on his own Jewish brothers. He had caused much trouble for Jewish families (in the *shtetl* of Rokishuk [Rokiškis]). During the Russian period, Serebrovitz was "looking after himself in prison."

When the Germans invaded Lithuania, when blood, Jewish blood of course, was flowing through the streets and the houses, when partisans were shooting at children, women, and men at the Forts[133]—then Caspi's star shone. He was taken out of prison and allowed to go free. He didn't wear any patch and he didn't live in the ghetto. He was a Jew—though, in fact—he was not. He would walk around the city, eating and enjoying himself all day long. What kind of role did he play? People said that his role in the ghetto was to be the recipient and distributor of rumors in the ghetto.

---

132 Josef Caspi-Serebrovitz, born in the town of Rokiškis, Lithuania, taught Hebrew and literature and was principal of the local school. He was a journalist and member of the Beitar movement before the war and apparently also served as a plainclothes policeman in the Lithuanian police. In the Kovno Ghetto he served as a Gestapo agent. This permitted him to not wear the yellow star, and also allowed him to live in the city, although he visited the ghetto frequently and influenced events there. The various sources depict a restless, loud, and unstable personality. In the summer of 1942, he was sent to Vilna where the Germans killed him, his wife, and his two daughters. For more information see Schalkowsky, ed., *The Clandestine History of the Kovno Jewish Police*, pp. 302–311.

133 Kovno was surrounded by a network of forts which were used later by the Germans as murder sites.

September 1942

Recipient: he had special agents in the ghetto (some official, such as Bayder,[134] others, unofficial and unknown). Concerning the ghetto rumors: Either the "unofficial" agents would spread them intentionally or they spread randomly through the rich imagination of the ghetto people. Serebrovitch, the big shot, knew all the rumors.

That was one opinion about him in the ghetto.

The second opinion was that he is the Jewish ghetto representative vis-à-vis the German Gestapo agents. Some say that he did a lot of good for the Slobodka Ghetto; others say that, in reality, he is guilty of many unpleasant occurrences in the ghetto. One thing, however, is a fact: that until a month ago he lived in the city, travelled with the Germans in a taxi, would come to visit the ghetto and that's it. Once, actually, the ghetto was grateful to Caspi. He had reproached the Jewish police standing guard at the ghetto gate (known in German as "the gate watch") that they should not behave so brutally toward their own brothers, their own Jews (at the gate, the Jewish crowd of workers were beaten. And who did the beating? The Jewish police, of course. Caspi apparently took an interest in this).

In short, a rumor spread a month and a half ago that Caspi had put on patches, and that he and his family had gone to live in the Vilna Ghetto. A short time after the abovementioned settled in the ghetto, news arrived that he had been shot, along with his entire family. This cast fear over the ghetto: people reflected on various things. A sign that Serebrovitz had agents in the ghetto, because Bayder, the official (first unofficial, but later the ghetto discovered that he was an agent of Caspi and working for the Gestapo), lost his position (he didn't go to work, didn't go into town to work, and so on) and became a senior policeman in the ghetto.

---

134 Zefania Bayder (1893–?), was the assistant of Gestapo agents Caspi-Serebrovitz and Lipcer, and was appointed in August 1943 as sanitation officer of the ghetto police at the request of the SD. Arie Segalson knew Bayder from the days when he studied with his son in the Hebrew Gymnasium in Kovno and their membership in the Beitar movement in the city. In his words, "Bayder was a good friend of Lipcer and because of this Lipcer put him in a work group in the Gestapo. Bayder also became very close with Gestapo officials and received from them special treatment, and in addition to this was the assistant of Caspi-Serebrovitz." See Segelson, *Belev Ha'ofel*, pp. 177–178.

Additionally, a man named Dr. Auer,[135] one of the best Jewish doctors in Kovno, who had a good reputation even among the non-Jews, and who had lived for the entire time in Kovno with his family and received Lithuanian and German patients, was now also sent to the ghetto. This, at the same time that Caspi went to live in Vilna. Now Dr. Auer lives in the ghetto. He was beloved by the Lithuanians and had a reputation among them as a good doctor, so they lobbied that he, Dr. Auer, would see them in the ghetto and treat them there... Right by the ghetto gate is a one-story brick house, beautifully renovated, and this became Dr. Auer's office. He sits inside, while at the gate, on an iron cot, sit a line of Lithuanians, who are waiting for "Herr Pani Dr."... Is this not comical?! Lithuanians from the city come to the ghetto, to a Jew, to be healed...An x-ray machine has also been sent from the city to Dr. Auer, so that he will be able to better diagnose the illnesses of the [Lithuanian] citizens...

Among those caught and sent for work at Palemonas was also my friend Beke Kot.[136] Beke was my school friend, a cheerful guy. While still in the city he lived near me, on the same street. His family had a bakery on Nemuno Street. His sister was killed in the city when she was run over by a car. In the ghetto, during the Great *Aktion*, his mother, who was sick, was sent to the Fort with his father. Beke remained alone. His father had

---

135 Dr. Auer, a Jewish orthopedic specialist, arrived in Kovno from Vienna a few years before the outbreak of the war. Dr. Auer attained an excellent reputation among senior Lithuanian officials who used his medical services. As a result, he was one of the two Jewish individuals allowed to live outside the ghetto. In mid-August 1942, the Germans ordered him to move into the ghetto. See Tory, *Surviving the Holocaust,* pp. 125–126; see also Garfunkel, *Kovno HaYehudit Behurbana,* pp. 51–52.

136 Dov (Beke) Kot (1924–?), was a graduate of the Hebrew Gymnasium in Kovno. In June 1941, after the German invasion, he was orphaned: his parents were among the first Jews killed in the city, and Dov remained alone in the Kovno Ghetto. He joined the anti-Nazi underground in the ghetto, succeeded in escaping the ghetto to the forests of Rodniki, and joined the partisan unit "Death to the occupiers." He fought in battles for the liberation of Vilna and, the day following the liberation of the city, was severely injured in a weapons' accident. He lost a hand and an eye, and his leg was crushed. He was hospitalized for many months in a military hospital and underwent several operations that helped him recover. After his relative recovery he left the USSR, reached Germany, and from there immigrated to the U.S. See Boris Kot testimony, YVA, O.93/14508.

September 1942

money, and had buried it. Beke didn't know where, but he did not despair. Furthermore, he supported his aunt. He even fought against the Jewish police and therefore often sat in "the ghetto prison"—he could not bear their injustices. Since people living alone (without families) were, for the most part, sent to Palemonas, he was dragged from his bed in the middle of the night and sent there.

The following day, in the morning, the day after they put Beke in the ghetto prison (from there they were taken to Palemonas), Izke went past the so-called "prison."

"Izke, help me! Try to get me out of here! Save me!..."

Izke raised his head to the iron-grated window. A pair of dark, sad eyes looked out at him. The two school friends looked at one another: one with a plea, with a look calling for help, and the other—with surprise, astonishment, and sympathy. Izke, however, couldn't help Beke. How could he have helped him?! With what?! It was impossible at the moment! Beke is an unfortunate [man] and had no *protektsie*. He was taken away...

Apparently, the work in Palemonas is difficult. A few Jews manage to escape from there every day. A few days ago, a group of ten Jewish men arrived in the ghetto—a new party of "hares." They report that the work on the highway is difficult and a regime of whips rules. A new party of escapees numbering sixteen men set out for Vilna. There are fewer Jews around Palemonas by the minute. People disappear in broad daylight and "they're gone." The escapees from Palemonas who arrived here are now going to the airfield. While in Palemonas they chose from among themselves a group leader who should represent the interests of the workers there. He came to the ghetto (I think the day before yesterday). It is Yoske Epshtein.[137] He doesn't have it bad: he doesn't have to work, he's not beaten, and, as a representative from Palemonas, he can "travel" from time to time outside of the ghetto.

---

137 There is no extant information available on this individual.

World News

Eastern Front: (From the newspaper *I Laisve* No. 212 (373) September 11, 1942)

From the Führer's headquarters, on the tenth of the ninth month, comes this report:

On the South-Eastern Front from Novorossiisk, following a blow, the German battalions have pushed forward a little.

The army's heavy artillery sunk five transport ships near the Black Sea coast.

Alongside the Terek River[138] [Caucasus], a German armored division pushed back a Russian offensive and broke through the enemy positions.

With the help of the air forces, a few fortifications were seized on the borders of Stalingrad. Remaining there, during a strong attack by the Russians, the latter lost fifty-nine armored vehicles.

Battle planes bombarded the facilities at Astrakhan.[139] Air attacks in the same place were directed at the airfields, east of the Volga [River].

In the Rzhev region the enemy began its assault with heavy infantry and armored vehicles. With the support of air forces, in great battles and with great efforts, the Russian attacks were driven back with a loss of seventy-seven tanks for the Germans.

---

138 A major river in the northern Caucasus, which flows through Georgia and Russia into the Caspian Sea. During World War II, German forces reached the Terek near Mozdok at the end of August 1942. This comprised the farthest extent of German conquests into the Soviet Union—but, aside from a small bridgehead, the Germans were unable to forge further toward the oil fields of Baku, which was Hitler's objective.

139 A city in southern Russia, situated across two banks of the Volga River, close to where it flows into the Caspian Sea. In the fall of 1942, the region to the west of Astrakhan became one of the easternmost points in the Soviet Union reached by the invading German Wehrmacht.

September 1942

In the region of Lake Ladoga[140] and in Leningrad, a few Russian assaults were warded off.

Thirty-six enemy ships were destroyed in an attempt to cross the Neva River.[141] (Continued on p. 397 in my notebook).

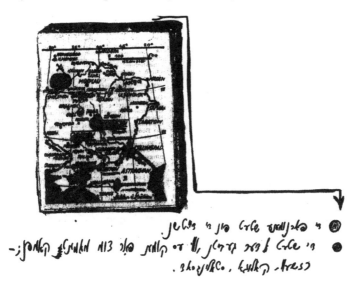

[Translation of original legend created by author]
- Cities taken by the Germans
- Cities or regions where battles are currently underway: Rzhev, Kaluga, Stalingrad

The previous night Russian airplanes with destructive aims flew over the German eastern regions.

Yesterday, the Russian air force lost 128 airplanes in one attack. Eight of our [German] planes did not return from a flight over the Russian regions.

---

140 Lake Ladoga is a freshwater lake located in the Republic of Karelia and Leningrad Oblast in northwestern Russia, in the vicinity of Leningrad (Saint Petersburg). During much of the Siege of Leningrad, Lake Ladoga provided the only access to the besieged city because a section of the eastern shore remained in Soviet hands. Supplies were transported into Leningrad with trucks on winter roads over the ice, the "Road of Life," and by boat in the summer.

141 The Neva River was one of the lines during the siege that the Germans imposed on the city of Leningrad.

On September 9, during the day and in the evening, a number of planes flew over western Germany. They dropped a few bombs, which did little damage.

Two British planes were shot down over the Channel.

<u>Rome</u>

Rome officially reports that the German division leader General Georg von Bismarck[142] fell in Egypt following a battle which lasted a few days. He fell as a hero.

<u>Amsterdam, September 10</u>

According to the news from the English news agency, massive battles continue north of Port Moresby, and are intensifying. The Japanese are 44 miles from the port.

<u>Berlin, September 10</u>

On the ninth, the Russian forces did not launch any major assaults. Furthermore, it has been related that this month, between August 30 until September 6 alone, 3,128 Soviet tanks have been destroyed in the Kaluga and Rzhev regions.

Russian assaults are underway near Kaluga and Rzhev, however, these are immediately squashed by the Germans.

German planes bombarded railways west of Moscow.

The German artillery has shot at Russian positions to the north-west of Medin.

<u>Vichy, September 10</u>

News has arrived that the English assault on a few beaches of Madagascar[143] began this morning. A number of places on the island have already been occupied.

---

142 Georg von Bismarck (1891–1942), was a German general who commanded several divisions during World War II. Bismarck was killed by a mine while leading the 21st Panzer Division in the Battle of Alam el Halfa (south of El-Alamein), on August, 31, 1942.

143 The Battle of Madagascar was the British campaign to capture Vichy French-controlled Madagascar during World War II. The seizure of the island by the British was to prevent access to Madagascar's ports to the Imperial Japanese Navy and to prevent the loss of or damage to the Allied shipping channels. It began with Operation Ironclad, the seizure of the port of Diego Suarez near the northern tip of the island, on May 5, 1942. A subsequent campaign to secure the entire island, Operation Stream Line Jane, was launched on September 10.

Amsterdam, September 10

According to the Reuters agency, the following western beaches of Madagascar fell at once: Majunga, Ambanja, which is 120 miles south of Diego Suarez, in addition to Morondava, which is 340 miles south of Majunga.

The English air force launched attacks 100 kilometers into the depths of Madagascar. Innumerable war ships bombed the beaches. (Madagascar was a French colony).

Stockholm

The street battles in India [sic] continue. The English are using the strongest means to "calm" the raging crowds. They are shooting people in the streets and the prisons are full. Five hundred people have been shot in India [sic] until now.

Headquarters Reports: Rome, September 10

The anti-aircraft artillery at Tobruk, Africa, shot down two British planes.[144]

Italian air forces again bombarded the airfield at Mkovo.[145]

Our destroyers shot down four British planes near Scoglitti[146] (Ragusa). One of the pilots, an American, had to evacuate, and, after parachuting, was taken prisoner.

Two of our planes have not returned [from missions] in the last few days.

The Italian torpedo boat *Polluce*[147] sank an English submarine in the Mediterranean Sea.

The Stockholm newspaper reports that Alexei Stakhanov fell at the front.[148]

---

144 A port city on Libya's eastern Mediterranean coast, near the border of Egypt. A renewed offensive in November 1941, by Axis forces under Erwin Rommel, resulted in Tobruk being captured in June 1942, and was subsequently held by the Axis forces until November 1942, when it was recaptured by the Allies.

145 Possibly Mkovo in southern Rhodesia (Zimbabwe). The British were in possession of airfields there but there was no fighting in the area. Another option is Mikova in Czechoslovakia, but the Italians were not active there.

146 A southern Italian fishing village in the Province of Ragusa, Sicily. The Allies chose it as the site for their amphibious invasion of Sicily launched by the U.S. 45th Infantry Division during the war.

147 The *Polluce* was sunk by torpedo bombers on September 4, 1942.

148 Alexei Stakhanov (1906–1977), was a Russian–Soviet miner. Soviet propaganda considered him as the founder of the Stakhanovite movement in 1935. This was a

The Struggles in the Battles during 1941
(According to the German report)

May 23–June 24: preparation of the positions for the battle in the east.

1. The [double] Battle at Balstogė [Białystok] and Minsk:

    a) June 22–June 24: breaching the border positions

    b) June 24–July 2: Balstogė-Slonim battle

    c) July 2–July 5: The battle at Svisloch and Berezina (two rivers) and crossing them

    d) July 5–July 9: the battle at the Dneiper

2. The Battle near Smolensk:

    a) July 10–July 14: breaking through the Dnieper positions

    b) July 14–July 20: the occupation of Smolensk

3. The Defensive Battle near Elnia and Smolensk:

    a) July 20–July 26: the defense of Smolensk

    b) July 26–August 9: the defensive battle near the Dnieper

    c) August 9–August 18: the defensive battle in the Elnia arc [semi-circular Elnia salient. Jelnes kilpoje, in Lithuanian]

    d) August 18–September 30: the defensive battle near Desna

4. The Double Battle at Viazma and Briansk:

    a) September 30–October 21: the battle at Briansk

5. The Assault on Moscow and Voronezh:

    a) October 20–October 24: battles in the Efremov and Tula districts

    b) October 24–November 20: Making use of the time in the field of operations [Lithuanian follows]

    c) November 20–December 1: the battle for Tula and the advance to Riazan and Kashira

---

campaign intended to increase worker productivity and to demonstrate the supposed superiority of the socialist economic system. The information recorded in Gerber's diary about his death was incorrect.

6. The Defensive Battles near Moscow:

a) December 1–December 22: the defensive battles in the Efremov and Tula regions

b) December 22 [–] The defensive battles north-east of Orel (and the battle continues)...

Operations and security measures in the regions (this apparently means the occupied regions) and battles against the Russian partisans.

September 24, 1942

Rosheshone and *Yomkiper* are already over. They are already behind us. I will note that the people tried to be pious during the time of repentance: they arranged prayer quorums (*Minyen*, in Yiddish) in private homes (since the synagogue, the *Besmedresh*, was closed on August 26). So, for example, a *Minyen* was held at the home of the Santotski family![149] There was a prayer leader and the main thing: The *Pnei* (lords) of the *shtetl* were there, like Natkin,[150] Lipcer, and many other bacon-eaters. Some people

---

149 On September 20, 1942, Tory recorded in his diary that "despite the ban on praying in public, many *Minyonim* [a prayer quorum of ten Jews] assembled in the ghetto. The wording of '*Hazkarat neshamot*' [remembrance of souls] has been printed on a typewriter by the council because of the shortage of prayer books and orders of prayer for the holy days." See Tory, *Surviving the Holocaust,* p. 135.

150 Karl Natkin (1888–?), was born in eastern Prussia, lived in Berlin until 1939, and arrived in Kovno to obtain an entry permit for the U.S., but remained in the city following the outbreak of the war. In the ghetto he served as the person responsible for the ghetto gate

tried to fast, others really fasted, and others still, in fact, ate like in the good times.

They recited the prayers, pounded their hearts, and then people had something to eat [to break their fast]—and signs of *Yomkiper* are gone: gone, left behind, people forgot it...

The young people meet almost every evening to have fun like little children—and for us the ghetto is not a ghetto. We don't feel it in our *khevre,* and we don't want to feel that we are living behind wires, separated from the world and from humanity.

The Vocational School officially opened. I received a certificate today (with bold letters, with ornaments, dots, with dates, and with little check boxes and stamps. There were also plenty of Jewish signatures, too...)

Lyusya's birthday was on September 21.

Izke Bubtshik[151] (a nice guy of around 13 or 14, maybe even 15, who lives together with Izke Kagan in the same apartment) and I went to Lyusya's at 7:30 that evening. There were red lights too, just like at Ilik's and Ida's birthdays. And most importantly—the table was prepared beautifully, wonderfully, deliciously, interestingly, and richly.

On the table were two kinds of little stuffed buns, with jam or with whipped cream; dark and light biscuits with two different flavors; sweets of all different colors; two whole cakes: one was light, beautiful, neat, white, and creamy, in the shape of a garland, and, most importantly, one could lick one's fingers after enjoying it. The other cake was in the shape of an eight, and was round, black, extravagant, shiny, creamy, and delicious. In short, people ate it too, and the young people certainly didn't abstain from it. Additionally, there was coffee (of the best kind) with sugar. This was on the table. Our group of young people—all sat around the table, according to Lyusya's order.

---

on behalf of the labor office and the contact person with the ghetto administration. He survived the Holocaust.

151 There is no extant information pertaining to this youngster.

September 1942

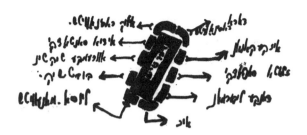

[Drawing of seating plan with names from right-to-left, clockwise:]
Dora Rabinovitsh, Izke Kagan, Zlata Santotski, Danke Liberman, Me, Lyusya Maniewitz, Bubtshik, Avremke Tiktin, Ida Santotski, Ilik Rabinovitsh

Within a few minutes the table was half empty. After another few minutes, there was really nothing left; but we left something, so that the Maniewitz family should also have something...

The tables were moved away, the chairs put on top of the closet, and Danke already stomped his feet, moving his hands in a lively fashion, bent his knees, and the room resounded with the stomping of shoe heels which beat the time of the "blow," "bang," and "whistle" orchestra, which our talented group created.... After the tap dancing (not a lot, because there was no record player so the dancing was to the beat of "our own orchestra"), a slow boxing match took place between Danke and Izke. People called for me to take part in the "comedy-boxing," but I refused. After the slow boxing, we played games, "deposits,"[152] and there was general craziness, but everything was joyful, good, beautiful—and everything was done so quietly, you could hear a gnat!

I was "lucky" in the "deposits": I had to hand over whatever I had on me. It had to be redeemed afterwards.

"What should the two depositors do?" asks Izke, the deposit holder.

"One of the two, whoever's deposit this is, must hold a short match between his lips and the other depositor must take the little match with his lips from the other's mouth," Danke suggested.

Everyone agreed. Izke showed the deposits. One deposit was Ida's and the other was mine. Ida and I looked at each other. Everyone erupted in

---

152 A game.

loud laughter. We also laughed. Danke broke a match into two halves and placed it in my mouth (between my lips).

"You can hold the match however you want, you can even pull it all the way in, but even then, she must take it out," jokes Danke. I wanted to obey him.

Ida got up and laughingly took a step toward me. I was in front of her. At that moment I noticed the happy-sad look on Avremke's face, who looked at Ida and then at me. My heart became uneasy. I took out the match so that it was more outside than in. Ida easily took the match with her lips from mine. People laughed.

"Oh, Lyuske, you are really no fun,"[153] Danke says to me.

"Come on, Lyusya,[154] you're a fool. You should take advantage of the opportunity," adds Zlata.

"Thanks, Lyusya," Ida calls out to me.

"You're welcome, Ida," I answer her, pretending not to hear the calls of Danke and Zlata. Shall I tell them that the look on Avremke's face stopped me from making a joke with a match? No...

A few minutes before 10 P.M. we snuck away from Lyusya's one by one.

Before leaving we heard the following:

"Esteemed *khevre*! This is a good opportunity for me now to remind you that this *Shabes*, September 26, the first day of *Sukes* [Sukkot, the Feast of Tabernacles], is my birthday. I invite you all to my home. I believe that you won't refuse me," Izke Kagan called out festively.

"And also, you won't forget to come to my birthday, which will take place this year on October 1..." called out Dora Rabinovitsh, beaming.

We went home.

---

153 The original Yiddish is not clear, but presumably this is the meaning. They are reproaching him for making it too easy for her.
154 Referring to the author.

September 25–26, 1942

Yesterday evening and today is *Sukes* around the world. Everywhere, in every land where there is even barely a *Minyen* of Jews, they are celebrating the festival.

Among us in the ghetto, people are celebrating this festival in the city or at the airfield.

Izke has postponed his birthday to October 13, because his mother is sick. Now we are waiting for October 1, when Dora will be celebrating her birthday.

Many illnesses have been spreading recently through the ghetto, for example jaundice, stomach typhus, dysentery, stomach flu, and food poisoning.

I met Heni on the street. I didn't notice her. I was standing with Berke Bek[156] and Kalter. She came up to me from behind and called me aside. I handed her a little flask (still sealed) with drops for the heart—this is the second time that I am giving her "medical" things. The first time was a Russian bandage for a broken bone.

That evening I went to visit her with Izke. We sat for a short while. Izke had already given her: plasters, tablets, four syringes of medicine to treat pneumonia, and now more plasters.

---

156 Boris (Berke) Bek, born 1925, was murdered in Dachau in 1945.

Ilya Gerber

September 27, 1942

Yesterday evening we went out walking, a group of friends. Before going home, I walked arm in arm with Zlata and discussed in a friendly way the good points and bad points of people, their character, and ideas. Not long ago I discovered that Zlata is not even eighteen yet! I was surprised—a strongly built girl with a good character, a good housewife, hands which can do everything, happy. She looks nineteen or twenty! It's not often one meets such a girl. And most of all—she is unassuming—I think—no hidden thoughts (so it seems) and sympathetic.

Recent Ghetto News

A month ago, the ghetto was talking about the eviction of residents from a few streets in the ghetto. Which? People were talking about the streets and lanes that are located behind Demokratų Street or Demokratų Square. People talked about it so much, until the residents of those streets were really frightened and, one night, the Jews from eight streets tried to move to the other side—to the ghetto area. For two days people got ready to leave quietly, they stole past the fence with pillows, with packages, and with suitcases.... And, in one moment, yesterday (*Shabes*, September 26), I look out of the window and I see entire caravans with wagons, possessions loaded on shoulders and backs: In short, we at home understood that the exact thing that people had been talking about for a long time was now taking place.

Putting on my work uniform, I went out in the direction of the Vocational School, which is located on the "fortunate" side which must move. On the way I encountered children, women, and men, all burdened, all dragging their remaining belongings. Imagine what a broken life this is.

September 1942

A while ago, when Jews lived on the other side of Demokratų Street, an order was given suddenly that within such and such a time, the Jews living on such and such streets, together with the main road there, Vienožinskio Street, should move out and free up the entire neighborhood on that side. In winter, during a big frost, the Jews moved, they toiled like ants, covered their noses, they dragged sleds and hurried over the snow, because within two hours the neighborhood around Vienožinskio Street had to be free of Jews. The deadline was later extended. The neighborhood, the eastern part of the ghetto, remained free of inhabitants. People in the ghetto said that the vacated quarter is designated for 1,000 German Jews who will be arriving.[157] We wait a week, another week, and they brought no one. They did not bring them but led them past [that area]! During that time, they took Viennese Jews, Rumanian, Czech, French, Dutch, and Hungarian Jews to the Ninth Fort, directly opposite our ghetto, on the hill.[158]

---

157 An order issued by the *Stadtkommissar* of Kovno on October 1, 1942, reduced the area of the ghetto, and the Germans began clearing the area around Demokratų Street and Square. However, rumors that the cleared area would be populated by Jews from Germany were inaccurate. German Jews were indeed deported to Kovno in November 1942, but were sent straight to the Ninth Fort where they were murdered. Tamar Lazarson-Rostovski noted in her diary that following the reduction of the ghetto area, her family were forced to take two more people into their home: "It will be very uncomfortable." See Lazarson-Rostovski, *Yomana Shel Tamara*, p. 41.

158 According to information provided by the Ninth Fort Museum in Lithuania: On November 25, 1941, 2,934 Jews, transferred from Berlin, Munich, and Frankfurt am Mein, were shot to death in the Ninth Fort: 1,159 men, 1,600 women, and 175 children. Another *Aktion* in which Jews from outside of Lithuania were murdered in the Fort took place on November 28, 1941. Two thousand Jews were deported from Vienna and Breslau and were murdered: 693 men, 1,255 women, and 152 children. Jews from Czechoslovakia, between 2,000–3,000, were fusilladed in the fall of 1941 together with Jews from the Kovno Ghetto. After the massacre, all documents of the victims were collected from the cells and burned in the Fort's yard. The Gestapo officers strictly warned Fort supervisors not to tell anyone about the massacre and threatened them with the death sentence for revealing the secret. In 1942–1944, the executions of small groups or individuals took place in the Ninth Fort. The last known mass *Aktion* (of foreign citizens' annihilation in the Ninth Fort) took place in May 1944. A transport with 878 Jews was sent from the Drancy concentration camp in France to Eastern Europe. Most of them were forced to get off at the Kovno railway station, and were taken from there to the Ninth Fort, where they were shot dead. Others were brought to the Pravieniškės forced labor camp and murdered in a nearby forest. The rest of them were transported to Tallinn. The lack of authentic information sources hinders indicating a precise number of Jewish foreign citizens killed in the Ninth Fort. However, it is apparent that there were no less than several thousand Jews who were murdered there during the period of the Nazi occupation between 1941 and 1944. My thanks go to Mr. Marius Peculis, director of the Ninth Fort Museum, for providing this information.

A while later—after the Jews from the eastern part of the ghetto had been sent away—the order was rescinded and the streets which before had to be evacuated could be settled again!

Jews did not hurry—no one believed the orders and their revocations. Slowly, slowly, Jews again tried to settle in the "fortunate part." In short, a group of about 1,700 Jews settled in the previously evacuated streets. Half the winter, and then the entire summer passed, and fall arrived. With the coming of fall there is a new order: On September 26, eight streets must be evacuated! Interestingly, before the order was issued, Jews already sensed something and two, three days beforehand, began to evacuate! From September 26, the German authorities allowed an entire five days for moving! One can understand the suffering of those who must move and mainly of those who already moved the first time and now again. I went to the Vocational School: it will be interesting to see if our school will stay or must also move its foundations... The mood in the school was, as they say, "distressed." The students and the masters were of the opinion that the school will remain in its place. Why? Because Hörmann[159] likes the Vocational School (I think that I have not written about that yet: it's true—Hörmann, the *SA-Hauptsturmführer*[160] is the real ruler of the ghetto, without his knowledge no Jews can be taken to work, without him no order can be given in the ghetto! This Hörmann, the party member Hörmann, is a very good person and had he not left Kovno for the moment, no Jews would be working in Palemonas. "He would not allow it!" say the Jews in the ghetto, repeating Hörmann's words.)

One fine day he came by taxi to visit the Vocational School. A civilian, a simply-dressed man, armed with a pair of little sideburns, he looked at the school. He stayed for fifteen minutes and then left.

People said that he liked the school. On this basis, people said that the school would remain the Vocational School and the fence would be [located] behind the building. Approximately something like this:

---

159 *SA-Obersturmführer* Gustav Hörmann, a Nazi officer, was head of the German labor office in Kovno. He treated the Jews well and fairly, and many Jews worked in his office, which was managed by Dr. Yitzhak Rabinovitsh. See Tory, *Surviving the Holocaust*, p. 70n1. During the war, Hörmann passed on a letter from Dr. Elchanan Elkes to one of his Lithuanian associates describing the Holocaust in Lithuania. Immediately after the war, Hörmann testified concerning German crimes in Kovno.

160 Should be *SA-Obersturmführer*.

September 1942

[Map showing from left-to-right, clockwise, with the following text:]
Demokratų Street and Square
This fence will be removed
The Vilija
The Vocational School will stay on this side of the ghetto and the fence will surround it on three sides
The fence will cut across Demokratų Street
The side of the ghetto which must be evacuated within five days

Thus, we students "planned" as did the school management. But it didn't help (more about that later). As I wrote earlier (on p. 414), the mood among us in school was not good. Most of the time we looked out of the window at how our brothers, Jews, were moving. Our hearts were gloomy. Some of the students from the school also had to move. People asked me to go and help, but Master Peres would not allow it. The Vocational School director, Engineer Freinkel, was outraged that we were pretending and not really working. So we began working. In the middle of everything someone came running, a student from the Vocational School who works almost opposite me in the carpentry, a refugee from Warsaw, with the family name of Klugman.[161] He is blond with blue eyes, and a good guy, and begged me: he is helping an acquaintance of his, a refugee from Warsaw, to move. The refugee has an airfield beam (a ghetto quota of wood) which needs to be rolled a few hundred meters but he can't do it because he has a wound on his stomach. Perhaps I can help him? I agreed straightaway.

---

161 Moshe Klugman survived the Holocaust, and lived in Kovno following the war. See list of survivors from the Kovno Ghetto, YVA, document no. 78782694.

Avrom Shafer,[162] another carpenter from our group, also went with us. The three of us left the Vocational School without permission and went in the direction of the log. This was a real and proper log. Klugman, Shafer, and I began to work. We labored a bit, we sweated a bit, and we pushed the log and rolled it until we reached the first single-story blocks, what was once the yellow workers' blocks, which the Russians built for the Lithuanian workers. This job took us half an hour.

September 29, 1942

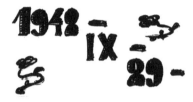

(Continuation from September 27)

After rolling the log, the three of us returned to the Vocational School. Before entering, Shafer called out:

"You know what, guys!" he turns to us, his face smiling, "you know what? You go in first and I will look from afar to see how Freinkel receives you... I don't want to get into any trouble."

We well understood and all three of us laughed our heads off. Klugman quickly opened the door of the Vocational School and went in. I followed him. And just our luck—exactly at that moment we encountered Freinkel...

"Where have you been?" we both heard the strong voice of the little engineer with the bump on his head.

"Where have you both been in the middle of work?" he asked us again and looked at us with acerbic eyes. I look at Klugman and he looks at me.

---

162 There is no extant information pertaining to this youngster.

September 1942

Klugman, the brave guy (I truly love his sincerity, happiness, and loyalty), as a result of his yellowness,[163] became even redder, his blue eyes became small and his voice shook, when he said:

"We were helping a sick person to collect…"

"Come into my office, I want to talk to you there," Freinkel cuts him off.

We went in. Freinkel tried to rest on a comfortable chair which was set aside for his honor, but he could not sit still for long: his custom of turning his neck from left to right when nervous and vice versa did not allow him to rest. He wriggled on the chair like a worm, pulled at his necktie with both hands while turning his head, and observed us sharply.

"Who allowed you to go?" comes the first question in our interrogation.

"No one!"

"Why did you leave the school?" second question.

"I called Gerber to help a weak, sick man to roll a log, here, just opposite the school."

"But you may not leave your place! When the school will be forced to move, where will you be then?" Freinkel cries, his voice ringing in the beautiful office, which was renovated according to his request. "I sit here, therefore it must be beautifully painted and arranged," he says all the time.

"Herr Freinkel, we know that leaving the workplace is forbidden, but to let a man get a stomachache[164]—I can't do it! I had to go and help him! He is a Jew and that is enough for me!"

I looked at Klugman with astonishment: to reveal so openly his thoughts, to answer and not fear the wrath of "Herr Director!"

"And regarding what you said, about when the school will need to move," Klugman continued, "I tell you that you will see me being the first at work. Then all arguments will be annulled."

Freinkel's face was enraged, his eyes were bloodshot, and he bit his lips with his teeth. I wondered at him. Not only I looked at the "yellow" one in this way, but also "him." He sat as though not himself, considered the one who spoke his mind, rolled his neck with his head from left to

---

163 Cowardice.
164 Perhaps a hernia.

right, nervously picked at his tie, and nervously put one lip on top of the other. He was anxious.

"I will remember you both! You will be first on my list to be thrown out of the school. You are free to go."

We left his office.

"Register them both," we still heard Freinkel's voice by the door, speaking to his secretary, Streletsky,[165] a tall, cold, slow person, with a hooked Jewish nose, and dark eyes, and all the while his head keeps moving, constantly shaking.

A few scrapes of a pen and our names were registered on a designated record.

We left the office. We looked at each other. Klugman embraced me happily and asked:

"You are scared of 'him'?!" I looked at him. Against our will we burst out in loud, happy laughter. Shafer, who had come into the school a little later, stood near us and not knowing why or how, also laughed. The laughter spread from one student to the next, who were waiting for us near the office, from them to Instructor Peres, and soon the entire corridor was filled with laughter, with "ha, ha, ha" and again "ha, ha." "Ha and hi, he, hi,"—in short, everyone was laughing so much they began crying and if one asked another why he was laughing—he could not provide an explanation. But suddenly, everything went absolutely silent, like in a grave. The door of the office opened and the "little one with the bump" appeared in the doorway.

"What is this crazy laughing here, why are you standing here? You should be working!" his voice grated in the silence. Neither dead nor alive, everyone ran from each other, helter-skelter.

Today, September 29, the school started to move from its previous place and into Block C,[166] a few steps from our block, where we live. As

---

165 This apparently refers to Yaakov Streletsky, a teacher in the ORT school in Kovno and one of the directors of the Vocational School in the ghetto. He was murdered in Dachau.

166 Block C was one of the line of buildings known as the "big blocks," located at 22 Varnių Street in the Kovno Ghetto; Block C was where the Vocational School was located.

September 1942

far as we can see, all the projects that were supposed to stay put have disappeared.[167]

People were saying that the school would move to Yeshuvatu no. 16. But then something happened, which more or less meant that it would move to Block C.

So listen to the story:

Almost every day, workers flee from Palemonas, where the Jews are laboring on the highway construction. Some of them come back to the ghetto while others flee to Vilna and in other directions on the way.

The committee, and most of all Hörmann, the *SA-Hauptsturmführer*, have taken measures against this. They want to stop the flight from Palemonas.[168] There's a note on the remaining ghetto fences: it lists the fifteen names and surnames of escapees from Palemonas and states that if they will voluntarily report back to their work they will not be punished. If not, and if they are caught, they will be severely punished. If they won't catch the abovementioned people, some of their family members will be sent off to do the work.

Apparently, over in Troki[169] they might have also heard this warning—but maybe not even there...

The ghetto inhabitants do not have one single night in which they sleep calmly through the night: in the middle of the night people go through the homes with lists and send people off to Palemonas in place of the escapees. Yesterday morning, Hörmann himself checked the passersby on Kriščiukaičio Street and whoever was not "kosher" was taken to the ghetto prison and from there—to Palemonas. That day alone he arrested (some say) twenty-five men (others say twelve) and thirty-eight women (some

---

167 On August 26, 1942, Köppen was appointed as commander of the Kovno Ghetto and published a list of new decrees, among them the order to close the Vocational School. However, the students continued to conduct group activities, and in mid-October 1942, when Köppen left his position and was replaced by Fritz Müller, the situation changed. See Oleisky, "Di fakhshul in Kovner geto," p. 27.

168 Over time the conditions in the forced labor camp at Palemonas, which were at first reasonable, deteriorated, and workers began to flee. Already in June 1942, Tory noted in his diary that ten workers had fled Palemonas, but apparently this number grew. Gerber's diary sheds additional and new light on the extent of this phenomenon and how the Ältestenrat and the German labor office reacted to it. Concerning the work camp at Palemonas see Christoph Dieckmann, *Deutsche Besatzungspolitik*, vol. 2, pp. 1090–1092.

169 Trakai or Troki, a small town in the Vilna district.

say only twelve!) and sent them away (the women were taken according to a list and they took those of the "better kind," with "professions").

Several workers have come from Palemonas to the ghetto a few times, taken the necessary things, and returned to their work.

This snatching of people in those areas near the ghetto gate had the effect that people are not moving to Yeshuvatu Street, because it is located near the gate. Block C is located on the side of lively ghetto life and less inhabitants live there. No serious police raids take place there.

At 7 A.M. this morning I was already at the Vocational School. There was real destruction and chaos in the school. The carpentry tables were turned upside down, the sawhorses thrown all around the room, many boards tossed around, half-finished work thrown aside, everywhere dust, a brouhaha and a racket.

"Look for boards that are 160 centimeters long, 4 centimeters thick, as many as you can find of that type." A group of us, four or five people, are given this order. We begin working. The rest of the students (there are eighty people working in the Vocational School!) helped move into the block. All the while Freinkel ran around, wearing his coat, with an empty folder in his hand (I am 100 percent sure about that), watched our work, hurrying along the work, calling us fakers and disgusting. He continued to run around from room to room like a whirlwind, like a little dragon, like a demon, [calling] "faker" here, "faker" there, and showing his power, which lies in his speech, in his voice, and he rushes on further, moving his head from left to right and that's it. While he was wandering around, people worked and as soon as he went off to the block, together with Instructor Peres, the mood improved, people whistled, and freed up material for firewood or, as we guys say, "it's for social aid"—meaning, for ourselves. And not only we profit from the S[ocial]A[id] (for short) but also the masters. The locksmith's workshop also has two masters. They, too, need wood. Master Peres also cooks a *Yushnik* on the wood. And Streletsky: he doesn't reject any carpentry wood. He has smooth boards: this makes a good impression, but when there are no smooth ones, he'll take whatever he can get. Berkman,[170] a former teacher, wanders around all day from one table to another and searches for refuse

---

170 This apparently refers to the Hebrew teacher at the Hebrew Gymnasium in Kovno, Zvi Berkman, born in 1888. He was deported to Dachau in 1944, and was murdered there.

[dregs]. He is a short man with a Jewish appearance, as well as Jewish glasses on a Jewish nose. He walks bent over, with his head forward, like he is looking for something (probably boards...), his stomach contracted, his legs a bit bent and, apparently, he suffers from flatfoot. He goes along dancing and whistling and he trips on a board. Then I come to help: I saw up the board for him and thereby earn a *mitsve* [mitzvah]... Berkman, the former teacher, is now something of a caretaker in the Vocational School. He must supervise that the prankster students don't pillage the materials. He records how many boards people take out of the storage room and his main occupation is looking for boards on the floor and asking everyone for a cigarette...

September 30, 1942

Tomorrow, the first, is Dora's birthday. She has already invited us this evening for tomorrow.

Today is the second day that the Vocational School is getting ready to move. I have looked at our new residence: a few steps behind our block stands the unfinished, large, three-story block. Its renovations stopped around the time that the Jews settled in Slobodka. It was previously enclosed with a large fence and window frames were stuck in the holes for the windows. However, the Jews had nothing to use for heating, so gradually, slowly, people stripped the wood from around the block and no remnant of a fence remains. Jews cut down a fence that was in place for non-Jews and burnt it and that's it. Later, the crowd took hold of the large, white, unfinished block, which briefly bore the title Block C. The window frames also disappeared, they too lived out their time and in their old age found a place in a Jewish oven. In short, Block C became free of wood.

Understandably, our new place can't be without windows. Simple, dark, four cornered holes looked from the block with horror at the Jewish ghetto. Now about the entrance. There is no stairway. Lift your feet high up and slowly put them on a high step which is an entire 75 centimeters higher than the ground. Then push yourself off from the spot powerfully and let us assume that we are now already in the entryway. Opposite, you see two staircases. One goes up, the other goes down—to the cellar. We will leave the cellar alone for the moment, but I will emphasize here, that if one is thinking about going and taking a look at what is underground, one must not lean on the handrail, which is not there, because then I can't guarantee your life... A few stairs (also without handrails) lead us to the first floor. Three doorways, on three different sides, look back at us. No sign of a door. Nothing there to help you choose which hole to crawl through because everywhere reigns the same chaos and destruction as downstairs. Each door leads to a few rooms. These should be so-called [unclear word...], unfinished. The floor is not the same in every room. For example, in one room the iron beams protrude. In another room there is already a concrete floor (that is, made of cement, probably for a kitchen, perhaps for a bathroom, I don't know...), in a third—a sandy floor. But there are no real floors, the way they should be, in the entire block. One) The walls—one can count the bricks one by one. Not yet whitewashed, not plastered—nothing done about this. You look at the walls and from the walls—whole and partial bricks, white and red, look back at you. Two) (How do the Jewish women say, and counting?...). Windows? Heaven forbid for Jews! Without panes and without frames. Now they have started to "glaze" the empty holes which jut out from the empty walls. Three) The ceiling? It is hard to say that this is a ceiling: If the ceiling was not hanging unsteadily in the air above my head—I wouldn't be able to say that the ceiling is a ceiling: you look up, raise your head upwards, and see above you twigs, intertwined with one other. And between them you see the second floor, if you are on the first.... But just imagine! God blessed the block with a roof. If not, it would have rained from the roof onto the third floor, from there onto the second, from the second the rain would reach us in the carpentry, on our heads. It is just good that there is a God and He protects us in the form of a roof...(so it seems, hence this is Four).

OCTOBER 1942

October 2, 1942

Yesterday was Dora's birthday. At 7 P.M. I went to Lyusya. She was already almost all set to go. She had bought sweets for forty-eight rubles and we went straight to Dora's. From outside, we could already hear them playing the music of a Russian romance. We entered the room and Mrs. Rabinovitsh came up to us. I expressed my good wishes to her and did not forget Dora. Those present already were: Dora, Ilik, Ida, and Izke. Dora was pleased to see us.

"Where is Avremke?"

"He is coming later," Izke answers me.

"And Zlata with Danke?"

"Danke is still at the airfield and Zlata won't come without him..."

I look at the covered table. The table consists of two small tables placed one next to the other. The table holds: A chocolate cake, creamy and shaped; next to it are a few plates with pastries; sweets of all kinds; a large garland, which looked like babke; and other desserts and nosh. Around this presentation of sweet things stood ready: cups, glasses, and more mugs for coffee. Next to each saucer is a little piece of white paper with the inscription of a family [name]. Each one had his spot, his place. Obviously, each couple sat down one next to the other. A red light was placed on a box. And a record player, placed on a chair, emitted beautiful, sonorous sounds: *The March of the Athletes* (a Russian record).[171]

Dora showed us what she received for her birthday. From Izke she received a brooch with a red stone and a special little box of four compartments for cosmetics. From others—from acquaintances—a mechanical pencil and something else. The mood was not so good. It wasn't so cheerful and everyone sat somewhat away from the tables, just like dolls.

Everyone was nervous and looked at the time.

"Where is Avremke?!" someone in the room asked every minute. "Why isn't he here?! And where is Zlata with Danke?!"

Izke suggested that he should go to Zlata to call them. He went off.

Avremke arrived at 8 o'clock. He took a "half"[172] and stood at the sideboard.

He defended himself saying that our clock is wrong. That it is actually running fast. Within a few minutes of arriving he had argued with Ida, his girlfriend. He offended her and she offended him. That evening they tried not to talk to each other. Around 8:30 the long-awaited people arrived: Zlata, Danke, and Izke. The mood improved and lightened up. People straightaway set about eating. Coffee with cake, cake with biscuits, coffee with babke—it wasn't bad. Right after eating people made space in the room. Chairs and tables disappeared like hocus pocus. Izke sat down next to the record player, "tickled" it, and it laughed out loud in the form of tangos, foxtrots, and rumbas. With the first dance, a tango, I got up and went over to Izke.

"Izke, get up. Leave the record player," I say to him, and wink in the direction where Dora, Izke's beloved, is sitting.

"You are right, my child," Izke happily jests and takes a step toward Dora.

I sat down. I looked at the record player. A commotion of voices drew my attention.

"No, I said! I won't!"

"But Dora! What's this? What's going on with you?!"

---

171 Probably *The Athletic Festival March*, composed by Sergei Prokofiev.
172 *Halbe*, which means half.

October 1942

"Girls, don't argue with me and that's it! Lyusya[173]—come dance," Dora turns to me.

I looked at Dora and did not understand: Izke had asked her to dance. Had she refused him? Indeed, how could that be?

"What's going on Dora?" I ask her, sitting where I am. She stands opposite me.

"Don't ask, Lyusya![174] Come dance!"

"I refuse!"

She looked at me. She became serious.

"Lyusya, do me a favor. Don't refuse..."

I gave in.

In the middle of dancing, I say:

"Dora, what does this mean?"

"Nothing...nothing...." She answered quietly.

Such scenes happen often among couples in love. And I believe that what happened on her birthday is also a product of female caprices, of making themselves interesting (I'm simply telling the truth), of wanting to be an object of attention. And perhaps, ultimately, she is not really responsible for this—this is a woman's heritage, it is passed on from woman to woman and in their [flirtatiousness], willingly or unwillingly.

I danced more than any of the guys: Avremke Tiktin says he is exhausted. Danke had come from the airfield—he also didn't dance. He tapped a few times but had no energy for dancing... Izke danced a few times. Ilik—the same. I missed almost none of the dances. One foxtrot after the other, one dance after another—I wanted to dance. I had to dance...it is hard for me to explain in words...

At exactly 10 P.M. the evening ended. I went to accompany Lyusya. It was a beautiful, starry night, like all the nights of birthdays.

Yesterday, October 1, the Führer spoke on the radio. When I get hold of the newspaper, I will try to translate it into Yiddish.

---

173 Nickname for Ilya. Not to be confused with his female friend, Lyusya Maniewitz.
174 Referring to the author.

A few days ago, the German newspaper reported that the Party House in Stalingrad[175] was stormed. Each house is a fortress, reports the *Kauener Zeitung*.[176] There were further reports yesterday and the day before from the Eastern Front that the German Wehrmacht pierced the northern part of Stalingrad and is slowly advancing.

Yesterday, they shot three Jews at the fence. They were either going there to trade or they were too close to the fence. One of them, a Jew of fifty years old, was killed on the spot. A bullet went through his forehead, the second hit him near his liver. The second victim was a woman. The bullet hit her hand, which had to be amputated. The third victim was a seventeen-year-old young man with the family name of Kaplan.[177] He was walking with his sister close to the fence. The bullet hit him in the leg. The woman and Kaplan are in the ghetto hospital.

Today, October 2, around 8 P.M., I met a few guys from the Vocational School. They tell me that we must also move out of Block C.

"Where to now?" I ask with "serious" resentment.

"Back to Ramygalos, to the former school, back to where we came from!" they explain to me in one breath.

"How do you know?" I don't let it go.

"Freinkel, the one with the bump, told me himself! And another thing, listen, the sawmill is also moving to our side, that means to the ghetto side, and Jews will operate it! Isn't that comical?"

---

175 The military campaign in Stalingrad began in September 1942. Initially, it seemed that the city would quickly fall into German hands. However, during the second half of September, the battle became difficult and brutal. More than once, both sides became embroiled in very close combat, fighting from street to street and house to house, turning the city into a pile of rubble. The battle continued until February 1943, when the Red Army finally won.

176 *Kauener Zeitung*, a German daily, was published in Kovno from July 1941 until July 1944.

177 According to Tory's diary, on October 2, 1942, Lithuanian policemen wounded seventeen-year-old Leib Kaplan and Mrs. Kanzer next to the ghetto fence. See Tory, *Surviving the Holocaust,* p. 138.

October 1942

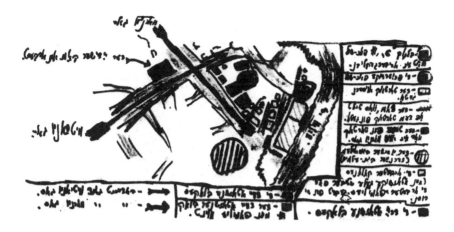

- 🔴 Block C—to where the Vocational School moved
- 🔵 The previous Vocational School
- ▭ The sawmill outside the ghetto
- ⤤ The fence which separates the sawmill from the ghetto
- ■ The door of the sawmill which is on Varnių Street
- ⓘ The Jewish cemetery (the new cemetery)
- ▫ The workers' colonies (one-story yellow houses for the workers' families, built by the Russians)
- ■ The three-story blocks
- ◀ The two-story blocks
- ■ The two-story block where my family lives
- ➡ Direction of Vytenio Street
- ➡ Direction of Varnių Street

The map on p. 438 [the previous page] should approximately show 1) the sawmill; 2) the former Vocational School; 3) Block C, to where the Vocational School recently moved; 4) approximate location where we hang out, for example the two-story block, which in fact stands on Vytenio Street and is considered Varnių Street No. 32 and; 5) the Jewish labor office or committee.

As I already wrote on p. 438 [previous page], the sawmill, which is currently outside the ghetto, will move over to the ghetto side.

- ■ Ghetto side
- ～ The fence around the sawmill
- ■-□ The sawmill
- ▧ Other side of Vilna [Vilija?]
- ▬ The gate to the sawmill
- ▨ The entry to the sawmill from Varnių Street

Up until now, the sawmill was closed to the ghetto. That means that the sawmill was encircled from three sides with a fence and from the fourth side the sawmill bordered the Vilija. Both peasants and Jews worked there. The peasants apparently had certificates to go in through the Varnių gate and, upon following the street straight to the Vilija they would come to the sawmill. The sawmill actually belongs to the Germans. The Jews who work there belong to the airfield. This, more or less, is how it works: At 5:30 A.M. all the Jews who work at the sawmill assemble at the square where all ghetto workers gather, that is at Arigalos Square. There, the designated workers are allocated a guard who takes them through the ghetto to the sawmill. The sawmill receives materials through the Vilija. Eighty percent of the workers in the sawmill are Jews; the rest are peasants.

If it is true that the sawmill will be inside the ghetto and its fence will be removed, then only Jews will work in the sawmill, because they will not allow any free Lithuanians to enter an open ghetto.

October 3, 1942

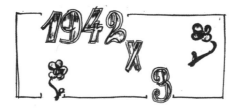

This morning I came to work, as always (like yesterday and today...), to Block C. I met Instructor Peres at the block.

"Go back home and put down your tools," he says to me. "Only keep your hammer, because we are moving back to the previous school!" he continues with a happy tone.

"And, master, I have heard that the sawmill will also move to the Jewish side?" I ask him.

"Yes!" he answers, "So Freinkel says."

Because today is *Shabes* and tomorrow is Sunday we must go to the airfield, so the master gave us an easy job: taking our own workstation back to the previous Vocational School and then we can call it a day. At 9 A.M., everyone had already finished their work. We, the young guys, gathered in a carpentry room on the second floor of our old school and gave concerts, harmonizing. It was happy and cheerful: in short it was a real musical concert... The greatest musicians of the Vocational School took part: first [soloist]—Solke Shukstaliski;[178] second soloist—Shleyme Finkelstein; support and rhythm—I present you: myself. The choir included: Bebke Khaytovitsh,[179] Zerubavel Rozenkrantz,[180] and others from among the audience.

---

178 Solke (Solya or Solomon) Shukstaliski was murdered in the Kovno Ghetto in July 1944, during the ghetto's liquidation.
179 Berl (Dov) Khaytovitsh was born in Kovno in 1923. He studied at the Hebrew Gymnasium in the city. His fate is unknown.
180 The diarist made a mistake in the surname. This refers to Zerubavel Rosenzweig.

At 12 noon we received stamped cards and we were finished. It is now 6:45. Enough for today. I must go to Izke to [record] the Führer's speech. "Bye bye," diary.

October 5, 1942

I will report here how the days passed for me and afterwards I will report the Führer's long speech.

Yesterday, Sunday, October 4, I was ordered by the labor office to go to the airfield. I went to work at Panemunė.[181] We went on foot up until the green bridge. There, a vehicle approached which was to take us to our workplaces. Around 100 men got into the vehicle and, with difficulty, we reached the Panemunė barracks. There we formed two groups and the foreman called out:

"Potters—forward!"[182]

Around ten potters, or ostensible potters, left the lines and went off with their supervisor.

"Whoever is a Zimmermann—come forward!"

I left the line.

"You are no Zimmermann! (Zimmermann is almost like a carpenter)," calls out an old supervisor.

---

181 A small town situated on the banks of the Neman River in Tauragė district, Lithuania.

182 A pottery workshop operated inside the ghetto. Tory noted in his diary that *Stadtkommissar* Cramer was very proud of this venture and spent long hours there. The family-owned pottery factory that had been active in Kovno for generations then became a German commercial concern, apparently also saving artisans from other locations. See Tory, *Surviving the Holocaust*, p. 264.

October 1942

"Supervisor, I am a Zimmermann, I know the trade well," I stammer to him in German.

In short, I became a Zimmermann. We didn't have much work, no one stood over our heads, and the supervisor was a fine little man. According to him, Hitler, together with the Russian Führer (the Stalin, as he calls him) should never have been born...

At 11:30, I went to a Panemunė German toilet, you will excuse me. I went inside. In less than a second, I was already sitting and I made myself comfortable. Thus sitting, lost in thought, I heard a soldier's footsteps. A German, a private first class, came into the big "office." My heart became gloomy and my stomach heavy: It has been known to happen that Germans would throw Jews out of the toilet and afterwards watch as the latter run with their unbuttoned trousers in their hands. I think to myself, "Nu, that's it, nothing to do...I need to move it." I consider the German. He is thin, somewhat bent over with sad eyes. Apart from that he has a half bald spot on his head... He doesn't say a word to me. He starts to pace back and forth, puts his hands on his back and pays no attention to me. I sit—he walks. I wait for him to go away and let me complete my business—but he has no intention of leaving... He goes this way and then back again and I feel that something is weighing on his heart, that he wants to talk, but he isn't brave enough, he doesn't know how to start. After a long time of contemplating from the side he stands exactly opposite me. I pull up my trousers, place one hand on top of the other and he stands in front of me, looking at me.

"How are you?" he asks me after a long silence.

"How should I feel? Sometimes good, sometimes bad, depends on what is happening," I answer cautiously, shyly, avoiding his gaze.

He looks at me, smiles, and begins his pacing again.

I watch him. He passes me by once, a second time, and then the third time he stops again.

"Are you buying something?" he finally says what had weighed on him the entire time and until now had been stuck in his throat. He blinks his eyes and looks at me.

"Are you asking me where I work?" I fix a pair of astonished eyes on him and try to understand his strange speech.

"No, I am asking whether you are buying something," he says, smiling, and now I have finally understood that his previous question also sounded something like that.

"What are you selling?"

The German pulls out a new red comb and shows me.

"Five marks (fifty rubles)," he says, "it's not expensive. This is a French comb and in Germany you can't get hold of such a comb."

"Five marks?" I repeat his words, "that's not cheap."

"So maybe you need a lighter. Not expensive, also five marks. A French lighter from the 'good times.'"

"Five marks? It seems…" I start to say.

"I can also add in ten flints as well. Five marks is not expensive…"

I look at him. The face of an honest thief with sad eyes, looking at me openheartedly. I don't feel good in his company and think that it will really be a miracle if he will go away.

"So, what's your decision: Are you buying something from me?" he asks.

"Yes, I would like to, but it's too expensive," I answer and at the same time fidget on my hollow seat, avoiding looking him in the eyes, and feel that my stomach is making terrible sounds. The German smiled happily but a moment later he looks sad again.

He stands in front of me, talking, begging me like one begs a *Rebbe*, to buy something, and I, like a great merchant, sit completely comfortably, and I might as well invite him to sit down next to me…

"If you don't like this," he keeps on talking, "perhaps you need a fountain pen?" And while he is talking, he takes out a fountain pen and shows me how it writes.

"Yes," I say, "this is good. How much for it?"

"Not expensive, eight marks."

"Yes! Eight marks is not expensive, even though the pen is a simple one, but where can one get ink for it?" I ask him a simple question to get rid of him.

"Ink, yes I have ink. An entire flask. I can sell it to you."

I begin again to fidget on my seat and feel my Jewish patience gradually cracking and my stomach cramping, oh the cramps, but I restrain myself… It is nevertheless not fitting in front of a German's eyes…

"I will ask my comrades," I tell him, "I will go in a minute and then I will ask them."

"But don't tell them it costs eight marks, rather ten marks!" he instructs me.

"Good," I answer him, "I will ask straightaway, right after I finish here…"

The German took a step to the exit. He left.

I breathed freely. I settle down and try to recover myself. Oh ho! He is back again! I see black! I find myself in a bad situation. But there is a way out! I sat back down and tried again the strength of the 5 centimeter thick piece of wood which was able to support half my body…

He again stands in front of me and his pleading eyes consider me.

"Maybe you need a silver watch?" And he pulls out of his small pocket a large, heavy, half-white watch…

"Why do you want to sell such valuable things?" I ask him, sitting and looking at him in wonder.

His voice trembles. His eyes look at an invisible spot on the wall and he speaks as though to himself.

"I have been away from Germany for three years now. I have a wife and children there. I have received five letters from her. I am going back to my homeland soon."

He stops. Tears fill his eyes. He is silent for a minute and looks at me and I feel that my heart sympathizes with him. I feel sorry for him.

"I haven't seen them, my closest family, in three years. Now I have an opportunity to see them…" his voice becomes nervous and rigid.

"I will come to her…, yes I will come to my wife with a thin body, with a thin face, and with empty hands…no I cannot do it. No, I cannot come to her, no…."

The last words receive less energy from his body and his willpower, because they sound weak and artificial. But in any case, I feel sorry for him!

He looks again at me; me at him; him at me.

"Maybe you need two new handkerchiefs?! Really cheap…" He shows me a blue piece of material […].[183]

"No, I have that at home," I answer. "I will buy the comb and the lighter."

I see how the man becomes cheerful. He takes the things out of his pocket and "praises" them, saying that they are good, that you can't get things like this in Germany…

---

183 Uncut, the edges not sown up properly.

"Whatever will be will be..." I think to myself and pull up my trousers...I pay him ten marks for the merchandise and run off quickly from the WC. I didn't return to my workplace but hid behind a tree, wanting to wait until he left the lavatory. He indeed left right away and I went back to the lavatory to finish my "anticipated plan"... I take off my belt...and then I hear steps and my heart beats wildly[...].[184] I stand up and prepare myself and, in that moment, he enters...the same sad look from the German stares at me again. He stands in the middle of the door like that devil from *Faust* and disturbs the other guy "at work."...

"Maybe you want to buy bread?! I'll soon get sweets from my wife, I will be able to sell those, too."

"How much is the bread?!" I ask cold-bloodedly and feel that either a catastrophe is happening to me or I will burst out laughing from pain.

"The bread costs ten marks!"

In short, I didn't answer: I ran past him from the lavatory and went to search for another WC among the "much-loved" Panemunė barracks.

This morning we tried to work in the original Vocational School, in the real school.

Around 11, a student came running to the school, out of breath, and stammered that Von Köppen had arrived with the ghetto commandant and another civilian German by the name of Dach.[185] Panic ensued in the school. The work gradually stopped. Work tools were silent. Chaos reigned on both floors of the school.

Von Köppen first, Dach second, and lastly, the ghetto commandant appeared by the window of the first floor.

"When I say 'Attention'—you immediately stand in line," Peres instructs us.

A few minutes later the slim figure of Von Köppen appeared. A handsome, thin face, young, a bit murderous looking, with a pair of

---

184 Illegible words.

185 This probably refers to Friedrich Karl Trampedach, born 1907, who joined the Nazi Party in 1931 and was commander of the political department (Gestapo) in Reichskommissariat Ostland.

arrogant eyes that considered us. For one minute he stood in the doorway and then straightaway strode with sure steps into our room. A tall figure, dressed in civilian clothes, a beautiful, well-fitting leather coat, well-pressed trousers, from the front and the back, with a border, with lacquered shoes on his feet, and on his head—a kind of grey hat with a green bow. Strong, tall, and neat—a true German. Dach is also in civilian clothes, but more simply dressed. The ghetto commandant is decorated with all his medals for "service to the Fatherland" on his green uniform with a pistol at his side, with a long nose like a [...],[186] creating a bad impression.

I can't say the same about Dach. Indeed, dressed simply, but he makes up for this with intelligence. His appearance suggested a mild character.

Only the first two came into the room. The commandant went off somewhere else. Von Köppen went through the entire room until the end then he turned around to face everyone and cried out, as is the German custom:

"Where is the *Achtung*?! When someone enters, you must say *Achtung*," he calls out loudly.

Freinkel, the small, insignificant person, at that moment a tiny man, looking at the big shot with fearful eyes, was really frightened and grated out ten minutes[187] later the word:

"*Achtung!*"

The students looked at each other and some even tried to smile. Everyone enjoyed the slight delay of the *Achtung*.

"Who is the director of the school?!" asks Von Köppen.

"Me!" Freinkel dances forward a few steps on his short legs to Von Köppen and remains standing before him in a frozen pose, like a cold mummy.

"What is your name?!"

"Frein-ke-e-e—l!" Freinkel draws out his own family name and opens wide a pair of glazed eyes, trying to compete with Von Köppen's height.

"Which Freinkel are you?" comes another question.

---

186 Some sort of derogatory comment. Like a snatcher, or a kidnapper.
187 Should be seconds.

Freinkel explains to him what he is, who he is, and where he comes from. Von Köppen cuts him off in the middle (he had the cheek to do so!...)

Von Köppen asked the "mummy" a few more questions, to which Freinkel routinely answered no, no, and no, again.

Von Köppen turned away from Freinkel, showing him his good side. The latter, however, continued standing like a soldier with straight, stretched out fingers and held himself nicely, none of his veins were moving, because... he had turned to stone out of fear. His look tried to penetrate the walls of the Vocational School, but the bricks would not allow it, they stopped the power of his glazed eyes. He made no movement: his look was focused on one point on the wall and apparently he really did not feel well.

Von Köppen left the room; Dach followed him. Freinkel looked as though reborn. Quickly and with firm strides his feet moved through the room, thereby showing his power, which is concealed in his quiet, majestic walk.

We, the carpenters on the first floor, remained below and the big shots went up to the second floor. The big shots went in order of authority. First: Von Köppen; second—Dach; third—the ghetto commandant; and fourth—the big shot Freinkel. And finally, after a long interval, Instructor Peres went up cautiously.

While "they" went upstairs to look at the second floor, we sat below waiting impatiently for the [finale]. No one worked. Everyone's gaze was focused on the door. A few minutes of complete silence. Suddenly, we heard a commotion above our heads and nervous, quick steps near our door. People were scared and started "making an effort."[188] Peres's pale face appeared at the door. He tells us the following:

When Von Köppen went up to the carpentry upstairs, Freinkel grumbled with a hoarse voice (just like someone put a hand over his mouth to stop him from talking):

"Achtung!" However, the *Achtung* came out so unsuccessfully, so cautious and quiet, that in the commotion of the banging his voice was lost and not every student heard the call. Therefore, some students stopped

---

188 *Terkhenen*—make an effort (in a display of working). See Kaplan, *The Jewish Voice in the Ghettos and Concentration Camps*, p. 28.

banging for a moment, others a bit later, and the rest carried on banging, as though it was not meant for them.

Von Köppen looked at all of them and his pale face became purple-red like the setting sun...his beautiful lips opened and a flood of curses fell on the heads of the students, the deathly frightened guys.

"Out of here, you undisciplined group!" screamed the big shot and waved his hands around.

Guys—neither dead nor alive—made for the door, where there was chaos and commotion, a rush and a struggle, until everyone had packed into the corridor. And only Freinkel remains: as though it is of no concern to him, his assignment is now to stand taut like an arrow, straight head, straight body, straight hands, straight feet. He stands and looks further at that invisible point, which, at the moment, is located on the white, beautiful ceiling. He stands and looks at the future. A cold sweat appears on his forehead. For him, the steam bath has only just begun... All the big shots again went past the small big shot—Freinkel—and did not even look at their faithful soldier. They went out into the corridor and ordered the students to go back to their carpentry. There, they found the director—Mr. Freinkel—as if frozen. The "pranksters" laughter is what awoke him from that other world to the reality of today and at breakneck speed, with hands stretched out, as though stuck to his little body, he ran from the carpentry and further stretched himself out before them at the locksmiths...

This is approximately what Peres related...noisy laughter erupted in the carpentry.

After looking at the rooms on the second floor, Von Köppen came back down to us. He looked at each room separately, until he reached the residence of the supervisors of the cleaners or, better said, the caretakers.

"No individuals may live here!" His command is heard in the carpentry. "By 12 noon the room must be vacated!"

From the Vocational School they went out into the courtyard. They looked at the old fence, looked here, looked there, and apparently considered where the new fence should be placed.

We guys looked through the windows at what is going on outside. Near the well we noticed Freinkel's big bald spot with the bump. Despite everything, he was standing in an exceptional pose. The Germans left the courtyard and went to their taxi, which remained stuck in the sand. Freinkel is still standing "at attention," an effect of the proximity to the big shots. Gradually, gradually, he recovered. Like someone who has been under hypnosis, he gradually returns to himself. His cheeks, which had become pale, regained color, the eyes regained their former sheen, that of a big shot, and the turning of the head from left to right revealed that there stood before us not a mummy, not a frozen figure—but Freinkel; Mr. Director, the leader, Engineer Freinkel! The big shot Freinkel! In short—the one with the bump on his head had pulled himself together.

Suddenly, there came an order: to help push the taxi out of the sand. First, cautiously and fearfully, a few students approached the taxi. After them, the first-floor students and after us—the second-floor students, the carpenters, and the locksmiths. Eighty people rushed to help. The first party reached the taxi and Dach sent back the remaining seventy people with a wave of his hand. The Germans, however, didn't want to travel further. At the corner of Ramygalos and Demokratų they considered the positions of the new fence. We stood a few steps away from them. I slipped among the closest to them to "catch" a few words of their conversation. They spoke about our school.

The ghetto commandant said that dangerous trade will take place at the corner of the school. He opposes the school remaining there. According to his opinion, the school should be moved to another place.

"No trade will take place here. And if it does occur—then I will flog the entire Vocational School." He repeated these words also to Freinkel. To hear their conversation better, I snuck into the first row among the men. I met Von Köppen's gaze.

"Bring a spade [German word]!" he orders.

I run back to the Vocational School. All the supervisors are standing in the courtyard with Freinkel, huddled together. I get hold of a spade and rush back.

"Dig a hole here, we want to see how deep the layers of the earth are."

I dig into the sand and make a deep hole.

"Enough!" I hear Von Köppen's voice.

I straighten up.

"Go, call your director," I hear a new order.

I call Freinkel. Von Köppen explains to him that from the hole, which I have dug, the fence must lead up to Panerių Street, through Demokratų

October 1942

Street. And from the other side the fence must be taken further along Ramygalos to the end and must turn behind the Vocational School. It looks something like this:

- Ⓓ The Vocational School
- ▬ The sawmill
- ✘ The hole which I dug on the corner of Demokratų and Ramygolos Street
- ▬ The path of the new fence

This means it's just like we students planned a while ago (see the plan on p. 415).

In short, all three of them got into the taxi and the engine kicked in. We began to push. Von Köppen drove with a weak motor (not completely on), sitting at the wheel, with us pushing.

Suddenly, the taxi began driving in a zigzag. Obviously, it became a lot more difficult for us, and it became even worse when Von Köppen turned onto a sandy hill and turned on the motor.

"Quicker guys!" we called one to another, "let's show what we can do…"

On top of the little hill it was a lot easier, but the engine stalled again. We push with all our strength—but nothing happens, they are not moving at all. Von Köppen […][189] a few times. We hear the sadistic laughter of the three in the taxi. The guys can't restrain themselves:

"Oy, a misfortune on all of you, on all three!" one shouts out loud while pushing.

---

189 Not clear, perhaps "tried to start it."

"You should slip whilst driving," one hears a second voice.

"What do you want from them?" comes a third, sarcastic voice, "I want to push them so far, even into the next world and wait, I'm not arguing with you, even to the next world, for the same money and effort...."

Apparently, the Germans in the taxi heard some of our conversation, because the taxi suddenly gave a lurch forward and we, standing behind, leaning on the taxi and pushing, landed on our stomachs.

In short, they drove off.

The Führer's speech on October 1, in honor of the Winter Relief campaign.[190]

In his speech, he first of all made fun of: democracy, Bolshevism, Jewry—in short, the entire world, except for himself. He, he is great— even greater; he is strong, even stronger, he is clever—a bastard! He surpasses all of them, compared to him they are all flies, and he doesn't give a damn about all of them, he doesn't care about anyone. This is the content of his speech. He has accomplished this and that for the people. Obviously, the Führer did not forget to mention the Jews. The difference is only that previously, in his former speeches, he didn't just mention the Jews. Quite the contrary: his entire speech was focused on the Jews. The Jew, and Jewry—is in every sentence of his, in every word. He started

---

190 On September 30, 1942, in his speech at the opening of the *Winterhilfswerk des Deutschen Volkes* (the Winter Relief of the German People), an annual campaign by the National Socialist People's Welfare Organization to help finance charitable work, Hitler said: "In Germany, too, the Jews once laughed at my prophecies. I don't know whether they are still laughing, or whether they have already lost the inclination to laugh, but I can assure you that everywhere they will stop laughing. With these prophecies I shall prove to be right. [...] On the first of September, 1939, we made two pronouncements in the Reichstag session of that date: First, that now that this war has been forced upon us no amount of military force and no length of time will ever be able to conquer us; and second, that if Jewry [sic] is starting an international world war to eliminate the Aryan nations of Europe, then it won't be the Aryan nation which will be wiped out but the Jews," see Ian Kershaw, *Hitler: 1936–1945 Nemesis* (London: Penguin Books, 2000). In 1942, Hitler repeated his "prophecy" four times in speeches concerning the fate of the Jews and their final annihilation. Many historians regard these words and their repetition as a clear and public expression of the plan for the Final Solution to the Jewish Problem. Apparently, the young Ilya Gerber (who read about the speech in the newspaper on October 1), understood the importance of these words already at this stage and included them in his diary.

October 1942

with Jews and ended with Jews. And now—now he doesn't talk so much about Jews, he doesn't say that the Jews are the misfortune of the German people and the entire world; he blames the Jews less now. Up until now he has blamed us enough for every misfortune and event which happens in the world—now he talks about the elimination of the Jewish people. He talks about mass destruction. He, the Führer, already speaks less about us. He says only a few words: he will destroy us. Here is the main section of his speech in which he mentions the Jews. He didn't mention us further in his speech. He only said this:

German text of speech [with one Yiddish comment].

[Translated from] The Yiddish:

> In 1939, on September 1,[191] I expressed my opinion before the Reichstag on two matters: first, after the war was forced upon us, no amount of force and also no amount of time will defeat us, and, second—if the Jews cause an international world war to destroy the Aryan peoples, the Aryan peoples will not be destroyed but rather Jewry (applause erupts in the hall after this section, as the Reichstag is roused to enthusiasm by the Führer's speech). He then mentions the English, who dragged one nation after another into the war, but at the same time the wave of antisemitism is progressing from one nation to another and it will, in the future, encompass all peoples; whoever takes part in the present war, will come out of it at the end an antisemitic state.
>
> The Jews in Germany also once laughed at my prophecies. I do not know whether today they are laughing or the laughter has already passed. I will certainly fulfill this prophecy, too.

---

191 This speech was delivered first by Hitler on January 30, 1939. However, for propaganda matters, he dated it to September 1, 1939—the day World War II started. According to historian David Bankier, this was purposely done to underscore the bond between the war and the extermination. See David Bankier, "Signaling the Final Solution to the German People," in David Bankier and Israel Gutman, eds., *Nazi Europe and the Final Solution* (Jerusalem: Yad Vashem, 2003), p. 35.

He did not mention the Jews any further in the October 1, speech. However, this was sufficient.

He spoke so much it filled up several pages of the newspaper. He spoke extensively and, according to his words, the redemption of the German people is already on Germany's doorstep, they must only usher it in. Mainly, they must be victorious following a hard-fought struggle. The Führer explains that as many victims and suffering that have already been laid down—they must give this many and even more in the future: and not spare any strength—and not spare even their own lives for the sake of the Fatherland. The victory will be won by means of a hard struggle, with suffering for and love of the homeland. This is approximately a brief summary of his long speech.

October 11, 1942

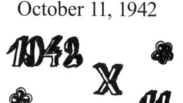

So there was Hitler's speech, and a few days later, Göring[192] also gave a speech. He spoke about the heroic bravery of the German army, about the brave deeds of particular fighters and emphasized that they are only brave and heroic because they know that they are fighting for a better future, for a secure tomorrow, for the Fatherland, for the Führer and most of all—they fight bravely for the little ration which each soldier receives…

According to the words of Marshal Göring, one could infer that the German soldier is worth a supplement and should be given an additional ration, exactly like the Jewish airfield workers, who work at the airfield all week long.

---

192 Hermann Göring (1893–1946), was a German political and military leader and one of the most powerful figures in the Nazi Party. He delivered that speech on October 4, 1942.

October 1942

Göring said:

"The German soldier travelling home from the front on furlough in the homeland receives separately a ration which he must bring for his family—first, he receives a kilo of sugar, three quarters of a kilo of black flour, 200 grams of butter, half a kilo of groats, and when the happy soldier crosses the border into his homeland, he also gets a bit of sausage.

The cities which have been bombed most heavily by the enemy will also be granted a ration: each family from the city receives 50 grams of meat per week!"

Since we are talking about products and rations, it is completely obvious that one then moves on to the theme of "the Jews," and Göring stated his opinion:

"Only one of the two can rule over the world: either the family of Romans or the Jews..."

The last words of his speech were:

"Today is good for us, but in a year's time it will be much better... why? Because in a year's time we will have the fruit of the Ukrainian earth. This year the fields were burnt by the Russian barbarians who want to starve the poor, unfortunate population..."

One thing I would like to emphasize: he believes that the Jews are dangerous to the German people, which takes pride in its physical strength and with which none can compare. But the Jew, the weak soul, the eternal hunched-over wandering Jew, with the eternal Jewish bag[193] and poverty—he, that same silent soul—he poses the danger to the German nation's downfall. In that moment, Göring increased the strength of the Jewish nation and put it on the same level as German power. Either the Germans will rule the world, or the sick, bent over Jewish beggars will. What a comparison... But probably he knows better, he isn't in such a senior position for no reason. If he talks about it, he must know what he is saying. The Jew—he poses the danger to the world; it is the Jew—in short, this is the meaning of the word: thief, swindler, robber, and destroyer of races. Destroyer of the cultural world, and so on and so forth...

A short announcement appeared in the Lithuanian newspaper:

---

193 For travelling.

"In France—300,000 Jews."[194]

Vichy: The general commissioner for the Jewish Question reported that, according to last year's registration, there are 300,000 Jews in both zones of France. However, it is known for certain that a great number of Jews avoided registering and apart from that, the number does not include the North African Jews.

A short announcement but an important one. This means that a year ago there were still so many Jews in France. Apart from that, there are also those in hiding, who do not declare themselves as Jews. What is their reason for printing in the newspaper and informing the world that there are still 300,000 Jews living in France—I do not know?!

According to the Germans' report—there are battles on the streets of Stalingrad.

The Russians have tried to cross the Don River, but nothing helped, the newspaper reports. In forty-eight hours, the Russians initiated twenty-four attacks in that sector against the Hungarians, Slovakians, and Rumanians—meaning, the ones pushing through launched an attack every two hours. The Russians yielded with great losses.

There are extensive battles raging near Voronezh.[195]

Also near Kaluga.[196]

Large battles raging at Lake Onega.[197]

---

194 On September 27, 1940, the occupying authorities published the findings of a census of the entire Jewish population in France, according to which 287,982 Jews were registered, 60 percent of whom were located in the occupied zone of France and 40 percent lived under the rule of the French government led by Marshal Henri Philippe Pétain (the Vichy government).

195 A city and the administrative center of Voronezh Oblast, Russia, straddling the Voronezh River and located 12 kilometers from where it flows into the Don River. The Germans used it as a staging area for their attack on Stalingrad, and made it a key crossing point on the Don River. In late June 1942, the city was attacked by German and Hungarian forces. In response, Soviet forces formed the Voronezh Front.

196 A city and the administrative center of Kaluga Oblast, Russia; Kaluga was briefly occupied by the German army during the climactic Battle of Moscow. It was occupied from October 12, 1941 to December 30, 1941.

197 A lake in the northwest European part of Russia, located in the territory of the Republic of Karelia (during World War II was the Karelo-Finnish Soviet Socialist Republic), Leningrad Oblast, and Vologda Oblast. It is part of the Baltic Sea basin. During the war, one of the major cities on the lake was occupied by the Finnish forces for three years and was the center of intense military activities.

October 1942

The newspaper reports that in the northwestern part of the Caucasus and south of the Terek River the German army divisions advanced with their allies.

Arkhangelsk was bombed again.[198]

Over the course of thirteen days, 816 planes were shot down in air battles, 131 planes were shot down by anti-aircraft batteries, twenty-two by the regular army, four were taken intact, and a further seventeen were destroyed on the ground. That means that in thirteen days 900 planes were destroyed. In that time, the Germans lost only seventy-seven planes.

The previous night, English fliers flew over the Baltic Sea.

There are battles at Rzhev.[199]

The Soviets are attacking around Lake Ilmen.[200] Within a month the Germans defeated fifty Russian attacks around the lake.

Extensive battles are also underway on the Leningrad Front. So it was on September 26, when the Russians tried to cross the Neva River. The Russian maneuver, the newspaper reports, was intended to save the critical situation at Leningrad. Despite the fact that hundreds of landing ships participated in the battle, watched over by eighty fast-shooting Russian artillery batteries, the plan failed entirely: the Russians lost [had] 800 prisoners of war, sustained more than 1,000 fallen [soldiers], 400 landing ships were destroyed as well as many armored ships in that area.[201]

Battles are taking place in the mountains in the Tuapse[202] region in the Caucasus.

---

198 During Operation Barbarossa, the German invasion of the Soviet Union in 1941, Arkhangelsk was one of two cities (the other being Astrakhan) chosen to mark the envisaged eastern limit of Nazi control. The German forces failed to capture either of the two cities, and also failed to capture Moscow.

199 For more information about Rzhev see the relevant footnote for diary entry from September 1, 1942.

200 A large lake in the Novgorod Oblast of Russia. The lake area was the location of an important battle during World War II.

201 During the invasion of the USSR, the German army besieged the city of Leningrad. The siege began in September 1941 and lasted until January 27, 1944, resulting in the deaths of more than half a million people. The Soviet campaign to lift the siege began only in June 1943.

202 A town in Krasnodar Krai, Russia, located on the northeast shore of the Black Sea. During World War II, the German military attempted to seize the town during the Battle of the Caucasus, which caused major damage to Tuapse.

October 14, 1942

1942.
X.
14.

The day before yesterday I got hold of the book *Dnevnik Kosti Riabtseva* (The Diary of Kostya Riabtsev) by N. Ognev.[203] The book describes the life of a schoolboy in the Soviet Union in the years following 1924. The book is a description of Russian students following the Revolution. It is a book of truth, no hidden thoughts and propaganda; it describes life with all its positive and negative sides. Interwoven are all the colors of life of the student's world. The book is very enlightening, and also adds a lot— because it presents only the truth: what happened is what was recorded. When I will have time, I will copy out a few extracts.

My sister Chaya (otherwise known as Mrs. Kalner), following a lot of struggles and a lot of running around and vexation, got into the large workshops. She is now working there for the fourth day as a "simple" laundress...and how much *protektsie* did one need for this, that she should work behind the firmly closed and locked doors?! How much of her health did it cost her until she was nonetheless allowed to work in the workshops for the important people of the ghetto? And for who do they work here? For the Germans, for our torturers!

The Jewish workshops (by this I mean the big ones, because there are also small workshops) occupy a big place in Jewish ghetto life. The ghetto workshops are located where the Slobodka–Lithuanian school was

---

203 N. Ognev or Nikolai Ognev was a pen name of Russian writer Mikhail Rozanov (1888–1938), who wrote the two-volume series about Kostya Riabtsev. The first part, *Dnevnik Kosti Riabtseva (The Diary of Kostya Riabtsev)*, was published in 1927; the second part, *Kosti Riabtsev v vuze (Kostya Riabtsev at University)*, was published in 1929. These books were also published during these years in Russian, in Riga and Paris; in Yiddish, in Moscow; in German, in Berlin; and in English, in London (N. Ognev, *The Diary of a Communist Undergraduate* [London: Gollancz, 1929]. In 1978, Progress Publishers that prepared publications for Soviet propaganda abroad published a new English translation: N. Ognev, *The Diary of Kostya Ryabtsev* (Moscow: Progress Publishers, 1978). Ognev wrote the first book about the radical changes in education in the Soviet Union in the 1920s from the perspective of fifteen-year-old Kostya Riabtsev, an independent and critical character.

October 1942

previously found—on 107 Kriščiukaičio Street. These are a few long, white-and-red buildings there. A group of Jewish policemen always stands guard around the workshops. Not everyone can get in there. Every person has a different certificate or a card saying that they work and are employed within the circle of the white-and-red walls.

These include the following:[204]

1. Clothing manufacturing no. 1
2. Clothing manufacturing no. 2 (tailors' department), no. 3, no. 4
3. Laundry (the laundry department also includes ironing and the drying room)
4. Leather workshop
5. Metal workshop
6. Brush workshop
7. Straw department[205]
8. Doll workshop[206] (also decorating)
9. Feather department (feather plucking)
10. Shoemakers' workshop
11. Woodturning (a section of the toys' workshop)
12. Carpentry
13. Smithy
14. Sock mending (embroidery)
15. Knitting section

It is apparent that Jews have become tradesmen (I don't mean to offend the former tradesmen) and everyone who was previously a member of the intelligentsia, who in all their years did not put a finger in cold water, has now taken to the work with zeal and the work burns under their hands. Why?

---

204 In December 1941, the Germans ordered that workshops be established in the ghetto. Over time, these came to include forty departments, and the number of workers in all departments reached 4,600 by the time the ghetto was liquidated. At first, the workshops fell under the authority of the Ältestenrat; later, they were transferred to the *Stadtkommissariat*. However, in reality, Moshe Segalson was the manager of the workshops. See Garfunkel, *Kovno Hayehudit Behurbana*, pp. 96–97.

205 Producing ropes.

206 Or possibly rags. There was also a toy-making workshop in the ghetto. See Tory, *Surviving the Holocaust*, pp. 156–157.

The city of Kovno has the SD, a general commissariat, and also many other high-ranking German divisions which wear underwear and make it dirty. The dirty underwear is sent to the workshops, to the laundry department. In short, there is enough work and [..][207] the workshops belong, in fact, therefore, to the [...][208] authorities and, till not long ago, a permanent German manager was there by the name of Peschel.[209] This Peschel left for the Caucasus Front. But this is not what I am getting at. Just as the workshops play a great role in our life, everyone respects the guarded buildings and understandably whoever has *protektsie*, gets in. Ninety percent of the former Jewish (Kovno) intelligentsia—not fit for work—are employed there. But they have gotten used to it and have already learned the job.

When a big shot arrives—he immediately goes to look at the workshops and this has helped us a lot in serious moments.

A few days ago, there was a report in the newspaper that the greatly esteemed *SA-Hauptsturmführer* Major Jordan,[210] the commander of all the bigger *Aktionen* in the ghetto, fell on the Eastern Front like a hero. In fact, he fell returning from the front—that is, behind the front—at the hands of Russian partisans. Before he left for the front, his laundry was washed in the ghetto workshops, in the laundry department. Apparently, the wish of the laundress was fulfilled.

Other former ghetto leaders from the NSKK have also fallen at the front some time ago. These include Shmikat, the "thief," and Hemfler, among others. Lewerenz was left without a hand and without a foot... (I won't wish them anything myself: the wishes of the Yekes—the German–Jewish men, women, and children—should be sufficient.)

There were "surprises" for the ghetto this week. As can be seen from the earlier chapters, they sent a certain number of Jews to Palemonas,

---

207 Unclear word.

208 Unclear word.

209 Martin Peschel was appointed by the *Stadtkommissariat* as the German overseer of the ghetto workshops.

210 *SA-Hauptsturmführer* Fritz Jordan was the first person appointed in charge of Jewish affairs in Kovno, as well as for the *Aktionen* and deportations for murder. In 1942, he left his post in Kovno and was sent to the front, where he was killed. Tamar Lazarson-Rostovski also noted this information in her diary: "The news about the fall of a few of those bloodsuckers from the NSKK, among them our worst enemy Jordan, who finally broke his neck, so cheered us up...." See Lazarson-Rostovski, *Yomana Shel Tamara*, p. 44.

October 1942

without the consent of *SA-Hauptsturmführer* Hörmann, the big shot from the German labor office responsible for the Jewish ghetto workforce. When Hörmann left for vacation, Von Köppen seized the opportunity and, without asking anyone's opinion, sent off a large number of Jews to work. When Hörmann returned from vacation, a rumor spread in the ghetto that he was not happy with Von Köppen's work and he would not have allowed such a thing.

It is evident that the work is very hard and generally conducted under difficult conditions. As Lurie, the Jewish airfield inspector (the inspector over the airfield workers) put it, one party of thirty-one men and a second of thirty-five men fled from there—all together sixty-six men fled! Sixty-six men fled from the work, fled from the guards, and from the murderous Hungarian supervisors. Some managed to flee to the ghetto and others set out for Vilna.[211] The Palemonas workers were divided into two groups. One went to work in Vievis[212] and the other remained in Palemonas. The work was difficult: providing all of Kovno and the surrounding area with gravel. Loading carts, and then, from the carts, pouring it into wagons. And the daily requirement is high: people say forty carts a day [per person] and one and a half wagons. When, at the appointed time, someone or other has not reached the quota, the "accused" receives up to twenty-five lashes from the Hungarian supervisors. Their provisions are next to nothing…

The situation in Palemonas is similar to that in Vievis.

Imagine, that one fine night, a cargo truck set out with the Jewish workers from Vievis! They took the Jews away from the work there and brought them to the ghetto. Among them is a lad I know—Bebke Shvartsman![213]

And imagine again, that the day before yesterday, around 5 o'clock, the Palemonas brigade arrived!

No more workers will be sent there, people say. The Jews will be replaced by Lithuanian "criminals" (they recently rounded up several

---

211 Concerning the sudden mobilization for the work camp at Palemonas, the reaction among Jews in the ghetto, and the role of the Jewish police, see Schalkowsky, ed., *The Clandestine History of the Kovno Jewish Police*, pp. 321–322.

212 A labor camp was established in Vievis, in the Trakai district, where Soviet POWs and Jews worked. In May 1942, approximately 700 Jewish laborers worked there paving roads and in construction under extremely difficult conditions.

213 Dov (Bebke) Shvartsman, born 1922, was murdered in Dachau.

Lithuanian black market dealers in the city). I need to stop by at Bebke's to see how he is doing.

A strange thing happened when they were about to travel from Palemonas to the ghetto. They were not informed, apparently, that the exhausted people were being taken back home, so they were afraid, and during the journey back to the ghetto nine men—Jews—fled from the moving vehicle! To where? No one knows...

There is a brigade here which travels to Yaneve to do forest work for two full weeks. Two weeks pass, and then the brigade people return to the ghetto. When the weather became colder recently, they distributed Russian heavy coats with boots to the Yanevers in Yaneve. The heavy coats did not have patches. On Sunday I take a look: Three "Red Army men" are walking around the ghetto, three young guys, talking, looking completely comfortable. I look at them in wonder. An acquaintance explained to me that these are indeed Jews but in heavy coats and without patches... It seems comical to me and I watch them until the last one disappears from my sight.

The day before yesterday a taxi brought two Jewish girls who had been imprisoned at the Ninth Fort to the ghetto gate. One of them went by the family name of Karnavsky. People relate that in honor of her arrival her family prepared a great celebration, which cost 25,000 rubles.

Recently two new "foreign" brigades were created: one left for Vilkovishk[214] and the second for Keidan [Kėdainiai]. Although it is forbidden to bring packages to the ghetto gate, nevertheless, somehow (with difficulties) they managed to bring them through the gate. Shultz, the "airfield's food minister" helped them. He's a good *Yeke*. He "takes" and he "helps"... There is another, similar brigade in Pren.[215] They work there for a week and then come "home" on Sunday...

---

214 Vilkaviškis, a town in western Lithuania. In September 1942, about fifty-five Jews worked in a forced labor camp which was established there. See Dieckmann, *Deutsche Besatzungspolitik*, vol. 2, pp. 1088, 1357.

215 The occupying authorities demanded that the Ältestenrat provide labor brigades to be sent to locations far from the city of Kovno. One of these was the town of Pren (Yiddish for Prienai) in the Mariampol district, where Jews built army barracks. Due to the distance from Kovno, the laborers returned to the ghetto only at weekends or even less frequently. See Garfunkel, *Kovno Hayehudit Behurbana*, p. 95.

October 1942

Yesterday, October 13, was Izke's birthday. The day before yesterday and the day before that he was ill, and his temperature was over 38 degrees. The day before yesterday, when the entire gang gathered at his house, he didn't mention anything about his birthday. We presumed that he would have to postpone the birthday a second time (see p. 409).

So then yesterday, in the middle of the day (at 4 P.M.), Avremke Tiktin came to me and told me that Izke will celebrate his birthday at 6:30. He suggested—and I agreed— that I was to come to Lyusya and we both should go to Ida, where Avremke would be waiting.

By the time I caught up with them it was sometime after 7 P.M. Ida, Lyusya, Dora, Avremke, Ilik, and I went to Izke's. My mood shouldn't have been so good, because I had heard enough that day about the latest news—and just what news there was that day.

On the wall, on the fence (a reminder of the destruction: I mean the word "fence"—how many fences are there here in the ghetto? You can count them on one hand...)[216] they hung notices in the middle of day:

"Report voluntarily for work in Riga! Looking for 150 women and 150 men to volunteer![217]"

A bad mood ensued in the ghetto.

After some time, the Germans went from notice to notice and, according to an order, tore them down. The Jews saw this as a bad sign.

They want to outwit us! People said that they don't need any people in Riga and that at night they will drag people from their beds! "We know them!" cries out a little Jew near the torn-off notice...

Ilik related that the order was cancelled by Hörmann. Others, however, are saying that Cramer, the commander of Kovno, was against sending Jews away from the ghetto.

Izke came toward us. Sounds of a Russian song could be heard in the room. I look around for the record player. There is no sign of it. My hearing ascertained that the sounds were coming from the sofa. I understood—the record player was hidden (so that it should not be heard outside) in the sofa and it was from there that the records were spinning.

---

216 It is unclear what the diarist meant here. He uses the term *zeykher lekhurbn*.
217 Regarding the call to register voluntarily for work in Riga, see Schalkowsky, ed., *The Clandestine History of the Kovno Jewish Police*, pp. 325–327.

For a short time we heard wonderful, solemn music from the record player as we sat around two circular little tables. We sat in the following order:

[Drawing of seating plan with names from right-to-left, clockwise:]
Izke's sister, Lyusya, Ilik, Bubtshik, Avremke, Ida, Me, Dora, Izke

The mood was not bad. We drank coffee and ate different kinds of baked goods (with cream and without cream, with raisins and without raisins). We had good treats, good company, we ate and drank, and didn't look at the time…

Avremke was truly in a bad mood. As soon as we left the table, he went out to the balcony, sat down on the handrail—and that's it. We didn't hear a word from him.

They put on a foxtrot, *Goriachi Bublichki*.[218] There were only two foxtrots and one tango.

"Go dance, Lyuske," the guys call to me (they themselves are limping along in their "dances"…)

"No," I answer, "first they should dance," I wink in the direction of Izke and Dora. "Put on the tango," I say.

Izke didn't need to be asked, he put on the only tango, and went right up to Dora. They danced a solo. The couple got angry, they demanded that another couple should dance too, but no one agreed.

After the tango we went back to the foxtrot which had been interrupted before.

I danced a solo with Ida.

---

218 Bublitschki meaning bagels/pretzels. For information about the Russian song see http://www.songsofmypeople.com/bublitschki.html, (accessed February 19, 2021).

October 1942

From among the guys, only Izke and I danced. Avremke sat outside on the balcony the entire time. Ilik did not try to "take a step" (he dances badly).

I went outside to Avremke and found him sitting where we had left him.

"Come inside, Avremke, what's going on with you today? Is your shoe too tight, is it pinching you?"

"I'm not coming in!"

"Why?"

"Because! I'm in a bad mood."

"You don't want to dance? So don't dance. Who's forcing you? But you can still come inside."

"I'm annoyed…"

"What about?"

My question remained hanging in the air without an answer. Outside the night is dark. A cool, autumnal wind blew, piercing through me. I leave Avremke alone. Around 9 P.M. more people arrived: Zlata, Danke, and Bebke Vidutshinski. The mood improved by 50 percent. The three girls (Dora, Lyusya, and Ida) forgot their toothache (each one of them had a tooth acting up…). They prepared the table again especially for the three of them, and, after eating, danced again until exactly 10.

I accompanied Lyusya home.

"You know, Lyusya, you are the only one whom I can confide in," she says to me. "Come over to me some time, I want to talk to you."

"What about?"

"You'll find out."

I remembered her words, from when we had gone to Ida's house earlier.

"I have no one here and hate everyone and myself, too. I feel like a sixty-year-old Jewess…" she said, and she nervously went out into the street. "You are my best friend here."

While writing these lines I remembered Ida's words to me while we were dancing a foxtrot.

"Lyusya, I dance heavily…ha?"

"No, the opposite, very lightly."

"No, don't mislead me, I feel it."

"I am telling you—you dance well. If you danced heavily, it wouldn't be easy for me to take a step."

"I know, I know…oh, don't tell me," she shakes her head. "I feel like I dance, and I know that I dance heavily…"

Why is she asking me such questions? Is she looking for a compliment, a good word? I don't understand…

I know, I don't dance too badly myself, I even dance well. However, I will never ask someone if that is true or not. In general, I hate compliments. I pay someone a compliment only when the person deserves it, when one has earned it. I really wanted to answer Ida, saying it is alright that she dances "heavily," but I can't insult someone (she was looking for a compliment). Even when someone is worthy of an insult (I am talking about girls)—I can't do it. I'm not capable of hurting someone. I feel struck sometimes by a sideways word, a small comment, I feel that the word goes through all my bones and in that moment, I suffer more for that person. Why? Because my nature is too sensitive. Just as a sponge draws into it the water together with all the microscopic little creatures, so an offensive word infiltrates my memory and blood, be it direct or indirect. I put on a good front, as if it doesn't bother me, but my first reaction is a shudder, I am not the same, and it takes a while until I am back to myself. I am too sensitive. I feel things deeply—and suffer as a result. Why? Because my nature is not built on firm foundations, on firm ground. I ask myself these questions: is my character firm and on a straight line? Am I a weakling in spirit? Am I able to struggle with life when I have such a character?

These are all daily questions for me and there are no answers. If someone was to ask me (whoever it may be, it's not important): is your character built on firm ground and is itself also firm? My answer would resound: "Yes!" But internally—I would waver between yes and no…

But back to the point. I avoid offending anyone (male or female) because I know that when I am feeling down, it hurts me, so it would pain the other, too. The other person is (possibly) exactly as sensitive as me. Why should I cause him pain? For a long time now—since being friends with the three girls and with the guys—I see that they don't mind fighting and insulting each other openly. This hasn't happened for me; either I give in (is this because of my irresolute character? I believe that

October 1942

in the moment one can catch sight of it)—or the other gives in. Fighting? That hasn't happened yet.

It is interesting, that in company I hate to fight or bicker with anyone about anything and my greatest failing—I hold people in high esteem and believe them more worthy than me. The other person is everything—and I am nothing. I hate to make myself stand out in company and be the object of attention (is this because of shyness?). In company—I am the third person (I bring this on myself), I listen more to the other person talking, observe the others well, and later draw conclusions. I know each one of us through and through. I understand each one's character and I empathize with them. Therefore, I earn everyone's trust in me, each one of the group pours his heart out to me, their sorrows. In such a moment I want to help the others, to unburden themselves.[219] As for me, for myself? I am more closed off in myself (from shyness?), I suppress my thoughts more that they should not become visible in the open, and find no counsel for myself... In a group which includes girls (in *The Diary of Kostya Ryabtsev*, N. Ognev calls them "chicks" instead of girls), I become somewhat uncomfortable and my movements become more "stiff," more restrained, in the framework of so-called "modesty" (*tsnies*) (don't laugh!) but I don't always "act haughty like that." With me it goes according to the atmosphere, according to the company, according to the way the wind blows.

This is how I am in the company of girls. Among boys—I am like a fish in water. In such company it's very cheerful, neither I nor someone else measure the words on a weighing scale. There, thought is free, words are free, there are no interferences: there, we are free men. At home? At home it is again different. I try to joke, to laugh, and here, too, I suit it to the atmosphere. Sometimes I receive a harsh reply, that is I encounter heavy resistance (one must understand this resistance in the context of the conversation) and then I again get more "highly strung" and, as they say, "stuck up." To tell the truth, for the most part, I am not the instigator of such incidents (a man is no angel—sometimes I also start it...) but mostly I stay quiet (perhaps because each one thinks he is right and not the other).

But in fact, at home I "more or less" get along with everyone.

---

219 The original is unclear.

Ilya Gerber

October 15, 1942

1942. X. 15.

It is now around half past six in the evening. Outside, a cold, sharp wind is blowing. It is very dark.

Recently, it has become popular in the ghetto to wear silver rings with a thin layer of gold at the top and a monogram. This is similar to the German fashion. It looks very nice. I was very taken with the idea. Each rings costs thirty-five marks or 350 rubles.

A few days ago, I sold my "clothing"—meaning my sketching tools—for forty marks. I immediately brought the money home. Yesterday, I broached the topic of the ring at home. My mother hinted that I should use the money from what I had sold. She simply expressed what I had not said out loud, what I had been thinking about and did not have the courage to come out with.

In the afternoon, Papa went with me to someone named Puke[220] (a family name). Puke is an old Jew with grey hair who trades in valuable objects and makes rings. He wants fifty marks for a ring according to my request! I had a good laugh.

"Come see his son," says Papa.

We go into a second apartment, opposite the old Puke's apartment. A handsome man with a noble appearance—the younger Puke[221]—greets us. My father and I explain the matter to him.

"How much will the ring cost?"

"Twenty-five marks!"

Exactly half of what his father asked!

---

220 Chaim Puke, born 1884, was a jeweler before the war. He was murdered in Dachau.
221 Yitzhak Puke, Chaim's son, born 1905, was a jeweler before the war. He was murdered in Dachau.

October 1942

"Come back on Sunday morning and we'll make a deal," he says to me. "Good," I answer, and in so doing forget that on Sunday I must go to the airfield.

The day before yesterday, the entire ghetto was resounding with the news: all Jews who are presently under arrest at the Ninth Fort will be released![222] People only discovered this at the last minute, that is, when they brought the Jews from the Fort past the ghetto under guard. Jews basically crawled onto the barbed fence wanting to see relatives, acquaintances…a large group of policemen and another few Jews were taken.

How did Jewish ghetto policemen come to be there?

It's a long story, but I will make it short. From the day that the ghetto was encircled with wire, trading began—secret trading. At first it was dangerous—people didn't trade on a grand scale. Later, the trade would take place in broad daylight. Jews approached the fence with an entire haberdashery shop, set up right by the fence, gave something to the guard—and the trading began. On one side were the non-Jews with their provisions—and on the other side the Jews, each exhibiting their merchandise, praising it, and showing it off from all sides: "Look, what beautiful merchandise—a real gem…." So it was, until they firmly outlawed large-scale trading. Trading became difficult. Now it has become a nighttime trade and indeed, at night, people traded on a large scale, including in the middle of the night. Jews would hoist sewing machines and other large valuable objects over from the ghetto side and the peasants would hoist over from their side cows and other livestock.[223] So it went on, and so it continues.

---

222 At the end of September 1942, six Jews (four policemen and two middlemen) were arrested in the Kovno Ghetto for smuggling goods into the ghetto and were sent to the Ninth Fort. The Ältestenrat, together with Benno Lipcer, intervened to save them from the death sentence. Three of the policemen were released, while one policeman and two agents, despite the promises, were murdered, along with their families, who were brought to the Ninth Fort for this purpose. On October 17, 1942 Tory noted: "Today thirteen Jews died in the Ninth Fort, including five little children." See Tory, *Surviving the Holocaust*, p. 147. See also Schalkowsky, ed., *The Clandestine History of the Kovno Jewish Police*, pp. 338–340.

223 There could have been a breach or an opening in the fence.

Recently the initiative of trade moved into the hands of the policemen. In the middle of the night they mobilized all the policemen from the third precinct, the policemen removed their patches, and walked to the fence. There, a few peasant wagons await with several *zentner*[224] of flour. One sack after another is hurled over to the ghetto side. One night the third precinct is mobilized, another night the second precinct, and the first gets a turn, too.

This is how they "buried themselves." The Lithuanian policeman may be guilty of this or not—I don't know—but they were denounced. Gestapo members came and arrested 90 percent of the Jewish policemen from the first precinct. An extensive investigation was conducted and a few were released. A few days later, people noticed that a group of Jews was going—under guard—up the hill which leads to the Ninth Fort. These were the policemen. People already lamented them and worried about them.

And then, suddenly, this news: they are bringing the policemen back from the Fort! A tumult ensues in the ghetto, and people run to look through the fence.

They didn't bring them into the ghetto but took them to the "yellow prison."[225] But this is a sign that they have already escaped from the claws of death.

This afternoon, I went to see a lad I know, Itshe Girzon.[226] A woman was sitting there and she related that apparently there is a new notice near the committee, stating that they are demanding 300 men for Riga. I didn't take a lot of interest in it—so be it what a Jewish woman says… I just went for a little walk with Itshe down Vytenio Street and then went home. There, I discovered that the story about Riga is true. A police officer we know (a Jew, don't worry) related that tonight they will take people for Riga.[227] A bit

---

224 One *zentner* = approximately 50 kilos in Germany, or 100 kilos in Russia (*tsentner*).

225 The large prison in Kovno. See Schalkowsky, ed., *The Clandestine History of the Kovno Jewish Police*, p. 66.

226 Yitzhak Girzon, born in 1924, was a student at the Hebrew Gymnasium in Kovno. He was murdered during the liquidation of the Kovno Ghetto.

227 According to an order issued by the *Stadtkommissar* of Kovno on October 16, 1942, the Ältestenrat was ordered to send 300 Jewish workers to Riga. See Tory, *Surviving the Holocaust*, p. 144.

October 1942

later someone from the committee came to us and told us that immediately as one enters the committee, turning left at the first door, there is a notice:

"Interested parties who want to register for the Riga brigade can sign up here..."[228]

A short notice which says a lot. People say that eighty volunteers already registered. One party of 5,400 men is already in Riga at work (it truly pains me that I have not been able to describe this, and even though a great deal of time has passed since then, I will write it all down at the right opportunity). Now they are sending another 300 Jews. People say that one can sign up until tomorrow at nine in the evening.

Today I discovered what the dear Köppen wanted to do to us (until now I have written Von Köppen, but that is not right. The correct writing is Köppen, without a Von).

I discovered from trustworthy sources, that Köppen had created a few projects to persecute the Jews.

First project:

Dress the entire ghetto in Russian heavy coats and give the civilian possessions to the Germans.

Second project:

Send away all the Jews from the ghetto for a designated period of time and then search all the Jewish homes. This smells 100 percent like theft of the household possessions.

In the meantime, his projects have been rejected.

This Sunday, October 18, Köppen must leave Kovno.[229]

I repeat the words which someone had uttered (one of the students from the Vocational School) about Köppen, while pushing the car (see p. 463): You should slip while you are driving...!

Today I finished reading *The Diary of Kostya Ryabtsev*. It left a deep impression on me.

---

[228] Regarding the order to leave for Riga voluntarily and the difficulty in mobilizing the inhabitants of the ghetto to do so, see Schalkowsky, ed., *The Clandestine History of the Kovno Jewish Police*, pp. 325–326.

[229] Köppen, who was in charge of the ghetto, completed his term of office and was replaced by Müller. For more information on this see the relevant footnote for diary entry from September 29, 1942.

October 16, 1942

1942. X. 16.

Today is the eighty-fifth day of the battle for Stalingrad. The Germans write about the following battles:

The German military is in Stalingrad. The battle goes on in every house, quarter, and street. When the military goes forward even a few steps and takes a house, they must leave new soldiers behind at that place, with the task of destroying the Russian partisans who hide between the stones and ruins of the house with machine guns. The battle continues! Each stone shoots.

The German newspaper reports a victory, a triumph by the army, which is located in Stalingrad: on such and such date, the German Wehrmacht took captive…three Russians! This is indeed a great victory and the newspaper reports it with really big letters (a fact!)

Apparently, last night passed calmly in the ghetto. I discovered that the deadline for signing up is Monday, October 19.

People are saying that now they will not go through homes according to lists, but every designated person will receive a special invitation with Hörmann's signature, ordering him to report to the German labor office. In Vilna, too, they are also using such a method for recruiting people.

People say that among the arrested Jews who were imprisoned at the Fort were the three Jewish ghetto policemen from the first precinct. Three of them have been freed and the remaining three will apparently be sent to Riga. Is this really true? I don't know, but this is what people are saying.

A small, brief quote from *The Diary of Kostya Ryabtsev*:
"Life: In literature it is one thing, and in reality—completely, entirely different. It is easier to live in fantasy and not in reality. But one must fight this."[230]

* * *

What is life?—A novel. Who is the author?—Anonymous. We read haltingly, laugh, weep...and sleep.
(These lines were written by Karamzin in the eighteenth century).[231]

* * *

A young woman—milk
A bride—butter
A wife—cheese...

October 17, 1942

I went out an hour ago to hear news. I went to Izke's. He has now been in bed for three days. On the way to him I noticed an unusual movement on the streets. I take a look: coming toward me is Bubtshik who celebrates[232] together with the Kagan family in the same apartment.
"How is Izke?" I ask him.

---

230 This is a translation from Gerber's Yiddish. See the English translation by Fainna Glagoleva: "Life as presented in literature is one thing, but in reality, it's quite different. It's easier to live in your imagination than in reality, but this is something a person has to resist." N. Ognev, *Kostya Ryabtsev's Diary*, p. 156.
231 Nikolai Karamzin (1766–1826), was a Russian historian and writer.
232 This, presumably, is meant sarcastically as a reference to the cramped living conditions.

He doesn't answer me but calls me over to the side.

"I met Avremke Tiktin. He says that his parents—his mother and his father—were arrested. They are candidates for Riga..."

I am beside myself! The devil only knows what they have hooked on them.

Bubtshik was not lazy and listed many more names of those arrested. Among them a family which works in the workshops! This shocked me! Every ghetto worker and inhabitant considered the big workshops so secure, this is a moral blow to the minds of the Jews.

I went off to Izke. Oh, I forgot. While I was talking with Bubtshik, Izke's father approached us. He told me that they are snatching people among the workers arriving at the Kriščiukaičio gate. The Jewish police apparently refused to "snatch" the people from the brigades and take them to the prison. The commander there got involved and took people himself.

"But I don't believe it," Kagan concluded his news.

Arriving at Izke's house, I told him what I had heard. I sat with him for about fifteen minutes and went off to Dora Rabinovitsh, because only there can I find out something (Ilik, her brother, works in the SD, that means the Gestapo).

Before going into the house, I met Avremke.

"Avremke! What's going on with you?"

"Nothing, what should be going on?"

I look at him in wonder.

"Nothing happened? Bubtshik said..."

"Nu, yes," he cut me off, "my mother and father received 'invitations' with Hörmann's signature."

"And you? And what about Chaim? Chaim is sick!²³³"

"My mother is still at home, but my father is already in the prison. She is taking care of him."

At that moment Yatl Kapelushnik²³⁴ came running in (Mrs. Tiktin's sister was married to Mr. Kapelushnik. However, Mrs. Tiktin had already died in Kovno).

---

233 Chaim Tiktin (Avremke's brother), born 1921. He was murdered during the Holocaust.
234 This apparently refers to Naftali Kapelushnik-Ayalon (1915–2000), who survived the Holocaust.

He reports the following to me:

"Ika Grinberg[235] (police chief of the first precinct) went to Margolis," (the Jewish brigade inspector, the inspector responsible for the Jewish workers who work in the city. The airfield belongs to Lurie).

"Ika tried to defend the Tiktin family. Margolis answered that it is nothing. He says that they sent out 700 'invitations' and they may release Mr. Tiktin tomorrow at 4."

Avremke stayed downstairs and I went up to Dora.

There were several people in the room: Mrs. Rabinovitsh; a man who is always with them, whom Dora calls "Dziadzia" (Uncle in Belarusian); and Dora.

Dora told me the latest news:

"They took seventy people from the big workshops, with their families, to Riga. They also took the Vayner family, the ones from the former fruit shop on Nemuno Street. It's interesting that they are taking entire families and not single individuals, as they have done until now. This doesn't seem to make sense..."

"And what's happening with the policemen who were brought to the ghetto?" I ask.

"Three of the six were released, and the remaining three...one can say..." Dora did not finish her words and looked at me.

I understood.

"At the Ninth Forth?" I ask her quietly.

"Yes, there, together with their families..."

"How did their families come to be there??

"They were rounded up at night...three families, women, children, babies...they were all there..." and she became silent.

"Shot?" I ask, and I end her thought.[236]

---

235 Yehoshua (Ike) Grinberg (1917–1944), was commander of the first precinct of the ghetto on behalf of the Jewish police. He was a member of the Zionist Youth Movement (Hanoar Hatzioni) in Kovno and the underground movement Irgun Brit Zion (ABZ). He ordered that the archive of the police be secreted in a hiding place which had been prepared in advance. He was murdered in the Ninth Fort on the eve of the *Kinder Aktion*, together with forty policemen from the ghetto.

236 See the relevant footnote for the October 15, 1942 entry, relating to the Jews who were arrested in the Kovno Ghetto for smuggling goods into the ghetto and were sent to the Ninth Fort.

She is silent. It's pointless to talk about it. People lived, they had dreams, they wanted to live and to let others live, until...until suddenly they were exterminated before their time, because they wanted to eat, because they wanted to live, because they wanted to survive... I believe it's senseless to say more: everyone understands everything and, I'm afraid to say, everything has become completely natural. One now looks at such facts—like at a fact, like a thing which is inevitable. So it is and there's nothing to be done about it. One looks at such facts with eyes wide open, sees what happens to this person, to that person. For a moment the heart is saddened but underneath, every person smiles [i.e., that it is not them]. Why? Why is it so? Is the human heart already so hardened and unable to feel for the other? I overheard a conversation:

"They can break their heads,[237] they can send away whoever they want and how they want! It doesn't matter to me. But they won't move me..." Each one bewails his own tragedy and isn't interested in the misfortune of others. Should I take to heart that this Yoske or that Mishke was taken away? Who will worry about me, who will sympathize with me, if they, God forbid, will take me away?

"Tfu, may it come to pass," concludes that person, "they can break all their heads on the wall one by one, it doesn't matter to me."

These are the feelings of not one or two Jews in the ghetto—all the Jews in the ghetto think this way. "As long as the misfortune doesn't know me—I don't know him [the victim]. And if I do sympathize with him, how does that help him? Will it make things easier for him? No! Not at all! On the contrary—it can also harm me! What do they think, that I have less troubles than him? It's better not to take it to heart at all. I won't lament for anyone else and I don't want anyone to lament for me and I just want to be left alone." This is what every Jew in the ghetto thinks and as one can see—each one lives a selfish life, a life for himself. And so one lives...

---

237 Meaning: let them do whatever they want.

October 18, 1942

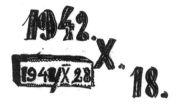

Today it is exactly one year (according to the Jewish calendar, two weeks after *Simkhes Toyre*) [Simchat Torah] since the Great *Aktion* was carried out. It was October 28, 1941.[238] In the first volume of my diary[239] I described more than half of the events which took place on that miserable day. I don't know, in truth, why I didn't describe it in full. I regret it. But now to remember what happened to the Jews who were selected in the small ghetto, how they tragically spent the night in apartments with no heating, apartments which had belonged to the Jews of the small ghetto who were previously sent away, who had ended their lives at the Ninth Fort. All this is now a bit difficult for me. But at the right opportunity I will record either my written account or a copy from the diary of Lyusya Maniewitz. (It was I who asked each of the three girls to keep a diary. They jumped at the idea and straightaway equipped themselves with writing paper. But in fact, only Lyusya M. followed through. All the dates in her account are exact, even more exact than in mine. A few times I have had the opportunity to read her diary. I will now borrow it from her for a third time.)

Today I found out from Lyusya that Avremke's parents were released. May it be with good fortune and with good luck! This is now the third time.

---

238 On October 28, 1941, the German authorities conducted a large-scale murder operation in the Kovno Ghetto. All inhabitants of the ghetto were ordered to gather in Demokratų Square (located within the boundaries of the ghetto) and an SD officer, Helmut Rauca, conducted a selection. At the end of the selection, 9,200 Jews were sent to the Ninth Fort, where they were murdered. A third of the inhabitants of the ghetto were murdered in this *Aktion*, and it greatly affected the Jews remaining in the ghetto.

239 This refers to a notebook that is lost.

Ilya Gerber

October 13, 1942
The date when the Jews were taken to Riga.

They wanted to "put them in chains" but they escaped. Thanks to whom? I believe that this is thanks to Ilik's help (*protektsie* with Lipcer) and Mr. Santotski, who also works in the SD with Lipcer.[240]

(I didn't see Avremke today yet and therefore I don't know for certain, but probably this is the case).

Lyusya tells me that Ida announced that they will not send the people to Riga, but somewhere else... Her father was standing near her and didn't say a word. That means Ida heard it from her father and her father doesn't deny it. And if he says so—he knows.

In general, something about the process of taking workers to Riga doesn't sit right with me. Why? Until now they would take one person from a family. In this way they would take the designated number of people and be done. Now? Now they are taking entire families. Entire families obligated to work, comprising three, four, or even more people. Additionally, they took sick people! They took cripples! They arrested an old man, elderly, with grey hair! Are they also taking these sick and crippled people to work in Riga? Is it possible?

Today I discovered the details of the last moments in the lives of the Jewish policemen's families:

Next to the ghetto guards on Stulginskio Street, at 9 A.M., a large, black vehicle arrived, with a cover on top. Then, a few small taxis with Gestapo big shots arrived. In a few minutes, more big shots arrived, but from our direction—from the Varnių gate. Also summoned were: Lipcer, Natkin, and other senior Jewish officials. Furthermore, according to an order, the women and children of the three Jewish policemen, who had been taken away previously to the Fort, also appeared there. The little children, frozen by the cold wind and wet weather, had to stand on the street in front of the big shots with bare heads, holding their hands outstretched. They trembled with cold and clung to their mothers. In the

---

240 Gerber frequently notes the power that Benno Lipcer wielded and his great influence on the fate of the ghetto population. He even notes the names of ghetto inhabitants that supported Lipcer and enjoyed his help in arranging a comfortable workplace and immunity from various decrees imposed on the general population.

middle of this they brought out a stretcher on which lay the body of a Jew. The Jew—who is sick, now suffering from pneumonia—was lying on the stretcher and did not know what they were going to do with him. Before the illness, when the German guards in the ghetto guardhouse were from the NSKK—this Jew was hand in hand with them, that is, they used to do business together and he used to bribe the NSKK guards. The Gestapo demanded this sick man be treated no differently, dead or alive (so the order stated!) and they had to take him out of the Jewish hospital and bring him on a stretcher to the vehicle.

Natkin got into an argument with the Gestapo officials, that they should let the sick man go.

"Anyway, his days are numbered," he defended the "interests" of the sick man.

After a long deliberation and looking at the sick man, they no doubt understood that this Jew is not worth the effort because the bed remained standing outside with the sick man while the families, that is the wives and children, were loaded onto the cargo truck. Surrounded with a large guard, the black truck drove to the Varnių gate, and from there—straight to the hill, the way to the Ninth Fort!

The wives and the children travelled the same way and to the same fate as their husbands.

The three men were shot upon arrival at the Fort. And a day later, they took the wives into the gas chamber[241] at the Fort and there they were "put to sleep"...the three men, the three women, and the children, they died or perished in two different ways, however they met again in one place, in one grave...

---

241 This information is incorrect. A gas chamber during the interwar period was placed in the First Fort, but due to reasons of secrecy it was published in the press that the gas chamber was located in the hard labor prison in the Ninth Fort. My thanks to Mr. Marius Peculis, director of the Ninth Fort Museum, for this information.

October 19, 1942

Yesterday evening I went to see Heni (yesterday, Sunday, the Vocational School, [words missing] I didn't go to the airfield). Misha Yatkunsky was at her house. We talked a bit. He told me that the people that were selected will not only be taken to Riga but also to Shavli (to Fritz-Müller, the airfield firm, which moved a while ago to Shavli,[242] also to build an airfield) and to Pskov![243] This means they will send the Jews to three places:

I Shavli (to Fritz-Müller)

II Riga (to the firm Windschild und Langelot, which moved to Riga a long time ago)

III Pskov (also for construction work)

We moved on to the topic of books. He will come to me on Tuesday to get a couple of books to read. I took the opportunity and took two Hebrew books from him: *Ben Hur*[244] and *Gesharim* by Z. Shneur.[245] Heni arrived in the meantime. I went into her room with her. We hadn't seen each other in a long time so first she asked for news about what's going on with the *khevre*, and, finally, we moved on to serious questions. We talked in a friendly tone and had a pretty good and agreeable conversation.

---

242 A German construction company that did construction work at the airfield in Kovno using laborers from the Kovno and Shavli Ghettos. The work in this company was extremely difficult and the managers were cruel and brutal. See Schalkowsky, ed., *The Clandestine History of the Kovno Jewish Police*, p. 166. Likewise, see Yerushalmi, *Pinkas Shavli*, p. 139.

243 A city located about 20 kilometers east of the Estonian border, on the Velikaya River.

244 *Ben-Hur: A Tale of the Christ* was a popular English novel by Lewis Wallace that was published in 1880. It was translated and adapted into Hebrew in 1924.

245 Zalman Shneur is the pen name of Shneur Zalkind (1887–1959), a Yiddish and Hebrew poet and author born in Russia. He published a collection of Hebrew songs and poems in 1922, entitled *Gesharim* [Bridges], among his other works.

She expressed her insecurity about being in the ghetto (regarding Riga) and was afraid that the police can "arrest" a family such as hers (of two people)[246] and take them to the ghetto prison.

We parted in good spirits.

"Come over and drop in again!"

"If I won't be embarrassed!" I joke.

That evening, I thought about dropping in on the guys, but, involuntarily, I went in the direction of our block and so it remained.

I found out, sadly, that a few of "them" lost their lives. Nevertheless, I also want to be a Lenstolnik.[247] I don't want to be a passive spectator but an active participant.

Today the ghetto is very troubled. There are various rumors. It is interesting who is responsible for these exaggerated rumors—it seems to me that the Germans are better friends of the Jewish people than the Jews themselves. If a freezing wind blows through the ghetto, before the Germans have even thought about what to do with us, a rumor immediately spreads through the ghetto, issued by the Jews themselves: an *Aktion*! A misfortune! Anything at all—immediately becomes: They're digging graves at the Ninth Fort!

I remember a while ago that the mood in the ghetto was so bad, it could simply drive you crazy. People imagined things, from the smallest thing to an *Aktion*. Just then a big shot arrived at the committee. Jews, obviously senior officials, had the audacity to ask him about the painful question.

He laughed at them and answered: "It's interesting that you Jews know better than us! We don't know anything about the question—yet among you the date is already set...."

So, today, people started a rumor (so said the Jewish women in the line queueing up for bread) that in the jail at 107 Kriščiukaičio Street (where the workshops are located) the Jews being held there broke down the doors and windows and escaped.

---

246 Heni Shpitz had arrived in Kovno with only her father. See the letter she wrote to the ITS (International Tracing Service database, TID 124582).

247 Presumably an active fighter.

"How many people escaped?" one asks another.

"What do you mean, how many?" comes the answer. "All of them! As many people as were there!"

"What are you saying? How many people escaped?" asks a third Jewish woman.

"You just heard!" a fourth woman gets involved, "five hundred men and women! All of them, down to the last one, escaped."

The first woman, the one relating the entire "story," seeing that the attention of the Jewish women in the line was focused less on her and all were turning to the one who had uttered the number 500, got angry, and burst out in a single breath:

"What 500 people? Why are you bothering us if you don't know! I have come straight from there. Seven hundred men escaped! And imagine," she adds, wringing her hands, "when the Germans will find out about this, then—woe! Woe is me!—they will carry out an *Aktion*! They will snatch people in the streets, they will take people, neighborhood by neighborhood!!..."

Complete silence enveloped the Jewish woman. In a few minutes a commotion began at the back of the lines. The commotion became greater and louder and there was the sound of fast running with loud cries: "They are snatching people in the streets! They are taking people, neighborhood by neighborhood! They are dividing people left and right..." It looked like a bomb had dropped on the line: all of them ran off in all directions. The Jewish woman, who wanted to draw everyone's attention to herself, remained standing alone in the corridor and whispered in a flustered manner: "Can it be true?...Can it be...?"

Apparently, she herself was persuaded that the news, which she delivered, is true and she believed her own lies, because, with frightened eyes and fast steps, she left the dark corridor.

I heard all this from a student who was standing right there in the line.

Since today all the students were working in Block C on a renovation job, and the block is a few steps from the block where I live, I went home to see what was going on. It is interesting how a rumor spreads: faster than a telephone conversation. I go into the corridor of the building. A female neighbor is a standing there.

"What's going on?" I ask.

"Don't you know, the people arrested in the jail escaped, only 130 people remain there…"

"Pst," I think to myself. "We're getting through this pretty well. There are still 130 people remaining?! Very good." And I leave her with a smile.

At home I didn't ask about this. Why create panic?

I went back to my workplace. Berkman—the "caretaker," the former teacher, the cigarette snatcher—was standing there. He relates:

"As soon as I heard the terrible news, not dead and not alive, I ran off to find a policeman I know, so that he should explain the situation to me: Is this an *Aktion* or not? What kind of misfortune do we have here?… So listen to this story." Berkman meanwhile grabs a hand-rolled cigarette from an onlooker who is listening (when Berkman tells a story, he moves his hands and his entire body more than with his tongue, therefore, when he speaks, people look, they don't just listen), spits right on the floor, removes his glasses, and makes further gestures with his hands:

"So, are you listening?" he looks around, to see whether the circle is growing. "I went to the policeman to ask him. 'Hey,' I say, 'explain to me what's happening. If not, if not—I'll absolutely lose my mind…'"

"Hey! You rascal, can you be a bit quieter over there and let an elder speak?" Berkman shouts and adopts a more severe demeanor. When it becomes quiet, he continues:

"So, he explains the entire story to me. He said, "I look at him… 'Nothing happened,' he assures me, 'no *Aktion* has taken place and none will take place! Someone indeed tried to escape from the prison but he was unlucky! They found the Jew hanging from the balcony of the prison trying to reach the ground, but they caught him and flayed his skin! He will have something to remember now!'" Thus, Berkman ended his talk with the policeman, and it is entirely possible that this is correct.

And this is what is called a rumor: someone tried to escape. The Jewish woman increased the number to 700 people. Someone said that if the Germans will find out about the escape of 700 people from the prison, they will conduct an *Aktion*. Jewish women merely heard the word *Aktion*, they pondered it a few times, until they themselves were persuaded that a police raid is underway on the streets and they are apprehending people, neighborhood by neighborhood! Jewish women in the line heard the word

October 1942

Aktion and twenty Jewish women ran off in twenty different directions, so in a moment the rumor spread throughout the entire ghetto. This is what makes people nervous, frightened, and to not know where to hide themselves. These are rumors and this is how they spread in a moment to all four corners of the ghetto. I believe that there is no better example...

It is already a week since I saw Ida. I have seen Dora once in that time. The same about Lyusya. I remain at home today, again. It is now after 8:30 P.M. It rained today, and the cold goes through one's bones. As it is in the heart—so is the weather.

Pnina Sukenik[248] came up to me at lunchtime today. She had previously borrowed a Hebrew book from me, *Yerushalayim Mehaka*.[249] She now asked for two more books: 1) *Oliver Twist*[250] and 2) *Zikhronot*. I have her book *Zutot*.[251] A lad from the Vocational School brought me a book—*HaShiga'on HaGadol*.[252] I gave him the Lithuanian book *30 Metųmoteris*[253] which belongs to Itshe Girzon.

I got an additional three books from Girzon—all three parts of the trashy books by [Mišelis] Zevakas: *Ragastenas*, *Primavera* and *Sidabro Taurė*, so I have four books from him. Girzon has the following of my books: 1) *Madame Bovary*[254] 2) *In [der] tkufe fun revolyutsye*[255] and 3) *Rūpestis,* another Lithuanian book (which actually is Ida's).

---

248 Penina Sukenik-Gofer, born 1925, lived in the Kovno Ghetto. In January 1944, she escaped the ghetto and hid until the Germans left the city in the summer of 1944. She survived the Holocaust.

249 The book *Yerushalayim Mehaka* (Jerusalem is Waiting) was written in Hebrew by Yehoshua Heschel Yeivin in 1939.

250 The first Hebrew translations of *Oliver Twist* by Charles Dickens were published in 1924 and 1935.

251 The book *Zutot* by Yaakov Klatzkin was published in 1925.

252 *HaShiga'on HaGadol* is a book by Avigdor Hameiri describing his experiences as a fighter in World War I, as a junior officer in the Austro-Hungarian Empire who fought on the Eastern Front against the armies of the Russian Empire. It was published in 1929. The book was first published in English as *The Great Madness*, in 1952.

253 *A Woman of Thirty* by Honore de Balzac.

254 *Madam Bovary* was written by the French author Gustave Flaubert and published in 1856.

255 Apparently referring to the Yiddish book edited by Eliyahu Tsherikover, published in Berlin in 1924.

October 23, 1942

Today, the Jews who had been arrested had to travel to work in Riga. All the while the Jewish police tormented the crowd with their nighttime police raids and searches. People were still missing.

A policeman expressed himself regarding the gathering of people for the Riga brigade in the following manner:

"Imagine a railway station where people come and go. There is constant turnover and movement. This is called in simple Jewish language *Dabokle*,[256] or prison."

How does the movement take place there?

It is something like the following:

One member of a family is arrested after having received the "invitation card" with Hörmann's signature on it. This means that the entire family must go to Riga, and, in the meantime, as insurance, they take one of the family members and put him behind bars. The remaining family members, who are free, try to have the order revoked, so that they won't have to go to Riga, and therefore search for all kinds of *protektsie*, approaching all forms of authority, pressuring all the officials, but it doesn't help—only the power of gold takes effect. It goes something like this: a Jewish woman comes running to Lipcer or another Jewish big shot with a cry and a scream, that they should release her son from prison, indeed—how can it be that they should take such a family as this for work somewhere...

---

[256] In Lithuanian: prison cell. See Schalkowsky, ed., *The Clandestine History of the Kovno Jewish Police*, p. 235. This term, in the local Jewish-Lithuanian jargon, was widespread also in the Shavli Ghetto. See Yerushalmi, *Pinkas Shavli*, p. 97.

October 1942

The outcome can be as follows:

1. If the family knows Lipcer or other senior Jewish leaders, who have a say in the matter, *protektsie* can help a lot. They receive a release note and the prison doors open to let the chosen one go.
2. If they have no *protektsie* there is only one choice: that is, to sit in the prison, cursing the day that he was born and the day "the other guy" was born...and waiting for the day when they will be told to leave.

Whoever has no "P" (short for *protektsie*) and wants to get out of prison, that is, he doesn't want to go to Riga, must apply the best and strongest protection money. One gives a bribe to a Jewish official, the latter takes it, puts it in his pocket—and makes change by giving a release note... So, who remains in prison? The one who has no *protektsie* and no dough [money]... Who is the most unfortunate? Mostly the airfield worker, who, from the very beginning, has been going to the airfield, suffering all day long in the cold wind and rain, and has the good fortune to be called by Lurie, the Jewish airfield inspector, names like: murderer, sloppy, underworld, and other similar choice words he uses for the airfield worker. At the workplace he drinks boiled water, eats one and a half little shreds of cabbage from the bottom of the pot, and at the real bottom, at the base of the pot, lies hidden a kernel, a little one, alone, with no father or mother, with no brothers and sisters. This is who remains in the prison.

Yes, in truth, I can't deny it, they also "mistreated" many distinguished people and "imprisoned" senior people, who work for example in the big workshops,[257] or even in other important workplaces.

How can this be?

Truly this person is an important person for the ghetto, a good craftsman, and has other virtues. He has, however, one failing and for this reason his virtues are not apparent...he once had a fight with a certain Jewish big shot! He once offended him, he reproached the labor office's incorrect and inhuman behavior toward the simple ghetto people. This is enough that the one sitting on the bench[258] will eliminate his ghetto enemy, he prefers to have him far away so that he won't be

---

257 The ghetto featured both large and small workshops as discussed earlier.
258 Meaning the one in power.

able to harm him. The big shot writes out a note, sends it to the home of this or that enemy, and that one "leaves" the ghetto. Here lies the power of the labor office and everyone is afraid of starting [a fight] with them. One may, God forbid, be sent far away from the ghetto to who knows where...

So why is there such turnover? Someone who has *protektsie* will be released from the prison and his place is freed up. And so, as they let a lot of people go, they are lacking people to make up the designated number which must be met. Therefore, they go and grab more people from their homes, send out more "postcards," and the prisons are full again. And so the story repeats itself, in and out, just like a train station...

Today they left [for Riga]. At around two o'clock.

October 26, 1942

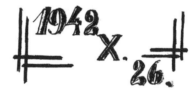

Izke is still sick with jaundice. He says that he is already healthy, but they make him wait at home... We, the guys, come to see him every evening. We try to solve "serious problems," assuming serious and rigid postures, as is fitting in such company, disputing, clicking our tongues, looking from one to the other with such seriousness and integrity, that laughter erupts, sparked by all the calculated maneuvers...

Two days ago, when we were at Izke's as usual, Lyusya sat down next to me and wrote me a note.

"Lyusya! Why have you changed so much? I no longer recognize you. I have changed—but I can't compare to you. Thank God, compared to a few weeks ago, my feelings toward X [sic] have changed entirely. I am very pleased by this."

October 1942

I tried to understand what she is getting at. "But I must answer," I think to myself. "Let's see what will come out of this..." I, too, answer on a little note:

"I have changed because I wanted to. I had to change and get out of the 'dead end' because I was not indifferent and was too sensitive. For myself—this is good. For others—?! Explanation to follow..."

Lyusya Maniewitz writes further:

"Lysuya (this means me!)! The truth! Do you still love Ida or Heni, and how are things going with Heni?"

"You ask me such questions, which I myself want to forget..." I respond.

Lyusya M. does not understand my last answer. She wants me to explain. I won't explain in full, and instead write:

"....And these things are forgettable..."

Lyusya did not answer.

After the Jews were sent away to work in Riga, a bad atmosphere settled over the ghetto. People started saying that now they will gradually send the entire ghetto away to work. People are saying that they need people in Shavli, Minsk, Pskov, Smolensk, Mariampol, and so on. Now people are saying a new thing: They will select from the ghetto 5,000 skilled male and female workers and employ them here in Kovno or [elsewhere] in Lithuania for work. The remaining Jews will be sent away to who knows where. There will be no *Aktionen*. If there will be, they are only for work.

The Lithuanians should have received their independence today, officially, on paper. Consequently, the Lithuanians shall present 20,000 soldiers for the front. They have been talking about this for a few months and now it is confirmed.

Ilya Gerber

October 28, 1941–1942

October 28, 1941–1942
Exactly one year since the Great *Aktion*!

October 29, 1942

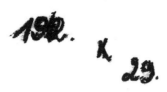

It has now transpired that the Jews who worked in Palemonas did not return all together. Last week a group of eight men and twelve women arrived and the day before yesterday another three men arrived! Imagine my happiness when I found out that among these three are my school friend Beke Kot (see p. 392—under the line) and Sholemke Layzon.[259] Beke lived together with Sholemke around the same courtyard during the good old times in Kovno. They always played cards together and went to the cinema together. They came into the ghetto together and languished together. They suffered together, toiled together, and together were taken to Palemonas. There, Beke found himself a place in the kitchen (this cost him a gold ring). On more than one occasion Beke was the recipient of blows from the Germans, but he had food [...].[260] And now, they are among the three lucky ones, both these guys: Beke and Sholemke. Both of them went away and both came back. I met them both near Block C. We clapped each other on the back in the street and parted in a friendly manner.

An *Aktion* took place last week in Oshmene [Oszmiana].[261] And I was informed (from trustworthy sources) that the *Aktion* was conducted by... Jews!!!

---

259 No information has been found concerning him.
260 Meaning unclear.
261 Oshmene [Oszmiana] is a district capital in the Vilna district. In October 1942, the Germans announced that they intended to reduce the population of the ghetto and execute 1,500 of its inhabitants. The task of choosing those fated to die was given to the Jewish order police in Vilna. Following negotiations with the Germans, Jacob Gens, the head of the Judenrat in Vilna, managed to reduce the number of victims to 406 Jews. On October 21, 1942, around twenty Jewish policemen from Vilna entered the Oszmiana Ghetto, led by Salak Dessler. There, they conducted a roundup and handed over 406 Jews to the Germans, mostly from among the elderly and the sick. These were taken to nearby Uglejewo and murdered by Lithuanians. Gens took upon himself responsibility for the act, claiming that there were 4,000 Jews in the Oszmiana Ghetto and that he was sacrificing a few lives to save many.

Even now I cannot calm myself about this thought: Jews carried out a death sentence on their own brothers, on their own Jews...no, I do not believe it! It is difficult to believe such a thing! But is it possible? Who knows? Today's times! A German prank... A hammer bangs on a nail on an anvil. The hammer is made of iron, the nail is made of iron, and the anvil—it is also made of iron and, nevertheless, iron bangs on iron, the second, the third, and so on. And [it carries out] the will of the one who wields the metals—the hand, the will of man! So, too, here: the one wielding—the German—commands the first Jew to beat up the second Jew and he is merely a tool in the hands of the German and is forced to carry out the order and save his own life at that moment... Who knows?! It is hard to say. But nevertheless! A Jew against another Jew? Is it possible?

The story, which sounds like a legend, goes like this:

Fifty policemen from Vilna, led by the Gens brothers[262] (who were, according to available information, armed with revolvers at their sides),[263] arrived in Oshmene [Oszmiana], where there has been a ghetto until now. They selected 2,000 men—and it's like they never existed. Two thousand Jews lived there and the black earth covered them...

People say that there are ghettos in: Kovno, Vilna,[264] around Vilna—in its environs, Lida,[265] and Shavli.[266] Apart from this, there are Jews in Lithuania in hiding; in villages (100 percent fact) and in cities or towns where Jews—sent out of the ghettos or who come from abroad (like Poland)—work.

---

262 This refers to the Gens brothers, Solomon and Jacob. Jacob Gens (1900–1943), served first as commander of the Jewish police in the Vilna Ghetto and was later appointed as head of the Judenrat. He managed the operation in Oszmiana but was not personally present. Nothing is known about his brother's involvement in the operation.

263 While serving as commander of the police and head of the Vilna Judenrat, Jacob Gens carried a pistol.

264 The Vilna Ghetto was established at the beginning of September 1941 and existed until September 23, 1943. Most of its inhabitants were murdered in Ponar, while some were sent to the camps in Estonia and Poland, and others remained in various locations in Vilna to be exploited for forced labor.

265 The ghetto of Lida, in the province of Nowogródek, was established in December 1941, and existed until September 18, 1943.

266 The Shavli Ghetto was established in mid-September 1941 and existed until July 1944. Its inhabitants were deported to the camps of Stutthof and Dachau together with the inhabitants of the Kovno Ghetto.

October 1942

This week, Rosenberg,[267] the famous "friend of the Jews," spoke. He spoke, obviously, about the Jewish Question. I did not read his speech. People gave me a verbal report of his speech. A few say that Rosenberg expressed himself about us in the following manner:

"The existence of Jews in Europe is highly undesirable."

Others say that he proclaimed: "Next week, the Jewish Problem in Europe will be solved permanently."

And others go on, saying other things. Rosenberg apparently expressed himself thus:

"The European Jew must be purged from public life and the public world…"

In short, it doesn't matter what/how he said it, we can understand one thing:

"Jews in Europe are undesirable."

About the Kovno–Riga Jews[268]

I don't know the exact number of Jews who were sent for work from the Kovno Ghetto in the direction of Riga. I heard numbers that do not seem plausible. People say that they took more than 300 families and single people from the ghetto, which brings the number to almost 1,000. Others say it was only 600 Jews.

From the ghetto they took the Jews to the airfield and packed them all onto wagons. Many of them escaped during the night and returned to the ghetto (a family of seven, with young children, returned that very same evening, to the ghetto. A fact!) From the airfield they took the Jews by train to the train station next to the Green bridge.

---

267 This refers to Alfred Rosenberg (1893–1946), among the leaders of the Nazi Party, its ideologue, and, from 1941, Reich minister for the occupied eastern territories. He was tried in Nuremberg and was executed.

268 A second group of Jews from the Kovno Ghetto was recruited for labor in Riga (the first instance occurred in February 1942) between October 16 and 23, 1942. The Jewish police managed to round up 500 people, but they were required to supply a larger number. For more information, see Schalkowsky, ed., *The Clandestine History of the Kovno Jewish Police*, pp. 325–326.

People relate what happened there: All of those designated for Riga were placed in the yard. Germans arrived and began to sort them. The young and strong were separated onto one side and the older people, who made a bad impression with their appearance, together with the young children and babies taken along by their parents, were placed on the other side. Two groups were created, one opposite the other. Here stands a young person who is capable of working—and opposite, the not yet fully-grown generation, that is small children, and right next to them the generation that has lived its life, the dying generation, meaning the older people. The young, those capable of work, took the front positions in the train and the second group sat in the back, last carriages, next to the carriage that contained the belongings of those sent away (people also relate that they dressed them all in Russian military clothes). The train moved off with the sealed carriages.

But then the following happened:

The front-most carriages stayed connected to the train, while the last carriages, containing the older people with the little children and also the carriage with their belongings, remained standing in place. The young, strong generation departed, leaving at the train station the old, weak people with small children in sealed up train cars…what will they do with them? A non-Jewish woman told my brother-in-law Shleyme that they were digging graves at the Ninth Fort. Were they intended for the old, sick people?

I won't go into it and everyone can understand whatever they want. I leave the question open.

According to the latest news, 265 people arrived in Riga! And the rest?! Those taken away included: Grafman, the chief editor of Warsaw's *Der Moment*,[269] and A. Shafer, our fellow student from the Vocational School. He, with his brother, left for Riga while his parents, together with a young sister, remained in the ghetto here. So people are torn apart!

---

269 *Der Moment* was a Yiddish newspaper that was published in Warsaw from 1910 until 1939. Avraham Yizhok Grafman was one of its last editors. Grafman left Warsaw when Poland was invaded by Nazi Germany and fled to Vilna and then moved to Kovno.

NOVEMBER 1942

November 1, 1942

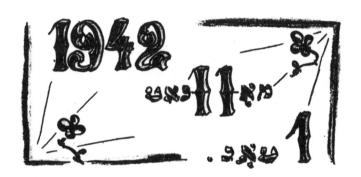

Yesterday evening, Papa received an appointment from the Jewish ghetto police to arrange the Hebrew song *Hatikva* for an entire orchestra.[270] This morning, lying in bed, Papa set it down in writing. Today at 10 A.M. (today, Sunday, the Vocational School is not open. This is the third Sunday like this, and I have the whole day free), we received two notes at home.

---

270 Boris Gerber, the diarist's father, conducted a children's choir in the ghetto. The Jewish police in the Kovno Ghetto asked him to prepare adaptations of songs (mostly in Hebrew) for the police choir which performed at the ceremony to mark the swearing in of the policemen. Later, he conducted and adapted music for the choir that performed together with the police orchestra.

The first one looked like this:
Mr. Gerber

Invitation[271]

The administration of the ghetto police cordially invites you to the official swearing-in ceremony of the police officials.

The party will take place on 16 Yeshiva Street, Sunday, November 1, at 3:30 P.M. sharp.

Entry by invitation only

[signed] The police chief.

October 31, 1942

That was the one note. The second note details the program:

Program

Of the official swearing-in ceremony:

November 1, 1942, 3:30 P.M.

1. Report for the Ältestenrat
2. Speech by the head of the Ältestenrat
3. Speech by the police chief
4. Guest speaker
5. Musical interlude: *Ki afar ata*[272]

---

271 On November 1, 1942, in a festive and elegant ceremony, members of the Kovno Ghetto order police vowed ("swore") to be loyal to the public and its leaders, and to act with righteousness, according to the values of justice. The ceremony, which was held at the initiative of the deputy commander of the police, Yehudah Zupovitz, a Beitar member, took place in the hall of the former yeshiva which had been converted into a concert hall, and was attended by public leaders and other dignitaries. The police orchestra and policemen's choir accompanied the ceremony and the swearing-in ceremony was conducted in Hebrew. For a detailed description of the ceremony see Schalkowsky, *The Clandestine History of the Kovno Ghetto Police*, pp. 359–361.

272 "In the sweat of thy face shalt thou eat bread, till thou return unto the ground; for out of it wast thou taken; for dust thou art, and unto dust shalt thou return." Genesis 3:19 (Philadelphia: JPS, 1917).

November 1942

6. Public reading of the swearing-in statement
7. Signing of the swearing-in declaration, to the music of the orchestra (*Prelude* by Perlmutter)[273]
8. Speech by a police representative
9. Concert
    a. *Yidisher kloglid*, conducted by M. Hofmekler
    b. *Eli, Eli*, music by Guravitsh
    c. *Kol Nidre*, music by Levandovsky[274]
10. Closing speech
11. Marching sequence to the sounds of *Beshuv Hashem*[275]

I would like to go to the official swearing-in of the mister [sic] policemen. I must try, perhaps they will let me in using the influence of Papa's *protektsie*.

Recently there have been arguments among the girls and the two guys, Izke and Avremke. I feel 1 percent responsible for this.

It is now exactly 3:30. Papa has gone to the yeshiva. I did not go. Something is hurting my throat. I took *The Diary of Kostya Ryabtsev* back from Heni today. Short, cut off words, silent, dull glances, a short handshake, and that was it, like there had never been anything.

---

273 Apparently, this refers to Jehudah Perlmutter, the principal cantor at the Kovno Choral synagogue at the end of the nineteenth century.
274 Louis Lewandowski (1821–1894), a composer of synagogue music, was a Jew of Polish–German descent.
275 "A song of ascents," Psalm 126: 1–6.

For the past two weeks I have been wearing a silver ghetto ring with a flat gold plate, with a monogram inscribed on it. The monogram looks something like this:

It cost me 250 rubles together with a little light fitting from a Singer [sewing] machine. The ring came out well.

The words which I write now under the horizontal line, I am writing at 9:30 (according to the new time. They turned the clocks back in all of Germany. So, too, in the ghetto).

My father relates his impressions from the ceremony of the police officials at the yeshiva. Everything went off successfully. The police swore before the labor office that they will carry out honestly all orders that they receive from the higher authorities, without being sidetracked by personal requests—because this is what is required of them. They swore that should a serious incident occur in the ghetto, they will not look to see whether the person involved is their brother, or sister, or a stranger—in such a moment, everyone must be equal. No *protektsie* should be used. This is the obligation of the Jewish policemen. The rights and responsibility of the policemen will become much greater and stronger as a result of this. Soon, there will be no groups standing guard at the gate. Rather, Jewish police officials will let the workers from the ghetto leave and only they will check the workers when they return through the gate. This is both good and not so good: the Jewish policemen from Vilna had also received full authority and also took an oath: as a result of their obligation they will be forced to obey the "highest echelon" and conduct an *Aktion* in Oshmene [Oszmiana]… But I won't get into that now…

November 2, 1942

Today I received a notice that I must go to work in the city as a carpenter at the Boston[276] factory. Generally, in recent times, they have sent a lot of people from the Vocational School to work in the city. For example, thirty locksmiths and twelve carpenters. I am pleased, but at the same time, my heart is sad:

I am pleased because this is one way that I can bring in some products and thereby help my family; but I am also saddened by this because I must part from the happy group of young people with whom I have, for a while, spent my time happily and joyfully in the Vocational School. Tomorrow is the first day that I will be going to work in the city.

The Kėdainiai brigade has just arrived, right now, at 8:30, from Kėdainiai.[277] Two large vehicles loaded with bags and with people. The bags, suitcases, and rucksacks were, knock on wood,[278] really big.

November 5, 1942

I have been working at Boston since November 3. Boston is the name of a factory which has been in existence since the good old times. When the Germans came, the factory's machines were taken deep into Germany and the factory was transformed into a large car workshop. Thirty Jews, more or less trained professionals, and about five Lithuanians work in this garage. The man who oversees the work is a German supervisor, a

---

276 Boston, a former cloth-weaving factory, operated between 1920 and 1941.
277 A forced labor camp was established in Keidan (Kėdainiai), a town located 51 kilometers north of Kovno. In September 1942, there were forty-eight Jews working there.
278 Literally: "no evil eye."

party member, but nevertheless a nice little guy. He doesn't shout at you, makes a joke sometimes, and understands your soul. I, as a tradesman, as a carpenter, have now had a chance to enrich my knowledge in the matter of locksmithing and have also become a mechanic here, fixing a car, turning screws this way, turning and pulling wire from the car's belly. On my first and second days of work at Boston I worked at carpentry and as a locksmith, I became an auto mechanic, a blacksmith (heating up and beating iron parts of the car's mechanism), and an iron builder...a true jack of all trades...

We leave the ghetto gate at 6:45 A.M. No guards accompany us as we walk. There is no supervision along the way. The procession of thirty men draws out over two entire streets. We each walk at a distance of a good few meters behind the person in front of us. When we arrive at Boston (a ten-minute walk from the ghetto) all the "little" Jews go to the window where the German supervisor stands and hands each one a note. The note has the name and number, in digits, of each of the workers (my number is 146). All the factory workers are required to complete the answers to these questions at the end of the day:

1. What he worked on
2. How many hours it took, what work was completed, and other similar matters

People get to working. They work until 8:30 A.M. From then until 9 A.M. is breakfast. At the specified time a gong rings and everyone stops working. All rush up the hill, to the special room that was designated for the Jews. The kitchen is located there, with the dining hall. Two women work in the kitchen. One is our neighbor Mrs. Britfeld, and the other—everyone calls Sheynale. I, too, call her this. After breakfast everyone goes back to work, and we work until 12. Lunch time is from 12 until 12:30. Three long tables hold cups with coffee, standing ready for a coffee break at 3 P.M. The pots with pig swill are already prepared in the morning. The lunch costs two marks per person. When one is hungry, one eats it and also digests it. Few people are picky here: today, an old, grey Jew sat opposite me. While I sat and waited for the pig swill to cool down, he had already received a second portion. By the time I had finished eating he had started a fourth portion and his neighbor finished what the old guy had left, which had remained in the cup... A few minutes later I hear the old guy's hoarse voice coming from the kitchen:

"Say, Sheynale is there no more soup? I thought that you would find a bit more for me in the pot…"

At lunchtime people here conclude business transactions. A few daring guys made a hole in the fence and from there go off in different directions. These guys bring back with them *zentners*[279] of flour, beets, potatoes, macaroni, as well as other odds and ends. Obviously, they want to earn something for the risks they take. And truthfully, this isn't such a bad thing, for this is what one pays here for the following: fifteen rubles for potatoes; twenty rubles for beets; 700 rubles for butter; 140 rubles for macaroni; sixty rubles for rye flour, and 130 rubles for 2 kilograms of bread.

We finish working at 4 P.M, and arrive back at the ghetto at around 6 P.M. The inspection at the gate (we go through the Varnių gate) is relatively low profile. The Lithuanian policeman received forty marks and the brigade went through safely. The policeman (a senior official) pawed everyone but took nothing. I went through last. I had on me 3 kilos of rye flour, 5 kilos of potatoes, and 2 kilos of beets. The flour I somehow attached around my stomach, the rest I carried in a bag. The policeman groped me from head to foot. He felt the bulge[280] around my stomach. He had a good feel and pushed me toward the ghetto without saying a word.

November 7, 1942

This morning, when I left for work, I encountered a grey-white dawn. The world was white from the first, cautious snow, which fell during the night

---

279 See footnote from diary entry for October 15, 1942, regarding the measurements.
280 The original word in Yiddish is *kompres*, see Kaplan, *The Jewish Voice in the Ghettos and Concentration Camps*, pp. 75–76.

between November 6 and 7. How sad, grey, and depressing the ghetto appeared today—on this great day, on this historic day.[281] A cold wind blew, piercing my body with its cold breath. It lets me feel my catarrh which has not left me all year long and which has cheerfully taken up residence with me...

Today, *Shabes*, we worked at Boston until 12:30. From then until 2:30 P.M., they squabbled and quarreled over the products until they reached a general opinion that we should go home. I, together with another Jew, remained to finish some work on a car and we returned to the ghetto at 6 P.M.

November 10, 1942

My father has a new job in the ghetto, one that has never been heard of and one that was not hoped for. He has become the conductor of the policemen's choir which is now being established. As the newly appointed conductor, my father must now assemble a four-voice choir made up of 100 ghetto policemen. It sounds like a dream: Jews in the ghetto, people sentenced to death, not so much people but rather shadows of people, living corpses, future "bagel bakers,"[282]—they are to form a choir in the ghetto? For whom? To entertain the embittered public? For whom? For the Germans? Hebrew songs, *Khazonish*[283] [cantorial] laments, *Yomkiper*–style songs—all for the Germans?! For whom are they making this choir? For the labor office? For Margolis, for Lurie? For the people whose friends, brothers, sisters, and relatives have been taken to the Fort?! For whom?...

---

281 The Gregorian calendar date for the October Revolution, which gets its name from the Julian calendar date of October 25. The Bolsheviks stormed the Winter Palace on this day in 1917.

282 Meaning unknown.

283 Cantorial.

November 1942

Hitler spoke today. The same voice, the same speech,[284] with the same content which we have already heard a thousand times—a short report on his old opinion regarding the poor Jews, and that's it. At the end—old, worn out, sickly applause from people who already beforehand knew the content of "his" new speech.

Stalingrad continues to hold tight. Today is the 110th day of the battle over the city. Hitler, in his speech, emphasized that Stalingrad will be taken not because the city has such a "beautiful name" but because it is an important point on the Volga. With the conquest of this important point, the trade and traffic on the river will be stopped.

The English offensive in Africa continues. According to the rumors from the ghetto and the city, the Germans, and mainly the Italians, are sustaining great blows. The English are advancing forward at fast speed.

Algiers (French Morocco), has been occupied by the American war forces.[285] People say that the Americans have seized or appropriated from the French and English a few bits of terra firma. People say that they have also occupied Palestine. I believe that if the rumors are correct, it is merely a weakness of the English, that is: they must withdraw their military from there, from the lost areas, in order to strengthen the weak places.

The English radio reported last week that:

"The English king deemed it correct to express his thanks to the English soldiers who heroically fought and won a victory in Africa."[286]

The transmission continued:

---

284 On November 8, 1942, Hitler made his annual speech in Munich on the nineteenth anniversary of the Beer Hall Putsch. Hitler claimed that Stalingrad was in German hands with only "a few small pockets" of resistance left and repeated his "prophecy" regarding the Jews.

285 At the end of October 1942, the American authorities told the Algerian resistance about their plans to land in Algeria and Morocco, and asked them to participate in the battle by seizing control of strategic locations in Algiers and Oran. The underground was not successful in Oran, but was fully successful in its part of the capture of Algiers on November 7–8, 1942.

286 Between October 23 and November 4, 1942, a decisive battle in the North African campaign took place at El Alamein. The German forces, led by General Field Marshall Erwin Rommel, were defeated by the British troops, under the command of Field Marshall Bernard Montgomery.

"Roosevelt expressed his wishes to English patriots and African fighters, may they always have such victories…"

The German newspaper reports:

The Führer happily received the news that the German fighters, in concert with the Italian fighters, together won a great victory in Africa and, on this basis, the Führer sent out a congratulatory telegram to the German–Italian fighters in Africa."

The same newspaper reported:

"The Dulce congratulated the heroic armies who won an Italian–German victory in Africa…"

So now—go figure out the real truth from all these congratulations: I believe it's not worth the effort…

November 15, 1942

Last week the following tragedy happened:

There is a city brigade called Yung. Its guards are partisans.[287] The guards vary. Obviously, there are different people there and so there are a few different opinions and different characters, so too among the guards. One has a harsh, evil character while another is different. Among these guards there was one partisan, a dangerous antisemite. He did not hesitate to state explicitly his bloodthirsty opinion: the day before he leaves for the front he will kill a Jew. And indeed, this is what he did. One day, when the partisan was standing at his guard post, the Jews from the Yung brigade noticed a change in the soldier: he became soft in his nature, let himself talk, and even tried to tempt a few guys to trade with him. He noticed that one had a pair of nice shoes, another had something else. He liked everything and wanted to trade with them. The young guys, who knew him from before, did not really want to listen to his talk and moved away

---

287 Meaning: Lithuanian auxiliary serving the Germans.

November 1942

from him as quickly as possible. The soldier noticed a young guy with a pair of good boots. He immediately stood in front of him. He tried to persuade the young guy to exchange the boots, offering him money and other goods for them. The young guy was doubtful. He asked a few Jews from the brigade about it. They advised him to stay away from the trade.

"Don't you know who you are dealing with?" they asked him. "He will cheat you."

However, the lad decided to make the exchange.

"Come with me, not far from here, we will make the exchange there and I will give you the items right away," the partisan said to him...

So off went the two.

Two days passed. The lad was seen no more. The brigade made inquiries. It became clear that the lad who went off with the partisan did not return after the "exchange." People inquired about it with the Gestapo. Gestapo officials came to the brigade's workplace to investigate the matter. It was evident that something was amiss. The investigators asked questions about the partisan. After the "trade," the partisan was no longer seen with the brigade.

They put another Jewish lad in a taxi with the Gestapo officials and they all drove off to the Šančiai barracks, where the partisans live. The Jewish lad recognized the soldier. After the Gestapo questioned him the following became clear:

The partisan took the unfortunate Jewish lad to a farm, ostensibly to exchange the boots. When the lad took off his boots, he grabbed them and pushed the lad into a deep well[288]... They say that as soon as the Gestapo officials heard his confession, they tore off his epaulettes with the diagonal leather belt strap and sent him to the Ninth Forth. The day before yesterday they pulled the drowned lad out of the well and brought him to the ghetto for burial...

A shabby, starving Jew without patches was searching for a family in the ghetto. People showed him where the family lives. These are his friends.

---

288 On November 12, 1942, Tory noted in his diary that the body of a Jew by the name of Blecher, aged eighteen years old, had been discovered. He had been kidnapped by a Lithuanian partisan who guarded the Jewish workers. "This partisan took off Blecher's shoes from his feet, shot him dead, and hid the body." See Tory, *Surviving the Holocaust*, p. 152.

Yesterday, November 14, (*Shabes*), I got up at 5 A.M., and at 6 A.M. was already at the ghetto gate on Kriščiukaičio-Arigalos Street. Sheynale, our cook from Boston, was already there. We went through the gate and on the way she told me the following story:

The ragged Jew, who arrived in the ghetto without patches, is Sheynale's friend. He comes from Druskininkai. He set out from there on the second of this month. Why did he leave?

Until not long ago, he relates, life was very good in Druskininkai. People put together good packages of products [289] to bring into the ghetto and they did not know of any *Aktionen*. About 700 Jews lived there, until...until November 2, 1942. An *Aktion* was conducted there on that day, among all 700 Jews...but he had managed to flee. He has been wandering since then. Now he is among friends.[290]

It is now 7:30 P.M. Up until now I wrote in the morning, but now night reigns outside. Ten minutes ago, Fanya Dembovitsh[291] came running to our house, and reported the following:

Half an hour ago someone attempted to assassinate the ghetto commandant. This is what happened: a watchmaker with the family name of Meck[292] (people say he is a weak lad, but a revisionist) tried to crawl

---

289 Gerber uses the term *makhn a pekl* (make a little package). For a detailed explanation see Kaplan, *The Jewish Voice in the Ghettos and Concentration Camps*, p. 65.

290 The Jews were deported from the town of Druskininkai, close to Vilna, at the end of August 1942. They were sent to an assembly camp at Kiełbasin and, from there, at the beginning of November 1942, they were deported to death camps, apparently to Auschwitz.

291 Fanya (Feyge) Dembovitsh, born 1921, was sent to the camps of Vaivara and Kiwioli in Estonia, and later to Stutthof and Bergen–Belsen. She was liberated in 1945.

292 On November 15, 1942, Nachum (Noach) Meck, a Jewish inhabitant of the ghetto, shot at one of the commanders of the ghetto's German guard while trying to sneak through the ghetto fence to the other side. No one was harmed but Meck was caught, sent to prison, and sentenced to a public hanging. The entire episode caused great horror and anxiety among the ghetto inhabitants, who feared future consequences. Regarding the development of the episode from the perspective of the Jewish police see Schalkowsky, ed., *The Clandestine History of the Kovno Ghetto Police*, pp. 327–331.

November 1942

through the fence with a little package. The commandant noticed Meck and wanted to arrest him. Meck shot at him but did not hit him. Meck was arrested.

A few minutes later, Arnshtam[293] the policeman from the gate guardhouse (nickname Mapu), and another policeman ran to the labor office. They were overwhelmed. As soon as the higher echelons of the labor office found out about this they shut down the committee and gathered the council members for a meeting. Fanya adds that the Gestapo also arrived in the ghetto.

When Fanya had finished relating this, her husband came in. He said: "I was sitting with acquaintances and we were passing time together. Suddenly, an acquaintance of mine, a doctor, came in. He asked us to leave because the situation in the ghetto is tense: Meck, a Jewish watchmaker, shot the ghetto commandant…"

When I returned home my parents were not there. Those at home were: Rokhele (a friend who had come to visit me), my sister, a guy we know, and me. At any rate, the words made an impression on us. However, we all wondered: that a Jew should have a weapon? Such a thing has never been heard of! It is difficult to believe that a Jew would have the courage to hold a revolver in his hand and moreover shoot it!! It is more likely that it is a provocation; either by the ghetto commandant or the Lithuanians. I am reminded of the moment of the first provocation, which also sounded something like this:

Someone shot from the ghetto at the then ghetto commandant Kozlovski.[294] I remember that after the provocation (one or two days

---

293 Tanchum Arnshtam, born 1907, was a policeman in the ghetto. He was renowned for his cruelty, served as deputy commander of the gate guard, was a close associate of Benno Lipcer, and among the most corrupt and repulsive characters in the ghetto. After the Jewish police was dismantled in March 1944, Arnshtam joined the new police force, which was established by the Germans, the Ordnungsdienst. At the end of the war, he was captured by the Soviets, tried, and sentenced to twenty-five years in prison.

294 In actual fact, Paul Kozlovski was one of the German police guards in the ghetto. On September 26, 1941, shots were heard next to the ghetto's main gate. Although no one was harmed, Kozlovski decreed that an assassination attempt on him had been made. Following this, a roundup was conducted in the ghetto, and 1,200 Jews were taken to the Ninth Fort, where they were murdered. Later, it became clear that this was merely a pretext invented to justify the roundup and murders. See Garfunkel, *Kovno Hayehudit Behurbana*, p. 68; Dieckmann, *Deutsche Besatzungspolitik*, vol. 2, p. 949.

later) they carried out an *Aktion* in the small ghetto...and now again a provocation?! Will they again conduct an *Aktion*?

Everyone tried to wait patiently until my parents and Shleyme[295] would arrive. They came directly from the old city. They related the following:

"We were sitting at Mrs. Lerman's. Suddenly, her niece (Mrs. Lerman's) rushed in, and in one short breath told us that she has just come from the gate. Four men, carrying packages, tried to crawl through the fence. The commandant noticed them and shot three times in the air. Three of the four ran off and one was caught by the Germans. The one who was caught is a Lithuanian..."

My mother added:

"As we were going by I went into Feldman the shoemaker (he lives opposite us). I looked in: They were all lying on the floor and crying... I calmed them down..."

Papa also added:

"I went past the committee. A messenger runs out and asks me: 'Where does Lipcer live?' The lad is very worked up and gasping. I showed him."

My opinion:

Something is not right about the story. Whatever may be: if Meck fired the shot—it will not be good, if he didn't shoot and it is a provocation—it also won't go down well. I believe that days of great significance are ahead of us. We can only hope for the best!

All this happened earlier, around an hour ago. Now about ghetto rumors:

A week ago (and perhaps even more) a rumor spread through the ghetto that, based on a calculation by Madam Tabu,[296] on the sixteenth day of the eleventh month, something will happen. Either the destruction of the Jews in Germany or the defeat of the German government. That means one of the two is possible: 1) Either we leave the ghetto tomorrow, or:

---

295 Referring to Shlomo Kalner, Chaya's husband.

296 This refers possibly to Madame de Thèbes (1845–1916), a clairvoyant. The author hints at the phenomenon of fortune tellers' predictions and the expectations of miracles. Garfunkel notes in his memoirs that messianic stories circulated in the ghetto and there was "strange talk about dreams and visions," only after the Great *Aktion* (October 28, 1941). See Garfunkel, *Kovno Hayehudit Behurbana*, pp. 248–249.

2) They take us all to the Fort... When might this all happen? Tomorrow, according to the ghetto rumors, based on the predictions of the French Madam Tabu.

A second rumor. This rumor reigns at every step, in every house and shack:

A great *Aktion* will be carried out on the twenty-seventh of this month.

Zerubavel, a friend of mine in the ghetto, who is always weighed down with news and doesn't speak for no reason says that the *Aktion* will take place on the twenty-sixth, in the evening! (He already knows and gives us all the news before the news is even printed in the newspaper and before the newspaper comes off the print. His news up until now has been 100 percent correct.)

Fanya's husband says about this:

"I heard that the German labor office received an order from the authorities that on the twenty-seventh they should not allow any Jews to go out to work in the city, meaning to leave the ghetto! Why? Because on the twenty-seventh there will be a general mobilization of the Lithuanians and the authorities fear a pogrom by the Lithuanians against the Jews... In short—the German authorities are concerned for the wellbeing of the Jews, they don't sleep at night, and continuously think about how to safeguard and lengthen the lives of the Jews...laughable...I don't believe it!"

November 16, 1942

Today, Monday, the mood in the brigade was not so good. Yesterday's story had a strong effect on life inside the ghetto. A mass shooting was looming.

According to the Jewish police report, it was really not a provocation, but it truly happened: the young man Meck shot at the commandant or in the air—it's all the same. When it was clear that the commandant was approaching him, shouting "Stop! Stop!" he tried to scare him, shooting twice into the air. The commandant, however, was not frightened. Meck saw that he was in a dangerous situation and apparently did not want to shoot at the commandant himself a third time, so he simply shot himself. He was wounded in the cheek. He was arrested immediately. People say that when the commandant bent over Meck, the latter offered him a sum of 6,000 marks (60,000 rubles!) to let him go. When the Jewish police arrested him, Natkin came to him. Meck offered Natkin 20,000 marks (200,000 rubles) that he should persuade them to let him go.

They found on him:

1) A Lithuanian pass; 2) 20,000 marks; 3) gold and diamonds, and 4) a revolver.

Immediately following the episode, the Gestapo summoned three members of the Ältestenrat for questioning. Advocate Garfunkel, Golub,[297] and Goldberg[298] went off. The Gestapo tried to question them. People give the following report:

They took the three Jews into a room. They were ordered to turn around with their faces to the wall. The order was carried out and the interrogation began. They asked them, among other things, why Meck was crawling through the fence and how he got hold of a pass.

One of the three answered something like this (so they say in the ghetto):

"He apparently has connections in the city and wanted to hide from the *Aktion* which will take place on the twenty-seventh!"

The Gestapo officials hurled questions at the committee members, how such a date has come about, in the midst of everything, in the ghetto, who started the rumor, and similar questions.

Throughout the entire interrogation, Garfunkel, Golub, and Goldberg stood with their faces to the wall and with their backs to the interrogators. They did not know who was interrogating them. During the interrogation they gave the impression that Meck is psychologically ill, crazy, and so on. They wanted to remove any guilt from the ghetto Jews, who are

---

297 Gerber is referring to Avraham Tory (Golub), secretary of the Ältestenrat in the Kovno Ghetto. Quotes from his diary appear throughout this manuscript.

298 Yaakov Goldberg, a lawyer, was chairman of the organization of soldiers discharged from the Lithuanian army, a member of the Ältestenrat, and director of the labor office. He survived the Holocaust. He moved to South Africa after the war and died there in 1985.

November 1942

completely innocent (they say that the Gestapo demanded 1,000 men for this "assassination attempt"), and also to lighten Meck's crime. If he is mentally ill—he is not accountable for his actions... People say that the three reduced the number from 1,000 to twenty people (in my opinion, this is hard to believe!)

Meanwhile, all three Gs (Goldberg, Golub, and Garfunkel)[299] were arrested by the Gestapo until the twenty men would be presented. Twenty men were presented yesterday: these were old people from the local home for the elderly and three or four crazy people...then they let the Gs go free.[300]

I just found out that they also let the twenty people go. Why? Because Meck's deed will be reckoned only on his account, his *kheshbn*,[301] and, as he is not "normal"—no one is accountable for his actions, not even him... At the interrogation, people say, Meck behaved very insolently and made strange movements with his body...

Meck's family has been arrested. They are in the prison here.

People say that the ghetto commandant wanted to shoot Lipcer, because the latter defended Meck.

The mood in the ghetto became lighter during the evening.[302]

---

299 On November 15, 1942, the head of the SD in Kovno published an order for the arrest of Ältestenrat members Garfunkel and Goldberg and the secretary Golub (Tory), together with the ghetto inhabitant Meck. Additionally, a further twenty ghetto inhabitants were to be arrested and held as hostage in the ghetto prison. Eventually, all the hostages were released. See Tory, *Surviving the Holocaust*, p. 153. Likewise, see Garfunkel, *Kovno Hayehudit Behurbana*, p. 136.

300 Regarding the "Meck Affair" as described by the Jewish police and the decree to hand over twenty Jews to the German authorities, see Schalkowsky, ed., *The Clandestine History of the Kovno Ghetto Police*, pp. 327–331.

301 Yiddish: At his own expense.

302 The Meck episode generated significant aftershocks among the Kovno Ghetto inhabitants, who feared the ramifications of the act on the general Jewish public. Dalia Ofer's notes about the episode, as it is described by the Jewish order police, discerns differences in the versions provided by different sources. This is both regarding the number of people trying to sneak out of the ghetto with Meck and their intentions, and in the descriptions of Meck's personality. See Ofer, ed., *Mishteret Hageto Hayehudit BeVilimpole*, p. 421. Ilya Gerber, who was also informed by rumors that spread in the ghetto, provides at least two different versions of the event as related to him by different sources. However, Gerber expresses surprise at the possibility of Jews possessing weapons in light of the charge brought against Meck: "That a Jew should have a weapon? Such a thing has never been heard of!" His surprise sheds light on the situation of

Ilya Gerber

Four days ago, a Lithuanian doctor and professor of gynecology, Mažylis,[303] operated on the female doctor Dr. Oleiski.... She had a tumor. The authorities allowed the professor to come into the ghetto with his instruments and operate on her. Mr. Oleiski himself is a big shot in the ghetto and has broad shoulders...[304]

Last week, Dr. Elkes operated on a blind Jew in the ghetto. He restored his sight![305]

The battles in Africa continue. The English have taken back Tobruk[306] along with other cities, too. The Germans and Italians are having a competition to see who can run faster: Nu, they're running away to the Eastern Front, bon voyage...

Last week the English took the island of Jamacco, which is located between Spain and Italy.

The Germans have occupied all of France apart from the coast of Toulon.[307] Hitler issued an order that they should not touch the city of

---

the Jews who lived imprisoned in the ghetto, without any rights. Likewise, it may also indicate the hesitation that some young people felt to take up armed resistance.

303 Pranas Mažylis, professor of gynecology and a practicing physician, resided with his wife Antanina and their teenaged children, Jonas and Liuda, in a large apartment on Putvinskiu Street in Kovno, situated close to the hospital Mažylis established in 1935. During the war many Jewish refugees were hidden by the Mažylis' and their extended family and social circle. On March 1, 2006, Yad Vashem recognized Pranas and Antanina Mažylis as Righteous Among the Nations. See also Tory, *Surviving the Holocaust*, p. 153.

304 Someone with power and money.

305 This statement reveals, among other things, the great appreciation and esteem that the inhabitants of the ghetto felt toward Dr. Elchanan Elkes, chairman of the Ältestenrat.

306 A port city on Libya's eastern Mediterranean coast, near the border of Egypt. In November 1941, a renewed offensive by Axis forces under Erwin Rommel resulted in Tobruk being captured in June 1942 and held by the Axis forces until November 1942, when it was recaptured by the Allies.

307 Toulon is a city in southern France which featured a large military harbor on the Mediterranean coast, with a major French naval base. During World War II, after the Allied landings in North Africa, the German army occupied southern France, leading French naval officers to scuttle the French fleet based at Toulon on November 27, 1942.

Toulon, because the French governor of the coasts solemnly promised to guard the city from an English attack (if it is only possible), requesting that no German soldiers set foot in the city.

Latest news from Berlin about the Jewish Question: The day before yesterday there was a Party meeting in Berlin about the Jewish Question in Europe. They adopted the general resolution—to destroy the Jews of Europe completely. I don't know the appointed time for the destruction.

November 18, 1942

Yesterday evening, Dora told me that Meck will be hanged today in the ghetto. Today, we were told by the brigade coming through the Varnių gate that Meck is hanging near the committee (in fact we knew this already at 12, while at work at Boston).

When I came through the gate it was already very dark and although I searched for the place where Meck was hanging, I didn't find it. My heart wouldn't let me ask the people, other Jews passing by, how can one utter the words: "Where is Meck hanging?" I can write this, and tell only my diary, but to ask a living person the question, "Where is Meck hanging?" this I could not do; the words sound too simple and too horrific at the same time. Brrr...

My mother reports:

At exactly 12 noon they hung Meck. A lot of big shots arrived in taxis, riding on horses, on motorcycles, on foot, and they all came with one aim—to see the Jew hanging. They drove together those living nearby to the hanging square. Before the hanging they gave Meck a last request before his death. The latter said:

"I want to go as a sacrifice for my family. I ask: let my mother and my sister go."

The poor thing, Meck, did not know that his mother, along with his sister, had already been sent off to the Ninth Fort an hour earlier (11 A.M.)...

They brought Meck on a taxi. I say on a taxi, because he lay bound on the roof of a taxi... Thus, he travelled from the SD through the entire city, and thus he came into the ghetto, and there, opposite the committee, they lifted him from the taxi. Kopelman,[308] the head of the Jewish ghetto police, stood near Meck. Meck again asked where his relatives were. Kopelman did not answer.

Meck kept himself more or less calm. One could notice a few places with cuts on his face, covered with plasters. Bits of flesh had been torn away on his neck. Apart from that he bore on his "naked body" the markings of fifty solid lashes.

He stood on a table. The noose made of rope was put on him by two Polish Jews who were brought here by order.[309] The two Jews, not accustomed to being hangmen, did not put the rope around his neck but on his chin. At that moment Meck fell back a bit but righted himself. He was calm and cold-blooded. His face was white as chalk. The rope is already on his neck. His hands are bound behind him. At exactly 12

---

308 Michael Kopelman (1895–1945), born in Kovno, studied law and before the war managed one of the largest insurance companies in Lithuania. He was the first commander of the Jewish police in the Kovno Ghetto and left his post in December 1943. During the liquidation of the ghetto he fled, was caught by the Soviets and, despite the requests of survivors from the ghetto, was tried for collaboration with the Nazis and sentenced to fifteen years of hard labor. He died in a forced labor camp in the Irkutsk Oblast.

309 According to Tory, they happened to be in the prison in Kovno. According to the ghetto police they were a pair of thieves, well known in the ghetto. They were offered to be released from prison in exchange for carrying out the execution. See Tory, *Surviving the Holocaust*, p. 154; Schalkowsky, ed., *The Clandestine History of the Kovno Ghetto Police*, p. 330.

noon they took away the table. Meck lost the firm ground underneath him and remained hanging in the air. He could not stick out his tongue: his mouth was bound with a kerchief. His death took around three minutes. After that, when the body had jerked for the last time, Schtize [probably Heinrich Schmitz] (one of the senior people from the SD–Gestapo) gave a short speech. The main aim of his words: Do not to go the same way as Meck, because this path leads straight to the hangman's noose.

Immediately following his speech, many more taxis arrived. Many big shots got out of them with happy faces, shook hands with the others with great pride, looked at Meck's frozen, yet warm corpse, and left with great fanfare.

November 19, 1942

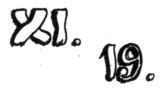

Today at 12 noon they took Meck down from the gallows.

Yesterday evening I wanted to go to him, but my heart would not let me. For a few minutes I looked from afar at the black swaying body and went away whistling. Why whistling? To cheer myself up? I don't know. Maybe!

This morning, when I went to work, I again saw the dead body hanging in the distance, but once again I went by without stopping. Today at 12 noon (exactly) they buried him in the Jewish cemetery.

The entire time, while Meck was hanging, two Jewish policemen stood near his body. They changed guard every two hours. It was a kind of *Garbe's sargyba* [guard of honor, in Lithuanian].

While they were holding Meck at the SD and interrogating him, Gestapo members searched his home. People say such exaggerated things about Meck's wealth, it is simply unbelievable.

They found:
1. Fifteen million rubles in money
2. Forty American half dollar coins (twenty dollars)
3. Ninety-five Russian tens (gold)
4. Three kilos of gold
5. And lots of gemstones

They didn't find any products in his home. The origin of the rumors is interesting. Germans conducted the searches, there were no Jews present, and the road was closed to traffic. From where do people get the numbers? It's all rumors.

As for the shooting itself, and what people say: is it really a fact that Meck shot a gun? Might this not be a second Van der Lubbe?[310] The revolver which they found near Meck was a German one…who knows?

Also, it is interesting they did not hang him for shooting at the commandant but because at the interrogation he gave an excuse which sounded like this:

They asked him: "What caused it, what motives led you to carry out this deed, that is—to try to flee from the ghetto?"

His answer:

"I wanted to run away from the ghetto only because there will be an *Aktion* on the twenty-seventh!"

Meck pronounced the words boldly and certainly. And they sentenced him because of this answer (not for the shooting), for spreading "false rumors."

It is hard to say that the hanging made a great impression in the ghetto. Some even laughed about it, some denounced and besmirched the name of Meck, the dead, hanging body of this Jew.

---

310 Marinus van der Lubbe was a Dutch council communist who was tried, convicted, and executed for setting fire to the German Reichstag building on February 27, 1933. Historians still debate who was responsible for this fire.

People say that in the Vilna Ghetto six Jews have been hanged (meaning in the entire time).[311]

Rosenberg, the famous "friend of the Jews", recently spoke on the radio. His words included the following:

"Jews in Europe are undesirable..."

There is a sign at the committee:

Whoever spreads false rumors about "relocations" [iberzidlungen]—will meet the same end as Meck...

Signed by Lipcer.[312]

November 27, 1942

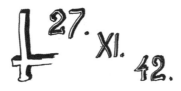

Today is the famous twenty-seventh, about which people have been talking for an entire month; the twenty-seventh, for which they hanged Meck...and, so far so good.

It is now around 8 in the evening (better put at night) and: nothing. We live and hope for better.

---

311 On June 5, 1942, the court in the Vilna Ghetto decreed the execution, by hanging, of six Jewish inhabitants of the ghetto who were involved in the murder of Jews. This sentence was carried out publicly in the streets of the ghetto by the Jewish police of the Vilna Ghetto. This episode is described at length in each one of the diaries written in the Vilna Ghetto. See, for example, the diaries by Kruk, *The Last Days of the Jerusalem of Lithuania.*

312 Lipcer tended to behave in this fashion. Thus, for example, on November 16, 1942, Tory noted in his diary that Lipcer "published a proclamation on behalf of the Gestapo, saying 'people who spread false rumors...will be punished. There will be no more *Aktionen*.' Everybody must work—and maintain quiet and order." See Tory, *Surviving the Holocaust*, p. 154. In November 1942, Tamar Lazarson-Rostovski noted in her diary that, according to a notice on behalf of the SD, no *Aktion* would take place in the ghetto and inhabitants were prohibited from arousing panic. "Whoever arouses panic—will be hanged." See Lazarson-Rostovski, *Yomana Shel Tamara*, p. 56.

Since they hanged the accused, innocent Meck, people in the ghetto have stopped talking about *Aktionen*. People's minds are a bit calmer now.

I have not written since the nineteenth because there has been no important Jewish news, apart from the fact that brigades no longer carry smuggled goods in their pockets nor in little packages—but in fact in big packs. Sometimes they succeed in getting through the Kriščiukaičio gate and sometimes not. Mostly, when the ghetto commandant stands by the gate, the packs or small packages are taken and people feel his whip, but if he is not there, it costs whatever it takes (someone puts something in the hand of the partisan or the policeman) and one goes through unimpeded. Things are different at Varnių gate. There, the commandant does not appear so often and obviously Jews exploit the opportunity and carry in *zentners*. A brigade which works in the city and which is loaded with goods goes around the long way and enters the ghetto through Varnių Street.

The Varnių gate is very expensive. I know from our workers at Boston. At first the Lithuanian police would ask for around 300 rubles to let something through. However, the Jewish policemen or the people from the labor office also want to be paid! They created a new system: you don't give the money directly to the Lithuanians but through a Jewish policeman.

Someone comes to the gate and the Jewish guard demands:
"You must pay 400 rubles to enter through the gate."
And a few days later:
"Today you need to pay 600 rubles!"
Another few days pass and there is a new demand:
"Today—pay 800 rubles!"
And we pay. Do we have a choice? What if they confiscate things? They have often confiscated goods. What good times we live in!

Because our brigade is very close to the Varnių gate, people exploit the opportunity.

Almost daily someone from the brigade has a package—and someone else doesn't. Two groups are created: A) one that has nothing and leaves straight out of Boston and heads for the gate. For having nothing—one pays nothing. The guards pat the workers' pockets, find them empty, and the people go straight into the ghetto. The column leader who goes along with Group A talks to the guards, agrees on a price, and goes back to Boston, where Group B, which is carrying things, is waiting. When Group B discovers that the way is clear and "smeared," they all run at full speed to the gate. Those who are carrying heavy things remain behind and this creates a caravan of carriers, which extends over one and a half streets.

Group B reaches the gate, where two Lithuanian policemen and three or four Jewish policemen stand, as well as people from the labor office.

"One by one!" shout the policemen [in Lithuanian].

But people don't obey. Even though the gate has already been "greased," all of them want to get to the other side of the gate in one go. They push in one throng with the packages while at the same time the policemen feel their pockets, turning a blind eye as they look at the packages on their backs.

When Group B is already in the ghetto, on that side of the gate, people are happy, and they rush away from the gate and from the cries of the Jewish policemen.

"Oh ho! You brought in packages! You still have to pay for it!" the policemen cry out to us.

They grab our column leader and demand a "supplement" from him!

And on more than one occasion it has happened that the column leader had to give money at the gate, or better put—to the Jewish ghetto police!

The following incident occurred:

The column leader Altman approached the gate to come to an agreement with the inspection. Only two Lithuanian policemen were standing there. He talked things over with them and they reached an understanding that he would pay 500 rubles (fifty marks) to go through. Altman informed Group B of this and the group immediately approached the gate. By now, however, Jewish policemen were also already standing there.

"You already came to an agreement with the guards?" they ask.

"Yes!" comes the reply.

"How much are you paying?!"

"Fifty marks," Altman answers.

"Oh! Less than eighty marks—and you won't be going through the gate!" comes the ultimatum from the Jewish ghetto police. With these words they stop the flow at the gate. Having no other choice—they paid eighty marks... The Jews "tore away" thirty marks from their own brothers—also Jews. And so it is with every brigade.

Recently, they are "flaying the skin from us," the people in the brigades: the Jewish ghetto police are already demanding up to 150 marks for ten people to go through the gate! And what will be later?! Even worse!!

DECEMBER 1942

December 1, 1942

Today is already the third day that winter has shown its true, gloomy face with its ice-cold character. Outside it is cold, the wind blows with all its wind and reed instruments, with the accompaniment of white snow. It is hard to keep one's eyes open and from time to time one's breath is cut off, taken away by the sharp wind.

I spent Sunday (today is Tuesday) very enjoyably.

We, the guys, gathered at Rochele Levin's[313] (I only just became acquainted with her) and danced the time away from 6:30 until 8:30. We were: Dora, Ida, Rochele Levin, Bebke Khaytovitsh, Shleyme Finkelstein, and me. The room was very big and three or four couples could move in the space (Solke Shukstaliski did not come, as a matter of principle, this evening).

(I will write more about this group which I listed above and how I became part of this *khevre* in a separate, long chapter.)

---

313 Rochele Levin (Regev) was born in 1924, in Königsberg. She was incarcerated in the Kovno Ghetto but survived the Holocaust.

Today I brought home the rations for my work in Boston. One gets the rations once a month: 2,800 grams bread, 300 grams of butter, a bit of sugar, and coffee.

People have been talking recently about significant victories of the Red Army. They are attacking on all fronts from the Caucasus to the White Sea. They broke the German lines near Terek. They are finishing up driving them out of Stalingrad. The offensive between the Volga and the Don brought good results for the Russians, the German newspaper reports. There are even rumors in the ghetto that they are already fighting on the border of Estonia and redemption for the Jews is approaching with quick steps from the northeastern side…

In Africa, people say, the Germans can't lift up their heads.

Now, one more day, two more days, and liberation is near. We must just not lose patience and then everything will be alright…

The day after tomorrow is *Khanuke* [Hanukkah]!

December 4, 1942
Khanuke

Today is the second candle. No miracles occur in the present century; they happened only then, when we were not alive. Apparently, the good fortune of the Jews who lived then was greater than ours. It is not our luck, unfortunately, that miracles should take place among us today.

December 1942

The ghetto creates many songs but sadly very few melodies: better put, almost none. Despite the fact that my father is a musician of the best kind and once composed a lot, now, in the ghetto, he has not composed any melodies. The music for the words is taken from Soviet melodies, and a few tangos, but no Jewish ones! The people create gradually, recording and expressing the pain of Jewish life in songs. In this way, they relate, recite, and sing about the life of the Jewish ghetto inhabitant at work. Every song is a fragment of life, embracing a unique epoch in our times. A ghetto song generally starts with the pain and misfortune of the Jewish people and ends with the hope for a better, lighter, and more fortunate future. Many songs of this kind were written by a well-known young woman, Sima Yashunsky.[314] She has a significant place in my poem notebook. Here is a poem by her, which was written following the First *Aktion*.

I Live!

My hand is almost unable to write
Thoughts in my head—barely a trace,
I am re-created, brought back to life
Both hands seize it in an embrace.
You sought to destroy all of us here
To shoot us all was your scheme
At times it seems like a nightmare,
An evil, terrible, ferocious dream.
I don't know what happened, what occurred
I only know that another day I live to see;
I so hope that a time will yet come
When I will be able to say: I'm free!

---

314 Sima Yashunsky-Feitelson was born in 1925. While incarcerated in the Kovno Ghetto she was active in the Jewish anti-fascist organization and wrote numerous songs about life in the ghetto, many of which survived. In March 1944, she fled to the forests and joined the partisan units. She survived the war. See Sima Feitelson (Yashunsky) testimony, YVA, O.3/11888.

Sima Yashunsky also described the Great *Aktion* but in a different tone, imparting briefly what happened on that terrible day and how it happened, without adding her own emotions.

The Great *Aktion*[315]

I. In the evening already notes appeared,
Causing sadness, suffering, and ache,
At 6 o'clock must all the Jews
In the big square stand and quake.

II. Be they men, women, or children
Be they old, weak, or sick—
In the eyes of every Jew is terror
What has happened here today?!

III. All night the ghetto was alight
Today light burns in the house of every Jew
Leaving open doors and gates
All poured out into the street.

IV. At the square the Jews line up
Everyone reassures his neighbor
Do not fear, nothing will happen,
It's only a counting for labor...

V. It is already light—one looks at another
"What will happen here?" the words rebound,
Suddenly soldiers are approaching
Encircling the square from all around.

VI. At eight o'clock the Germans arrive
Strolling through, looking everywhere
Already despondent hearts shudder
Eyes, afraid and silent, stare.

---

315 According to Yashunsky's testimony, she wrote the poem directly after the *Aktion*. Ibid.

December 1942

VII. Just look, now the policemen too are coming
     Labor office and magistrate beside
     Escorted separately and placed
     Here in Demokratų, just aside.

VII. And now there goes another column
     Women, children, old people, wide-eyed,
     But why are they taking them separately
     Putting them on the Panerių side?

IX. Look now, Jews! It is an *Aktion*! They are sorting here!
     Like slave traders the imperious German stands
     No need for exertion, just right and left,
     He deals out fate with his hand.

X. In fear and panic people surge
     Like calves to the slaughter toward him
     Right and left his hand directs
     No need to move any other limb.

XI. And on both sides a lament ensues:
     He tears apart families with a look of steel
     A mother cries for her child, a child for its mother
     Can such a wound ever heal?

XII. On the "good side" the question hovers
     Those on the Panerių side—what will be their fates?
     But suddenly, a glimmer of hope,
     For them the small ghetto awaits

XIII. And with visceral wildness people start running
     (to warm homes, so longed for all day)
     Yet several silhouettes remain lying
     No longer rising up from the way.

XIV. Early morning. The square is lit up
     Here and there corpses lie on the ground
     And on the hill the selected
     Those who for the Ninth Fort are bound.

XV. Oh world! The blood cries out to your conscience
     That of men, women, young, and old,
     And at the Fort stand mass graves
     Forever orphaned and united, behold…

Songs have been written with the following kinds of content: 1) going out of the ghetto and the way to work, 2) the sufferings, the moral and physical pain at work, 3) making light of the troubles when you have a burden to bear, and 4) the way back from work in a light, happy tone, or the opposite.

Sima Yashunsky described the way back from the airfield to the ghetto in a light manner and style. The poem is:

The Great Rain

Thick black clouds chase across the heavens
Swallowing up chunks of sky
"Oh, you clouds, black clouds,
Let us into the ghetto fly."
Yet the clouds will not listen,
Running quickly, in a rush, a hurry,
Wet drops begin to fall
Driven on by the wind in a flurry.
The clouds have become accustomed
Our misfortune they know so well
What we have now become
What we were before this hell.
Soaked to the skin
Completely alone we run
Woe to our bitter fortune
Big and small must cry, everyone.

December 16, 1942

I haven't written for a long time. I have recently been mainly in the *khevre* of the "well-known" Dora, Ida, Solke, Shleyme, and Girshke. Bebke Khaytovitsh rarely shows up; Izke and Avremke are also rare guests.

On the eighth of this month the English churches held a prayer service for the Jewish souls in Hitler's lands. On the twelfth they did this also in Jewish synagogues.

The English radio reports:

Within four months, one million Jews have been killed in Poland. Until now there were four ghettos in all of Poland. Now—there are seventeen! Why? Because they sent the Jews from the four ghettos to all four corners of the country so that their strength should be diminished and weakened.[316]

I heard today from someone who works in the SD that 700 partisans from Lithuania travelled to Poland. He reports that the 700 carried out among the Polish Jews not *Aktionen* but genuine pogroms. They killed people in their homes, and opened fire and shot them in the streets. They destroyed the Jewish community in that region.

---

316 Ilya Gerber's anxiety regarding Polish Jewry was very fitting. News from Europe revealed the horrific extent of the Nazi plan for the future of European Jewry, with the shutting down of the ghettos and the mass deportations of Jews to concentration camps in the East. The BBC reported the reaction in Parliament to this shocking new development.

December 20, 1942

Although the mood in the ghetto is not very good and people are exchanging whispers and talking about the *Aktionen* which are taking place in Hitler's lands, nevertheless, the musical ensembles are working at full steam, arranging concerts, holding rehearsals, singing, playing, and strumming their instruments. Last *Shabes*, there was a concert for the Jewish policemen. Last Sunday: for the better [sic] airfield workers. Even the German ghetto commandant attended, together with the Lithuanian one. They liked the concert very much and applauded greatly. When the program was over and everyone stood up from their seats, the above-mentioned big shots remained sitting and demanded more...

Today, Sunday, there is a concert for the committee members. The concert will take place at twelve noon. The concerts have always (until now) been held around 4 P.M., but as of yesterday it has been brought earlier, while it is still light outside (because they cut the wire and provide no more electricity, only important establishments and the workshops receive electricity. So, the ghetto remains in darkness).

The paragraph above was written around 11 A.M. I am now writing at 7 P.M.

December 1942

At around 12 noon I went to Solke's home. Solke was still lying in bed. When he heard that he could go to the concert—he was ready in ten minutes. At 12:45 we were already at 16 Ješibotų (Yeshiva) Street, at the former yeshiva... There were two policemen at the door. "Let me in. I have the notes for the soloist Zacks[317]..." I declare, and push Solke forwards.

"Shush, don't yell," replies a policeman, "give me the notes!"

I don't like the idea. I move away from the door and search for an idea of how to get in with Solke. I will hand over the notes inside myself...

I go to a higher-ranking policeman.

"I must, without fail, give these notes to Zacks," I say in a solemn tone.

"And who are you? Who sent you?"

"I am Gerber!"

"You should have said so before! Let him through!" he turns to the guard at the door.

We find ourselves inside. The concert space is a long and wide area, decorated with thick pillars in the middle. At the end—is a stage. Veneer images, representing two harps, have been created on both sides. In the middle of the stage are two Stars of David.

One looked like this: And the other like this:

One is the symbol of the Jewish ghetto police, the other features the ghetto's communal institutions.

We stuck ourselves in a corner: two *Yurgalakh*—high-ranking Lithuanian officials—were sitting on the first benches.

The orchestra played a few numbers which in general were well received by the audience. The conductor, Hofmekler,[318] bowed nicely for the applause and continued to wave his "baton."

Zacks, the newly appointed column leader of the airfield, sang two songs without a hitch. The last piece that the orchestra played was *Kol Nidre*. The concert finished. Solke and I then went to Bebke Khaytovitsh. He was not at home. Mrs. Khaytovitsh asks:

---

317 Tory mentioned in his diary that the singer Yaakov Zacks performed at a concert on July 24, 1943 (on 20–21 Tammuz). See Tory, *Surviving the Holocaust*, p. 433. He was murdered during the liquidation of the ghetto. This is possibly the same Zacks.

318 Michael Leon Hofmekler (1898–1965), conductor and violinist, conducted the police orchestra in the Kovno Ghetto. He was deported to Dachau, but survived the Holocaust.

"What's going on in those places? People are saying that they have begun snatching people again..."

"It seems to me that it's quiet at present," I answer.

"Why are they snatching people?" asks a certain Jewish woman from the side.

"The electricty station is giving out a very small amount of energy because there is no coal.[319] Wagons with coal are arriving now but there is no one to unload it at the electricity station in Petrasun. Toward this purpose, the Kovno city commissioner, Cramer, issued an order that the ghetto should provide workers to unload the coal. They are working at this task in three shifts: 1) In the morning; 2) during the day; 3) and at night there are 150 men. There are no available workers and also no volunteers—so they seize people," I finish the long explanation.

On Kriščiukaičio Street we meet Bebke. He tells me that today's meeting point for the gang is set for 4 P.M. at Rochele Levin's. The three of us parted.

The clock showed 3:30 P.M. I remembered that Lyusya Maniewitz asked for my song notebook with the first part of my diary. I took it to her. I reached Solke's before 4 o'clock. The two of us went to Shleyme Finkelstein. We meet Bebke on the doorstep.

"Shleyme won't go into the city," he jokes, "he is afraid that such a great find as him might get caught and taken for a night shift in Petrasun... it makes him feverish and that's it—he won't go."

All three of us laugh on the street. Solke, Bebke, and I are all dressed up in our best clothes and look like counts.

"You know, Lyuske," says Solke, "I don't want to get caught for the work today dressed like I am now. I believe that you and Bebke also

---

[319] The issue of lighting was one of the most difficult problems in the ghetto. Garfunkel notes that at first the electricity station in the city did not discriminate against the ghetto. Yet already early on, problems with lighting ensued because of the large number of inhabitants relative to the number which had lived in the area before the ghetto was established. Due to the lack of fuel for heating, the inhabitants used electricity not only for lighting, and the electricity network was not suited to such large usage. Additionally, at the end of 1942, there was a severe lack in the supply of fuel for the city's electricity station, and the ghetto was among the areas first affected. In the winter months, the ghetto was often in complete darkness. See Garfunkel, *Kovno Hayehudit Behurbana*, p. 107.

wouldn't want to. If I get caught and have to work with the coals," he continues, "I would take off my trousers and work naked."

I interrupt him. "On the contrary. I would work together with you and see your physique in swimming trunks…"

So we walk around, joking and laughing out loud. We mock Shleyme and his fear.

"Stop!" we suddenly hear a command.

Opposite us stand two policemen. I recognize the officer, it's Ika Grinberg.

He asks Solke:

"Where do you work?"

"In the Vocational School," comes the answer.

"And you?"

"Also in the Vocational School," says Bebke.

"And where do you work, Gerber?"

"At Boston," I answer boldly.

"Did you work today?"

"Today no, but all week—yes!"

"Give me your card!" resounds the order.

This surprised me. A good acquaintance, my former gymnastics teacher, a good friend of our family—he's arresting me?

I try to argue with him. It doesn't help.

"Solke—Go, go to my house, and tell them that I've been seized," I say.

The guys disappeared.

I walk near Officer Grinberg and I am surprised. At that moment I am angry with him, but later I considered: if all big shots were so conscientious, if there was no *protektsie* for anyone, just like him, it would be an entirely different matter. As a result of *protektsie* only the *amkoh*— the masses—suffer, because they have fewer acquaintances in the "well-known" circles. If there would be no *protektsie*, the "Jewish misfortune" would fall not only the heads of the unknown, but on everyone in general.

So, on this matter, I respected and esteemed Officer Grinberg.

On the way the "Officer" seized a few more people who were not working on Sunday and took us to the prison office on the corner of Kriščiukaičio and [?]. We went through a small narrow gate in a high, barbed wire fence and entered a narrow corridor of the former Jewish school. The low ceiling with the narrow entrance is perfectly suited to a prison. To the left is the prison office. A square room, the ceiling right overhead, and full of policemen. Opposite the door, by the wall, was a square table which held the weight of a white lamp, dozens of work cards belonging to the detainees and placed on the surface the two hands of the secretary, also a policeman.

The racket in the crowded room was immense.

"You're a provocateur! I brought in two people and you, you scoundrel, let them go!" one policeman screams at another.

"You yourself are a scoundrel! How can you accuse me of letting them go!? Did you see it? You pig!"

"Be quiet!" Grinberg says to the two opponents in a quiet and commanding tone.

It gradually became quiet. But then, in one moment, all the policemen go running to the officer, calling out:

"Write it down, officer, I brought in two people!"

"I brought four!"

"Me: one. Write it down..."

Grinberg once again shouts at the lack of order...

December 21, 1942

21. XII. 42.

Today, Monday, we started working at Boston at 8 A.M. The brigade's mood was both cheerful but also distressed.

It was cheerful because the senior overseer has gone on furlough and he was replaced with a German soldier who understands little about our work. The Jews obviously exploit the opportunity and don't overwork themselves. It was distressful because the announcer on the German radio (so say the Jews) communicates every three or five minutes that European Jewry must be destroyed. I believe that this is because London and Washington will use all means to save European Jewry by New

Year's.[320] I believe that if London and Washington will apply themselves seriously to this, it can have only the opposite results for us.

Today I heard that Leon Blum[321] was shot in France, together with the former French cabinet. To what extent this is true, I do not know.

(Continuation from p. 578)

Every minute, policemen arrived with "captives." Grinberg registered how many young men each one brought in and the other secretary–clerk registered the captives. Every three men which he registered were handed over to the policeman Iserles.[322]

My name was one of the three surnames called out. They took us out to the corridor. Iserles was already holding our cards in his hand. He looked vicious to me. He held a flashlight and a whip in one hand and our three cards in the other. He called us to him one by one. At that moment he opened the door of the corridor and tried to push us in. He found it difficult. On the open side of the door stood, squeezed together, were around ten men and many more faces protruded behind them. I understood that this is the prison's threshold. The voices of the "prison inmates" were not musical and no usual passersby could hear them. Iserles pushes us from behind and in front is a wall of Jews, which wouldn't let us in. Iserles

---

320 On December 17, 1942, the governments of the U.S., USSR, Britain, and their allies, including governments-in-exile, published a joint declaration, promising to punish the Nazi war criminals for the extermination of European Jews.

321 Leon Blum (1872–1950), a French Jewish politician, served three terms as French prime minister. During World War II, he was caught in southern France and tried in February 1942, accused of damaging and weakening France. The trial, which was a great embarrassment to the French regime, was stopped. Subsequently, in April 1943, Blum was handed over to the Germans, who imprisoned him in the Buchenwald and Dachau concentration camps. The information on Blum's murder was incorrect, and Gerber himself doubted it.

322 The policeman Nisan Iserles, born 1914, fled from the ghetto in January 1943. He joined the partisan units in the Lithuanian forests, and survived the Holocaust. In the testimony that he gave to Dov Levin in 1965, he did not mention serving in the order police. However, he stated that before fleeing the ghetto he was in contact with and consulted a number of people, including the commander of the order police, Moshe Levin, and his deputy, Yehudah Zupovitz. See Nisan Iserles testimony, Oral Testimony division (OHD), The Avraham Harman Institute of Contemporary Jewry, The Hebrew University of Jerusalem, reel 12/135.

screamed, beat with his whip on the ceiling until the Jews were afraid and let us in among them. The door closed behind us. The lock grated. I am in prison! Darkness surrounded me. Voices echoed in the empty space. Everyone was complaining, "blessing" the policeman and the big shots, cursing the day they were born. All this happened in darkness, with people stepping on each other's feet and corns. A bit of light penetrated through the bars and the long windows of the former school, but this was too weak to battle the darkness. I lit a match. Pale faces were standing around me and looked at the flame. I knew many of the guys there. It was interesting to me to look around the prison. Left and right, near the wall and near the window stood long and wide bunk beds. Six beds, three on each side, created between them a long wide aisle. In the middle of the room stood a miserable little stove. My heart was not happy.

"Where will they take us?" asks someone.

"To Petrasun, to work, unloading wagons with coal."

"Oy, listen, listen what kind of thieves they are," one hears a voice in the darkness. "I'm all dressed up to the nines, just like for a ball, oy, and now I'm going to do such a job?! No, I will run away. Run-a-way!"

"Sh, calm down Mr. Jew, where will you run to, don't get heated up, it isn't so bad, really, we should get away with such trouble as this? Is it such terrible work?"

"We're not talking about the work but about changing clothes!" comes a new voice. "My only good suit, my only pair of shoes, and my coat! This is dirty work! They should understand that it is impossible to work in such clothes! Tfu on them!"

We hear in the darkness a hateful spit and then it becomes quiet for a moment.

The door of the "prison" keeps opening and closing as new "captives" enter. The commotion increases from minute to minute. Everyone is arguing, moving their hands in the darkness, and a few even quarrel among themselves about why someone hit them with his hand on the back in the darkness...

"Guys, why are you fighting, let's sing something!" we hear a young voice.

"Come on! Let's!" People join in from all sides.

Someone starts singing *Ei ukhnem*.[323] He continues with other songs, starts coughing, spits, but it doesn't matter, the crowd whistles, stomps its feet and claps hands and it is very merry until…both ghetto commandants arrive. Then it becomes a bit quieter. To make the room a bit lighter (there has been no light in the ghetto for the past few days), they made a fire and everyone goes past in a circle according to a line, just like Indians in a death dance around a pyre, and people throw little scraps of paper so that the flame should grow. Suddenly a voice is heard:

"Gerber!"

The crowd repeated the name like an echo, each separate syllable: Ge-er-be-er.

Iserles called me. I went out of the prison into the corridor. I see Papa and Chaya. Solke told the people at my house that I was in prison, nu, so Papa came running straightaway with my sister. They brought my working clothes with food. I immediately changed my clothes and went back into the prison. Papa however did not rest. All the police and functionaries more or less know Papa, so it wasn't too difficult to get me out of prison. Arnshtam,[324] Iserles, the police inspector of the third precinct, and others helped with this.

Papa got his "jewel" out of prison and took me home. This was the first time that I had sat behind bars.

The men who were to be sent to work that evening indeed went to work in Petrasun: half of the "captives" were driven there, and the other half had to go on foot—a 15-kilometer walk. There, they were forced to load wagons with coal. They designated two men per wagon, and every two men had to load a wagon. When the work was done, they took the wagons to the train station in Kovno and there they unloaded the coal, again two men per wagon. Returning to the ghetto on foot they arrived at 7 A.M. They worked for twelve hours without rest, outside, at night, without food, fearing the whips. Most of them—90 percent—were handsomely dressed in clothes fit for a ball.

---

323 Song of the Volga Boatmen. A Russian folk song.

324 In spite of Arnshtam's particularly unpleasant reputation, there were occasions in which he helped the Jews, such as in this case. See also Samuel D. Kassow, "Inside the Kovno Ghetto," in Schalkowsky, ed., *The Clandestine History of the Kovno Ghetto Police*, p. 56 (n62).

December 25, 1942

The last week has been full of news. First: A Jewish State! Second: German Jews—American citizens! Three: The shot at Laval, and more, and more, and more...

A rumor had spread at one time in the ghetto that the Jews are receiving their own kingdom. Apart from *Eretz Israel*: Syria, the other side of the Jordan, and another bit of land will also belong to us Jews(!).[325] The Americans will be protectors of this land. This was recorded on paper following a decision by Churchill and Roosevelt, who earlier reported that they will solve the Jewish Question favorably by the new year. The German newspaper mocked the plan and, in general, no one took it seriously. So be it that people talk; there's a very long way between talking and doing. And here, unexpectedly for everyone, the news bursts out before the world: the Jews are to receive their own land! They will have ministers, senior officials, their own firemen and policemen. In short, a Jewish kingdom with Jewish rule! One down.

Roosevelt respectfully informed Hitler (a week ago) that if they will not stop the persecution of the Jews in Germany, he will begin persecuting the Germans in America and for every Jew—ten Germans will fall. The German people in Berlin became aware of the diplomatic note and demonstrated in the streets with slogans: "Destroy the Jews!" (so people are saying in the ghetto). The censor did "not" reject the slogans, but even

---

325 Concerning the rumors that were circulating in the ghetto at this time regarding the establishment of a Jewish state in the Land of Israel see December 22, 1942 entry in Tory, *Surviving the Holocaust*, p. 162. Likewise, on December 23, 1942, Tamar Lazarson-Rostovski noted in her diary: "There is good news. They are saying that **Palestine Received Independence**. The ghetto is rejoicing" (emphasis in the original). See Lazarson-Rostovski, *Yomana Shel Tamara*, pp. 66–67.

December 1942

endorsed them. They have started broadcasting from the German stations every three or five minutes the same phrasing: Destroy the Jews. This was the answer to Roosevelt's note.

Now Roosevelt has issued a new decree: all Jews in Hitler's territory will, from such and such a time, be considered American citizens. Because the Jews are now receiving their own land, they are in fact Palestinian citizens, and thus are under the protection of the English and Americans. That means—we, Jews from the Kovno Ghetto, are citizens of Palestine. Roosevelt is concerned about us and about our protection; for now, "temporarily," we are civil prisoners…let us say that it is so…[326]

I was told that Laval,[327] the important in-law from the Vichy regime, fell victim to an assassination, "may his memory be blessed."

And now I mention a story which happened some time ago and which I only recently discovered:

In the Riga Ghetto they "shot" at the commandant (they probably shot at him there exactly like we shot at our one here). The provocation there cost the Jewish community 200 people. And, the greatest number were mainly from the Jewish police. Others here among us say that 200 people indeed lost their lives but these were not Riga Jews, rather they were Kovno Ghetto Jews who were taken there last time. Who knows the truth?![328]

➤—?- ?-?-? →

---

326 These rumors were incorrect. They were probably intended to comfort the Jews in light of the alarming news about the extermination of the Jews. The Allied response to the news of the murder of the Jews, issued on December 17, 1942, and the promise that those responsible would be punished in due course, probably led to various interpretations and versions.

327 Pierre Laval (1883–1945), was a French politician who served three times as the French prime minister, on the third occasion in Vichy France. Following the liberation of France from the Nazis in World War II, he was tried for collaboration with the Nazis, sentenced to death, and executed.

328 A group of ten members of the underground left the Riga Ghetto on October 28, 1942, in order to join the partisans. However, they were caught by a German ambush. Following the discovery of the underground group, the Germans punished the inhabitants of the ghetto: on October 31, a unit of forty-one Jewish policemen was called for a regular parade in the parade ground and its members were shot by machine gun, without any warning. Most were killed immediately; the few that managed to escape were caught and executed after a short battle. An SS man was also killed during this incident. At the same time, the Germans also arrested approximately 300 Latvian Jews, interrogated them brutally, and killed them.

At the last minute, while writing, I discovered that Laval was not shot but rather it was Darlan.[329] Darlan fled some time ago from France with part of the French navy which was located in Algiers. Obviously, the Americans received Darlan well. He was supposed to reveal secrets of the German–treacherous French [i.e., Vichy] policy. Darlan was shot by a twenty-year-old young man, whose name is not known, while on his way to a meeting.

Goebbels spoke on the radio on the twenty-fifth. No word about the Jews.

December 28, 1942

World News

The situation on the fronts is not favorable to the enemies of the Jews. It draws out interminably. In Africa, together with the Italians, they got such heatstroke that it had a terrible effect on them. Night rules for them on the Western Front, and on the Eastern Front it's also hot, so hot that it's simply steaming and when night falls the air quickly cools and the horror dance begins for the Germans.

The German press reports that the Russians are attacking in the Don–Volga region, in the Caucasus, in Stalingrad, and other places.

---

329 Jean Louis Xavier François Darlan (1881–1942), was a French admiral and political figure. After France signed an armistice with Nazi Germany in 1940, Darlan served in the pro-German Vichy regime, becoming its deputy leader for some time. When the Allies invaded French North Africa in 1942, Darlan was the highest-ranking officer there, and a deal was made, giving him control of North African French forces in exchange for joining their side. He was assassinated less than two months later, on December 24, 1942.

"In the Don–Volga region the Russians have occupied our foremost positions. We have drawn back and occupied our old positions," the newspaper reports.

The Russian losses are enormous. They are attacking on all fronts, hurling the greatest and best forces and they are, poor things, forced to retreat with great, innumerable losses. "The Russians attacked in the Caucasus and broke through our positions, but we fought them back."

An acquaintance just visited us. We asked him about the news.

He doesn't put any stock in the English. "They are robbers, barbarians, terrible people under the mask of virtue. Pirates, under the mask which is called chivalrous. They are oppressors, cold-blooded murderers. And thanks to this, the English kingdom continues to exist.

The Germans—they don't use any masks; they show their true faces. They are basically all noble people—people with chivalrous behavior."

Regarding the Eastern Front, he says that the Russians will achieve a lot. Their aim is to drive the Germans back to the winter positions. Concerning the rumor that the Russians occupied Rostov again with an air landing—this, he says, is a lie.

Regarding the good Jewish news, about the Jewish country and ministers—everything is a lie. Why? Because the English and Americans won't stir up the Muslim world during the war. I believe that his last hypothesis is correct.

December 31, 1942

The notes for the choir which Papa is being forced to create are now ready. The voices have been heard; the list is also ready. The first rehearsal is to be held today. Many of the policemen have little desire for the entire matter and come to our house, one by one, seeking to get out of singing by using their *protektsie*. This one can't, and this one doesn't want to—his heart won't let him. "When the entire world is fasting[330] because of our destruction shall we go and sing?! The Pope too has been fasting[331] and we should enjoy ourselves?! No!"

My father listens to such arguments but is compelled to answer them all with one word: No! He cannot excuse anyone. He is being forced—and so he must force others.

We, Jews, are standing on the threshold of 1943. Regarding this year, people said that the Jews will not live to see it—they will not survive. At the beginning of 1942, people in the ghetto were already saying that, according to the Führer himself, in the year 1943 one will find a Jew only in a museum.

---

330 Between November 30 and December 2, 1942, upon receiving information about the murder of the Jews in Europe, the Yishuv leadership in Mandatory Palestine declared three days of mourning.

331 It is difficult to ascertain what was the source of this incorrect rumor referring to Pius XII. It is possible that it followed Pius' Christmas speech, delivered a few days earlier, which referred to "the hundreds of thousands of persons who, without any fault on their part, sometimes only because of their nationality or race, have been consigned to death or to a slow decline," yet he did not specifically mention the Jews. The reaction of Pius XII remains even today a controversial topic. See as quoted by Michael Phayer in David Bankier, Dan Michman, and Iael Nidam Orvieto, eds., *Pius XII and the Holocaust: Current State of Research* (Jerusalem: Yad Vashem, 2012), p. 34

JANUARY 1943

January 1, 1943

1943. I. 1.

This one, the nation cursed by *Der Sturmer*,[332] the perpetrator of all crimes, the one responsible for the World War, the betrayer of nations, the enemy of peoples, the parasite which lives at the expense of others, the Bolshevik, capitalist, and exploiter of everyone—this is the Jew, upon whose head all the curses of the world pour out, who is guilty of everything. He! He has survived to enter a new year, the forty-third year!

Therefore, indeed, our little Jews "broke glasses,"[333] wished each other *Mazltov,* and had a merry time. For an entire week they didn't stop, they really got into it, they drank a lot, ate well (taking their hand off their hearts), and didn't sleep well. It's superfluous to mention the young people. They want to consume the entire world hastily (an old tendency: *Der Sturmer* also reported that "The Jews want to take over the entire world, enslave everyone, and destroy...") and to act up, cause a great stir, dance and sing like in the good times...

This week we had a good time at Rochele Levin's home. Those present were: Ida, Dora, Solke, Bebke, Shleyme, Rochele, Mishke Tartak,[334] and me. A good snack at 11 P.M. was well worth it: the eating itself, with a few

---

[332] *Der Sturmer* was a weekly German–Nazi tabloid-format newspaper published by Julius Streicher, from 1923 until the end of World War II.

[333] A reference to the breaking of a glass under the *chuppah*, the Jewish wedding canopy.

[334] Misha Tartak was born in 1921. He was deported to Stutthof, where he was shot dead.

glasses of 30 percent [alcohol], was great. From 12 until 3 A.M. we danced to the record player. At 3 A.M. coffee with pastries and Napoleons.[335] I arrived home around 5:30–6.

I believe that it is already high time to describe the events in our old and new group. This will be very difficult for me, but it is high time.

About two months ago (see p. 533, October 26), Izke became ill with jaundice. Dora, Ida, Avremke, and I would visit him every day. I was then studying at the Vocational School. A group of us guys at the school separated ourselves from the rest of the students and created a separate circle, a cozy, happy one, which later became even stronger on the basis of our friendship. We would meet daily at the school, enjoy ourselves together in the carpentry workshop, and sing together.

Bebke Khaytovitsh was a cheerful lad, he would pour forth words just like the best orators, always encouraging others, and was also always joyful and happy. Shleyme Finkelstein was also a cheerful guy, musical, happy, and therefore everyone really liked him. Both him and Bebke. All three of us hung out (more or less) only in the Vocational School. I would sing, Shleyme would set the beat, and Bebke would be the MC. He would inform the respected audience of today's program and we would perform it.

Some time later, Solya Shukstaliski entered the Vocational School. We discovered a musical instinct in him. He became the fourth member of our group. Solke was now the second voice, I was the first, Shleyme would set the beat, and Bebke was the MC. We would hang out in the Vocational School but not outside of it.

I know Bebke more or less from the city. He was known in the [corporations] and mainly where one could drink a lot… I knew Shleyme less in the city, but he let himself be heard as the one who set the beat. Here, in the Vocational School, I saw that he has, in general, a lively and somewhat debauched character—he's quite a lad, a tongue on wheels (he can't compare to Bebke), and he knows Russian folk songs really well.

I like Solke more than the others. I remember him vaguely from the city. I reminded him at one opportunity that once, in the courtyard of the

---

335 Mille-feuille or vanilla slice.

January 1943

Choral Shul[336] on Oželskienės Street, we came to blows because he was talking Lithuanian on the street...

I felt an empathy toward him. A cheerful youth (who can also be serious), a handsome lad, and big hearted.

The four of us began to hang out together. I would be in their company until lunchtime and after lunch, from the evening, in the company of the girls and the guys—Izke and Avremke.

During my last period in the Vocational School we worked for a while in Block C and we would scheme so that our foursome would work together. In the same Block C, on the first level, is the *Parama*.[337] One day, in the middle of work, a lad came running to me in the room and told me that two young women were waiting for me outside. I ran outside at full speed. The two young women were Dora and Ida. They had come to see what Lyuske was up to... A few days passed. The girls would often come to see what I was doing... My friends noticed the girls and wouldn't leave me alone: I must tell them all about the girls and whether they already have someone. I informed them that they are taken, already spoken for. The girls also noticed my group and asked about them. Ida once stared at Shleyme, who was then in the ghetto fire brigade.[338] Now she wanted to get closer to him. Dora is also interested in getting to know them. Bebke, Solke, and Shleyme would exchange words with the girls... No serious conversations took place between them at the time. But we didn't work in Block C every day. The girls came...and we (I also include myself in this) weren't there. The girls would ask me again in the evening where we would be working the next day. I often misled them, saying that we were

---

336 The Choral Synagogue is located at 13 Oželskienės Street, in Kovno. The construction of the synagogue was funded by Levin Barukh Minkovski, a local merchant. Permission for building of the synagogue was received in 1872. See Aliza Cohen-Mushlin, Sergey Kravtsov, Vladimir Levin, Giedrė Mickūnaitė, and Jurgita Šiaučiaūnaitė-Verbickienė, eds., *Synagogues in Lithuania: A Catalogue* (Vilnius: Vilnius Academy of Arts Press, 2012), vol. 1 (A–M), pp. 224–228.

337 The name of a company that traded in food products and sewing notions which maintained a network of grocery stores throughout Lithuania. The company was nationalized during the Soviet era, and the premises served as a distribution point for rationed food products.

338 A special group of firefighters was formed in the Kovno Ghetto, with the necessary fire-extinguishing equipment. The firefighters also transferred the seriously ill to the hospital on stretchers. See Garfunkel, *Kovno Hayehudit Behurbana*, p. 239.

working at the Vocational School and not on the block. My instinct tried to alert me that at some point, something bad can come of this.

The guys started to "pressure" me:

"Lyuske, are they coming today?!"

"No!"

"Nu, tomorrow? Huh?!"

Such questions. They simply wore away at my patience.

Bebke laughed at them:

"These are girls? [Yes] These are girls! Chicks!"

I didn't answer. Therefore, whenever they asked about the girls I simply didn't answer. Shleyme also tried to laugh at it.

I saw that the guys were drawn to the girls and the girls were drawn to the guys... Nothing serious happened yet, but something wasn't right about it. This was a façade comprised of a plus and a minus: either they needed to unite or there would be a short circuit.

At that time our foursome was known as the "United States," and we were popular among the "well-known" circles, making up a two-voice choir. Izke was ill by then. I went to visit him daily. I told him about our quartet. I didn't "mean" anything by this. I was a member of the "quartet" until lunchtime and in the afternoon—a friend (a loyal one) in Izke and Avremke's circle.

Once, one nice day, Bebke (or another one of the three) made a suggestion—to get together once and for all in the evening at one of our homes and have a good time. Obviously, there would also be girls. Everyone leapt at the idea, because now we would have a chance to publicly show our "musical activities." From the beginning this was a problem: where can we get girls?! Bebke has a lot of acquaintances from among the "weaker sex." Perhaps he could bring some of them? This suggestion was rejected: the girls are too "used to it" in cheerful circles and would be bored in our *khevre*... Shleyme had no one to bring. Solke too. I was the only one who must or could provide a few girls.

"The girls won't go!" I say

"Why not?"

"The girls have a group. Dora is with Izke. Ida with Avremke. Nu, and Lyusya Maniewitz—their friend—must then come too."

"What does that have to do with anything? Are they married? Will they be cheating on someone?"

I explain to them that the girls won't want to come without the guys, they are used to one *khevre* and that the light of another circle, another world, can blind them and this can harm the girls and me too, as a friend in that *khevre*. "It will look," I explain to them, "like I am pulling the girls away from their guys to be with you!"

"How do you know that they will refuse? And second, it's just a one-time thing!"

January 6, 1943

[Extracts from a Lithuanian newspaper copied into the original diary]

Today, I noticed this bit of "happy news" in yesterday's newspaper. I believe that this doesn't need to be translated into Yiddish: it is completely understandable, sadly, also in Lithuanian.

A peasant who works with me at Boston reports:

Things are not going well for the Germans on the Leningrad Front. Seventy-six thousand German soldiers and several colonels have been taken captive. The Russians are now 80 kilometers from the Latvian border.

Stalin has now created a new Siberian army comprised of more than 7 million soldiers. With that, the peasant ends his news.

* * *

I am now reading a book by Knut Hamsun,[339] *Di Vogler* (The Vagabonds).

Solke is still sick with jaundice. The guys wanted to "take revenge" but it's not working out: Solke is sick, Shleyme is also in bed with a fever, Bebke has no courage now and I—I barely want to. I visit Solke like a friend and see the guys—I don't want to play a trick on Izke and Avremke. As for the girls—I sympathize with them, and, anyway, I don't dare to make a move against them. Why should I do it? In my heart I hold silent anger toward them, a feeling of annoyance because they have forgotten the past. But, so be it, how can it help?

[Continuation]

In short, the guys would not leave me alone and so I asked the girls. The girls were immediately excited about the idea but considered it a bit. I didn't want to ask them about it anymore. I filled my role with great difficulty and not very well.

At 6 P.M., we guys from the Vocational School would meet at Shleyme Finkelstein's home; he lives not far from Izke. That's where the rehearsals took place. After the rehearsals, I walked with Solke past Izke's home. A few times he "unwillingly" wanted to go visit him, because the girls would be by his bedside at the same time. Solke knew that I went to visit him after the rehearsals. I invited him to go in when we were near Izke's.

"No, I don't want to!" replies Solya.

---

339 Knut Hamsun (1859–1952), a Norwegian writer, was awarded the Nobel Prize in Literature (1920). He supported the Nazi regime during World War II.

January 1943

"Come on now, come inside!" I implore.

"Will you be staying with him for some time?" he asks, already relenting.

I felt that if I take him to visit the "sick person" my friends from the past won't look upon this kindly.

"Yes, I will be there for a while."

"I will go in with you for fifteen minutes, but afterwards we must go back home together!" he says to me.

"No, Solya, I will be staying longer, and you can go in, what's your problem?"

He refused to visit Izke.

I liked him, Solke, but despite this I didn't want to bring him into the girls' *khevre*. I believed that the girls would become flustered in his presence, together with the guys, because their conscience is, nevertheless, already not completely clear.

One evening Solke went with me to visit Izke. There I found Ida, Lyusya, Dora, and Avremke. The mood changed somewhat with our arrival. We got to talking about our rehearsals. I had to, and wanted to, hear the answer from the girls in the presence of their "cavaliers" and how the latter would respond to this. I went to Izke and explained to him that we, a few guys, were planning a "little dance" and if he, Izke, wasn't against the idea, we will invite their girls to the party.

"Please! Why not?" Izke agreed.

Then I openly asked the girls about it. Ida looked at Dora and the latter at her. They laughed with a strange, nervous laughter. Then they became serious.

"And the guys?" asks Dora.

The three words hit me hard. The three words reminded me and drew my attention to the fact that I was doing an injustice to the guys. But my conscience was calmed by the fact that Izke, had in fact, permitted me to ask them openly. Despite this I felt guilty and in a bad situation. The question also pained me. But it was, so to speak, throwing the truth in my face. I lost myself for a moment and after a short pause, said:

"Yes, Avremke, this means you, too!" My answer came out hesitantly and unnaturally.

Why did I not ask Avremke directly, why did I not invite him? Because, at that time, my new Vocational School friends had an indirect—not a direct—influence on me. Mainly Bebke and Shleyme—they rejected my proposal—to have an evening to which everyone was invited. "If they come, if you want to invite them—we will not come," they stated with finality.

At the moment of their ultimatum I decided how to handle it: ask the entire group of friends and the girls and see the effect it has. If they come—great. If not—then it's no use. Whether they come or don't come is obviously not my affair but entirely their own. It's their decision. With a person, who is sure of himself and stands resolutely by his own decisions and has a firm and strong character, one can try a thousand times to persuade him of something—but he will remain firm in his decision. One cannot dictate to a person (with a free will): he alone dictates to himself.

So it was in this case: If the girls would be resolute in themselves and their decision—not to go without the guys, or not to go at all—then they will not go and there would be no misunderstandings. At that moment, and in this case, I blame the girls the entire 100 percent!

I could ask them—and they could refuse! And then nothing would happen! But it's not our luck (better put—not my luck)...

Obviously, Avremke acted just as any clever person at such a moment: Him? No, he isn't going. What for?!

He was right. But I wanted to persuade him to take this step—he should go and enjoy himself with us. Izke lay in bed, looking serious. He didn't utter a word. This had a far greater effect on me than Avremke's refusal. A quiet accusation flowed from him toward me! A quiet reproach! I felt and sensed it—and could not bear it. The girls were talking quietly amongst themselves.

The room became silent. Following the "deliberation" the girls begged Avremke not to refuse, but to agree. Avremke however had decided once and for all—not to go! (I completely agree with Avremke on this. I would have acted exactly the same if I was in his place).

Avremke's refusal and Izke's silence and seriousness also affected the girls. They started to have doubts. Cautiously and uncertainly, as <u>always</u>, as <u>constantly</u> guilty, I again mentioned the evening that "we" want to organize a few more times and left with Solke.

January 1943

Solke didn't visit Izke anymore. He was my witness that evening.

The next day, and the day after that, I also sat by Izke's bed. We always talked about the same topic: about the time that the girls came dancing once with our group from the Vocational School.

Does it seem like a trifle matter? Ha?! After everything the girls had doubts: yes to go, not to go, yes to go, not to go...

If it became uncomfortable for me, then I would simply reproach myself: "You know, guys, I regret the entire matter. Do what you want: if you want to go—so go; if you don't want to go...!"

At that moment all of them would fall upon me from all corners with reproaches, why am I talking like this, I mustn't keep talking about it and thinking this way.

Avremke, I could see, was pained by the entire matter. It pained him—and pained him openly. Izke suffered, but did not show his feelings openly. He was serious.

Working in the Vocational School offered me the opportunity to be free for a couple of hours during the day. I spent those hours with Izke. After all, he was ill. I wasn't bothered as much about the issue and stated my thoughts openly about the entire matter. I wanted to apologize to him for stirring up the group with such an invitation and if he so wishes—I would not talk about it anymore, about the invitation.

But apparently, Izke is not against it! He actually wants the girls to enjoy themselves. It gives him pleasure, he says. He likes the whole idea. He persuades me that I should ask the girls even more to come to the party that we are organizing on Friday. He doesn't leave the question and desires only that I should pique their curiosity and interest, so that they should come. If it doesn't bother him and he is also interested that the Friday event should happen, what can I say? Certainly, and for sure!

That same evening, we were all sitting again with Izke. On the agenda: the old-new topic: "to go or not to go." I don't feel comfortable, despite having Izke's agreement. The latter was talking quietly with Avremke. Avremke can't sit still. He cannot contain his feelings: it is evident that all this is bothering him and that he is greatly interested in the coming Friday. He is a bit nervous. I feel that Izke, despite him saying "it doesn't bother me" is not behaving toward me in a friendly way. Now he is no longer talking with Avremke quietly, they are already writing notes to one another. The situation becomes more strained by the minute. The girls are a bit too confident. They see that the guys are staging a quiet protest about the situation that has arisen and they are delighted by it. They pester me, that I should tell them about the other group: what does Solke say, what does Bebke think, and what does Shleyme do. Gradually, it becomes a matter of pride for the girls. They raise their voices, are not bothered by the guys, and each one reveals their thoughts openly.

"What are we, their wives? Don't we have our own opinion?" says Dora and Ida supports her.

"Go, go to them," calls out Izke, "and later we shall see..."

This sounds like a warning, like a call to battle. The girls remain still. The serious tone makes an impression on them. But not for long. A minute passes and they speak:

"Indeed, we will go! What can you do to us!"

"We'll see later!" comes the answer.

I don't understand Izke. A few hours ago, he practically begged me to invite the girls, and now? Did he change his mind in that time? The atmosphere burdens me. I don't feel well. In fact, I am the one destroying their idyll, their good, yet normal and monotonous, life.

I now sit like an onlooker and consider the situation.

I withdraw openly from all of them and say that I will interfere no further between them and remove myself. The girls straightaway grasp at me, I should not talk that way, they will certainly go, it shouldn't bother me, I am not guilty... The guys say that they have nothing against me, that everything, the "going or not," is between the four of them and not me. I'm not to blame!

I see clearly that the two guys—Izke and Avremke—are indeed moving further away from me while with the girls—it's actually quite the opposite. For them—the "going" has already become a matter of pride. They want to go and indeed they will go. Therefore, they won't leave me alone. I spoke with the girls separately. I said to them that I see myself at the present moment as a destroyer of friendships and that I will not be joining the "carnival dinner" this Friday, because, without me, they would not go to people they do not know. I had to endure a redoubled attack from the girls and in the end yielded, but I removed the responsibility from myself.

I also spoke separately with Avremke. He has nothing against me, he talks a bit about the "invitation," saying that I didn't handle things properly in this case. I try to defend myself but because my conscience indeed feels guilty in this matter, my defense didn't seem very good. About Friday, he says, he can guarantee that Ida will not be going. He feels that he is in a strong position with her. He has great influence over her. I answer that he must not guarantee, because such things don't work in life and, second, no one can make guarantees for another. Especially not in times like ours. He stands by his opinion—nothing will happen.

The guys view Bebke as too much of a playboy, Shleyme is just nothing, and they don't want their girls to fall into "such hands." They are a bit right about this. They regard Solke as more of a good guy.

January 10, 1943

Solke went to Larik Lubetzki's nineteenth birthday today. It is supposed to start at 5 P.M.

January 11, [1943]

Today is Monday. I didn't go to work today because, very simply, I lay in bed. When I was at Solke's yesterday I had a terrible toothache. I started shaking with chills. I have not been feeling well for an entire week now but I haven't given in to it. Solke has been sick all this time. Shleyme has been in bed for a week with a high temperature, and Bebke has also been in bed for a few days. Now it is my turn.

Solke's visitors yesterday were: Bebke, Itshe Girzon, Zerubavel from the "half-yellow race,"[340] a lad I don't know, and me. We decided to hold a literary evening. The "yellow one" will be the editor. Everyone will bring material.

Avremke Tiktin joined us later. I accompanied him home. On the way we talked, like real friends, like we used to be. I asked him to use his influence (on his entire group) to include Solke as a member of his group. At present the *khevre* is made up of the following members: Izke, Dora, Avremke, and Ida. The new additions are: Heni Shpitz, Larik with his girl or his beloved (it's all the same) Riva'le Kaplan.[341] Everyone has a partner.

Izke — Dora; Larik — Riva'le

Avremke — Ida; ??? — Shpitz

Evidently, there is a free place opposite Heni.

Therefore, I say we should try to bring in Solke into the empty space and then we will be able to raise a toast.

I already spoke about it with Solya, but he, as a friend and member of our quartet, doesn't want to do it. I simply persuaded him that he should be a frequent visitor there, because if Heni, as someone who didn't know him, could visit him a few times while he was sick, he should take advantage of the opportunity. Heni is apparently interested in Solya. The first foundation of feeling is here, so why should it not go further?

This group can be a much more interesting one for him than our group! I say this to him, and it hurts me, I hurt myself: if Solya, the only loyal friend of mine leaves us and obviously also my group, what remains for me? Who do I have there?! Then it will be empty around me, without a friend. I'll remain friendless, just me alone with no one else!

And despite this, even though I know that with his departure I will lose the truest and dearest one—nonetheless, this is how I deal with it! I am not selfish! And in many previous cases in my life this has been a big mistake and a disadvantage for me, but when I devote myself to a person I will make sacrifices for him. He is dear to me, I like him—I also esteem him and seek what is good for him. I will help the person that I esteem

---

340 Unknown. Zerubavel was a member of Irgun Brit Zion, perhaps there might be a connection.

341 Riva (Riva'le) Kaplan (Verblovsky), born in 1926, was incarcerated in the Kovno Ghetto, from where she was sent to Stutthof. She survived the war.

however and with whatever means I can. I want that person to be happy. I see that the group is, in one respect, more interesting than our group. There, Solya can find that which he cannot encounter and find among us; why should he not go there?! I feel that it would be better for him there; if it doesn't appeal to him at present—it will in the future! He won't be able to avoid the new group, even though he assures me that he doesn't [...][342] with groups, that one doesn't exchange friends and that he can't do this because of me. (So he once said to me!)

I told him once and I repeated it a second time: man (by nature) does not dictate the feelings, but rather the opposite—the feelings are what dictate to the person; and feelings, which grow into love (for a girl). These types of feelings are often stronger than feelings of friendship. In short, feelings of love win out over feelings of friendship!

I say this because I see that Heni and Solya are growing closer very quickly. And as Solya will discover her and at the same time also that *khevre*, this very simply means his imminent departure from the old group. It is impossible to dance at two weddings at the same time. One goes where it is more interesting. And because I can foresee it in advance—I want, as his loyal friend, to speed up the entire process. Perhaps it is not good for me to think this way, perhaps my fantasy about the entire matter is a bit too extravagant. It is 100 percent possible since neither Heni nor Solya openly express their feelings and one cannot know what the future will bring. One cannot predict and draw conclusions on the basis of the first meeting.

I don't want to make myself stand out but only want to tell the truth—I base this on experience (don't laugh!).

The moment that Avremke brought me into the girls' group, that is these people, I noticed that Ilik Rabinovitsh could not find great interest here and could only be a distant friend, a spectator. As for Lyusya Maniewitz, this *khevre* wasn't appropriate for her, either. Had she found a close friend in the group, who could be more involved with her—then she would have been able to remain. Otherwise not. I myself immediately said that I don't fit in with the group—because I don't have a partner. And so I became the wagon's fifth wheel. As long as Ilik and Lyusya

---

342 Unclear.

Maniewitz were in the group, I could be a member there, but when the two of them left us and the group remained composed of Izke with Dora, Avremke with Ida, and myself, I predicted that sooner or later the time will also come for me to leave the group. And so it really was. And moreover, I foresaw it when the fuss began about inviting the girls to a one-off party with the guys from the Vocational School. I even foresaw that Heni would sooner or later come into Avremke and Izke's group. I had already suggested it to her when I was spending time with her. She refused. Why? She had nothing against any one member of the group but, when taken all together, all of them as a whole, she did not like them... Now she is a member of the new, reorganized group!

During the first days of acquaintance between Dora, Ida, and the Vocational School guys I foresaw that this was the eve of a storm. I predicted the new coexistence of the newfangled, newborn group (Solya, Bebke, Shleyme, Dora, Ida) and my last days in Izke and Avremke's group. I foresaw a short coexistence for the guys and the girls (because it flared up too quickly) and a quick expiration of the blind love. When I was already a permanent member of the "four-guy orchestra" Avremke came to me. He inquired about how things are going in our group.

"May the Jewish exile last as long as the illusions hold among them," I answer.

As a former good friend, I tell him (perhaps I shouldn't have said it) the latest news at the present moment.

"I tell you, Avremke, that the tragedy and the pain is so great, it is fearful to mention. You will see," I say, "that in a few days' time, the girls will come to a difficult situation and then there will remain only one way out: to hang themselves..." I laugh. "It's no life with the guys! Either the girls must reject the guys or the guys must reject the girls. And then," I say to him, "the girls simply deserve pity: where will they seek shelter? Will they be in such circumstances and come back to you? No, there is only one way out for them. In their place, I would have hanged myself a long time ago...!"

I more or less foresaw everything. But I was wrong regarding one thing. More about that later. Now then, in this case, even though Solya does not know Heni well and vice versa, I foresee a joint future between them. May it be good!

January 14, 1943

Today is the fourth day that I am lying in bed. The first three days I had a fever and today, if only it would continue… What? The world is waiting for me? Let it wait…

No one "dropped in" to visit me during the first two days. To tell the truth, I wasn't waiting for anyone. Who could visit me? Solke is still sick. Izke, Ida, Heni, and Dora—they will certainly not come (one only visits a person when one needs him!). So, the only possibilities are Bebke (Shleyme F. is still sick) or Avremke, who is more or less friendly to me.

This is what happened: Avremke came to visit yesterday at 11:30. He found out from my mother that Lyuske is sick. Truth be told, I was pleased to see him, first because through him I will find out the latest news from the "newly created front" and also other news from the group (his) and, second (only the truth!), I wanted to see him as he was to me in the past, in the "good years" when we shared a true and deep friendship. Despite the fact that he had promised to meet with the girls around that time, nonetheless, he sat with me. He saw my diary. He didn't ask for permission to read it, but I didn't stop him. Afterwards he told me how the girls had come back to them. Life with the others apparently wasn't good. Then he also gave a commentary about Larik's birthday (the tenth).[343] The mood there was not so good (as I understand it). But I couldn't be happier for them!

Lately, as can be seen from the previous entry, the guys are drawing Solke into their group. Good! I understand it. I see here the good intention which is directed toward Solya and the strong rebuffing blow directed at me. It is interesting to me: did they do this knowingly, and plan ahead? Perhaps yes, and perhaps no! I provided an answer to this myself: they could have blamed me (Izke and Avremke, since who else does this concern…) for destroying their good life with the girls. For this I have an answer.

---

343 Eliezer (Larik) Lubetsky, born January 10, 1924, was liberated in May 1945.

I. Before I brought up the question openly, I had received Izke's agreement. That means that when I approached the girls with the vexing question: "To go or not to go?" the responsibility for this did not rest with me alone, but on both of us equally: on me and on Izia [Izke], who agreed.

II. Had the girls not wanted to go—they would not have gone. That means that for their deeds, for their decision, which was made according to their will alone—the people who carried out those actions bear the responsibility.

III. The girls removed all responsibility from me, as did I myself, regarding the entire matter. Both guys apologized to me later and shared with me that the guilt was not mine.

Very simply, then, both the girls and the guys have absolved me of any guilt. That means, that they cannot have anything against me. I am clean.

So, who is guilty of destroying their former setup?! Either way it's not all my fault.

The girls, when one asks (better to say, when one asked them) why it came about that they separated from Izke and Avremke, had an answer: "It had to be this way," meaning—they don't blame anyone, or rather, they only blame fate (*Likimas*[344]).

Then, when the guys apologized to me, saying that I was not the one who destroyed their good life, the question remained between us "Who is really to blame?" The guys answered: "You're not to blame here (to me); only the girls and their frivolity are guilty!" Thus, my conscience is declared clean of everything by everyone! For the moment I am happy, but only for the moment.

Avremke started visiting Solya recently, as did Heni. I understood that they are aiming at something…people don't just come to visit for no reason. When one visits, one has an interest in doing so. When one has an interest—one will become friends, and this will lead to being accepted into the group. There, in Izke's group, they know that Solya is my only good friend. If they would have true feelings of friendship, if they would be considerate people, they would not behave this way.

---

344 In Lithuanian: fate.

January 1943

They see that Solya and I are two friends and if we are good friends—our wishes are as one; very simply put: two devoted people are in fact two bodies with one soul.

His last wish is—to take Solya for himself. That means, to take him away from me! To separate between the two of us; drawing him closer to him and further away from me (as a result of reasons which are unclear to me and demand an explanation). Do they know that this is a blow for me? Are they doing it consciously?! What do they have against me? My conscience is clear. And because my conscience is clear and innocent—does this make me feel better? Not really. Because if it is clear, it is so for me but not to them. Apparently, they believe that I am the criminal. And I do not write this to calm my conscience, but that my thoughts should be clear (simply said and written) in this...stupid matter!

Avremke came to visit again yesterday evening. Bebke and Lyovke Goldin came to visit after he left. We talked a bit about the literary evening which we guys had organized on Sunday.

A doctor from the committee came to see me today (at lunchtime). She told me that I am healthy and strong and must sweat a bit more. I received another two days furlough. That's great!

Avremke has only just left now, at 5 P.M. A nice guy. He tries not to forget me and pops in to see how the patient is faring. Because of his sincere kindheartedness and because I feel a true empathy toward him, I let him read the diary. He relates things that are difficult to believe: he is becoming distant from his group. An invisible wedge has been formed there!

Ten minutes ago I arrived at a decision: because there is only a little writing paper left in the diary and because I see that the matter I have been writing about recently takes up a lot of space, I will now end it as quickly as I can.

The first Friday event did not take place. It could have taken place, but I didn't bring the girls to Solya's where the dance was supposed to be held. Before the second Friday, I took both girls by the hand and told them that the Friday event would happen only if they swore that they would go back to their boyfriends, Izke and Avremke. They took the oath. I had a conversation with Izke before that. He asked me (in response to my speech) to avoid seeing the girls for a week. He thought that if I, "the initiator" of the "party," would not see the girls for a week, the girls would come back to them. I promised. And the girls promised me too, and took an oath. I simply tried really hard to ensure that the girls would go back to them. I told this to Solya, adding to him that I would not invite the girls to come anymore. If they want to, they could come directly to him. I avoid them. The first Friday didn't happen, the second was supposed to happen. At the appointed time I came to Solya. I did not invite the girls. They could come or not. But I had received their promise, and this reassured me.

That Friday, Ida, Dora, Lyusya Maniewitz, Bebke, Shleyme, Solya, and I came. The guys promised me to act properly... I noticed that Shleyme did not leave Ida's side, Ida looks at him in his eyes and Solke was the same with Dora. Bebke started to misbehave. I saw that the promise and the girls' oath was just a bluff and I, poor thing, found myself in a difficult situation with Avremke and Izke. I didn't know where to turn. I thought about writing them a letter. My conscience would not let me rest. This is how it goes:

Izke! Avremke!

You asked me to leave your group in the name of our friendship. In the name of friendship, I promised to keep my word 100 percent and carry it out as best as possible. In this coming week I will venture out as little as possible and avoid the group: I want you to live well and that the obstacle I have created should not be felt by you. I don't want to be a Mephistopheles for you. The price for this is very heavy for me but I will avoid you and my last word to you is to wish you both happiness.

L.G.

P.S. Don't forget that you had a friend who was loyal to you and is still loyal to you, just from afar...

Don't visit me—this is my last wish.

January 1943

They received the letter and came to me. They used their worst language and wanted to withdraw their demand from me (about the week) and that I should come visit them. ("That day he (Izke) gave me a pipe.")

I didn't go visit any friends for a few days. I walked around the streets on my own. The girls were still going around with Izke and Avremke. But, in fact, they already "belonged" to the Vocational School guys. I told Izke about this, how the girls had given me their word. I was loyal to them until the very last moment. Concerning what happened on Friday—neither Izke nor Avremke knew about it.

One evening, I was returning home from a solitary walk. I heard someone warily whistling "our" whistle. Near our house I recognized Dora and Ida, without the guys, without anyone. I understood that they wanted to ask me something. I broke my promise and went up to them. They were very happy. We talked among ourselves for twenty minutes. Dora wanted to know what Solya thinks of her. Ida wanted to know what Shleyme and Bebke say about her. I avoided answering. I saw tears in their eyes. The girls are in love! Dora with Solya and Ida—well, she is not sure with whom: either Shleyme or Bebke. I refused to mediate between them.

The girls came to me and tried to prevail upon me to be the mediator, but I would not be moved. "Only love breaks walls!" They themselves became the mediators.

Solke is with with Dora; Ida with Shleyme. However, Ida quickly changed her feelings and set her sights on Bebke. The love remained strong. Dora went around with Solke for a month. Solya acted up, which put Dora in such a situation that she had to move onto Shleyme.

But this didn't last for long. Dora, who had pushed Ida to leave Avremke, now felt regret and wrote a letter to Izke (she humbled herself!) asking him to "take" her and Ida back. And so, it happened. It had a great effect on Bebke! Because he was really in love with Ida. It also hit Shleyme like thunder and he had, poor thing, to stay in bed, sick. As for Bebke—he tried to hold on, and even composed a poem about it. Here it is:

Ilya Gerber

"Moto: Treue ist die Freundschaft
Und falsch ist die Liebe..."
[Friendship is loyal, and love is false]

1. Four friends, four like bears
   Once upon a time we were
   And where one turned, there,
   Like a wall of steel all would be.
2. One is of peasant stock
   An only son, a cadet
   His origin—quite a shock
   Yet he suits our quartet.   ← (Solke)
3. One of us is quiet and still
   An onlooker in the set
   People say writing is his skill
   He writes books like Hamlet.   ← (me)
4. One—looks like a count
   Puffed up he walks around
   "Any girl, I can hook"
   Such statements from him abound. ← (Shleyme)
5. The fourth is me, as all can see!
   I do not suit the quartet's ring
   Neryakhke[345] Solke calls me
   With a falsetto voice I sing.   ← (Bebke)
6. We lived happily indeed
   No trouble, no worry about the morrow
   Only some girls did we need
   And so, we decided to borrow.
7. Two girls we took on loan
   (It's just a joke, or so we thought)
   But three by love were overthrown
   Over the barrel, we were caught.
8. Thus, enemy out of friend was made
   Two even came to blows   ← (Shleyme and Solke)
   Over what?! Over a little maid
   Who wanted neither as her beau. ← (Dora)

---

345 From distorted Russian: meaning negligent, careless.

January 1943

9. And the two lads, for this belle,
   Don Juans of such great fame,
   Like high school students in love they fell
   Idiots and morons just the same.
10. And the girls—
    (Better put—like children they are)
    Played with them like toys
    Even a blind man could [see] that far.
11. And one bright night
    (It was New Year's just gone by)
    They sent them on their way
    Oh, how beautifully the moon shone.
12. And from this poem the moral
    Is very straightforward:
    Children of fifteen years old
    Are not a good match all told
    Let us continue to live in joy
    Like every good, pious Jewish boy
    Let us continue to sing and laugh
    And cause no more fuss on their behalf...
    (Bebke wrote this on January 1, 1943).

Solya and I made fun of it. We thought up a joke about it. I took a pen and ink and wrote it out on a piece of paper. At 8:30 P.M., when it was very dark, I hung the placard on a green fence. A day later we saw the consequences of this. Bebke screamed, made a fuss, said that he can't walk down the street without being bothered, everyone stops him to ask him, what happened with him and Shleyme... Why? Because there is a notice about them....

The notice, which Solya and I made, was written with large letters:

Our deepest sympathy for the dear friends Shleyme and Beba [Bebke], in the bloom of youth, separated from their women.

Signed: a group of sympathizers

I have lost the friendship of Izke and Avremke (it seems also the girls, why?! I don't know!) but I have received a good devoted friend in their place—Solya Shukstaliski! I value him.

The clock shows 7:30 P.M.

I think that I won't mention the topic of "to go, or not to go" anymore. So nice, but also too much. This was a "happy tragedy!"

Good night my diary! Until tomorrow—Auf Wiedersehen…

January 15, 1943

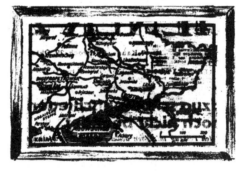

Significant Russian attacks are taking place on the arc of the Don River. The Germans report: great Abwehr battles are underway. Regarding Rostov[346] people already said some time ago that the Germans intercepted the Russian air landings there. But apparently it was a lie. The Russians are attacking in the Caucasus, and, according to the reports in the German

---

346 Operation Don was the Soviet offensive by the Red Army's Southern Front aimed at capturing Rostov in January–February 1943.

January 1943

newspaper, it appears that they are "tasting gunpowder." Things are also going "well" for them on the Northern Front (just like I'm limping...)

Today is the fifth day that I am sick. I am officially sick but, in fact, I am already dancing around the house and my mother cries that I am bothering her, and that lunch will only be ready at 3 P.M. because of me... I cannot say that I feel very good: my pulse is a bit too fast. But hush. I don't say anything at home, because I want to go outside a bit this evening. I am not used to sitting at home for so long. I must escape to "freedom" where snow, cold, and wind are presiding today.

A week and a half ago I made the acquaintance of a lad named Monik. He comes to Solke's together with Grishke Shalitan. He read out a few poems (which he wrote himself). He has a talent for writing. The poems were brimming with spirit and with the strength of battle and calls for liberation. He is a good guy. I like him. But why do the good guys keep to themselves? Why don't they get together and create a good guys' group? By them I mean only the more known ones, like: B.S., S. Sh., M. __, G.S., A.K., and myself. Do we not already have a further connection? And for us Jews—this moment is so important! I believe that everyone knows what he is and, sadly, is satisfied with this alone. My hopes to be more active rest only with M. And perhaps here, too, I am mistaken. We will see.

When I was sick, I finished reading the following books: *Di Vogler* by Knut Hamsun. It depicts the fishing life of the Norwegians in the fjords and is a book of close to 600 pages in Lithuanian. *Kim* by R. Kipling.[347] The book portrays the life of a "white" boy in India. The boy does not have a father or a mother, and the books describes how he is drawn to the free life, to the people among whom he ultimately finds his "home." This book has 394 pages. Then there is another Lithuanian book: *Petrasir Liucij* by Romain Rolland.[348] It depicts a love story between young people

---

347 *Kim* is a novel by Nobel Prize-winning English author Rudyard Kipling (1865–1936), first published in 1900–1901.

348 *Pierre et Luce* is a 1920 novel by the Nobel Prize-winning French author Romain Rolland (1866–1944). It focuses on the impact of the First World War on two lovers.

aged eighteen. The love of a rich boy for a poor girl—and there is no obstacle between them, apart from the world war. The war comes between them and their love and it also causes both their rapid departures from life, that is—they both fall victim to the war. This book has 112 pages.

Finally, a Hebrew book without a title by the writer A. Kabak.[349] A beautiful book with good content about the lives of geniuses. It has 246 pages. That means, I finished reading four books in five days, with a total of 1,352 pages.

For some time now a big shot has been wandering around the ghetto, an SA man. He is a bit disturbed, but still manages to make trouble for the Jews—he can do this because he need not apply any intelligence.

If I recall correctly, I already mentioned earlier that the little Jewish ghetto children used to receive 50 grams of milk from the few cows in the ghetto. When Müller (so the big shot is called) arrived in the ghetto as a *makher* he straightaway stopped giving milk to the little ones. He is also a big guy in the workshops. He demands that they greet him politely and stares at the Jewish women. Long ago he issued a command explaining how one must greet him and the ghetto commandants: when one sees a uniformed person, from ten steps away, one must remove one's hat, bow deeply, and in this way walk past the big shot. When one finds oneself five steps away from him—then the Jew may put his hat on. The frost can burn—it's all the same.

A week ago, there was a further order from Müller as follows: As he often travels to the workshops and the way which leads there is through Varnių Street, he ordered that from today onwards (from the day on which the order was issued) no Jews may walk around on Varnių Street, because when he, Müller, drives past, the Jews make him dizzy. He can't bear it… He has weak nerves with a weak head… Now, Jewish policemen stand on the abovementioned street and drive away Jewish passersby from the holy street, since Müller must travel past!...

Jews make him dizzy…have you heard such a thing? If only it would be true!

---

349 Avraham Aharon Kabak (1883–1944), was an author and a literature teacher at the Hebrew Gymnasium in Rehavia, Jerusalem.

January 18, 1943

Latest news from the ghetto.

Latest ghetto news: One of our four—Shleyme Finkelstein—is still sick. He has now been in bed for over two weeks with a very high temperature because his situation is not so simple: he is sick with pneumonia, indeed, in both lungs. He is hallucinating. The doctor's words: we must have hope! Perhaps he will hold out.... There has not yet been a crisis with him. This is something we are not acquainted with in him.

Solya is already walking around outside. Heni comes to his home almost daily. Despite the fact that Solya says he doesn't think about her too much—I believe that by the end of the week (tomorrow is Monday), we will be able to break not little glasses but big ones. I only wonder about this, since, nevertheless, I once loved Heni (an old story). It seems that one could not love more (I mean more strongly) and now? Now there remains in my heart for her an empty feeling—better put, I feel nothing for her whatsoever! Even the friendly feeling toward her has disappeared. My opinion about her is not bad and not good. I have no opinion about her— because I am completely disinterested in her now. I even try to avoid her.

Now a bit more to the point.

Since the ghetto was established, since "our" ghetto exists, an order has been in place that Jews are not allowed to have children![350] The Lord of the World commanded the Jewish people, saying to them: "Listen you, My chosen people, do what your Master tells you: If you want to live and derive enjoyment from your ignoble life in the world there is only one way to achieve this—have children and you will have pleasure."

---

350 At the beginning of February 1942, the German occupying authorities in Lithuania published an order forbidding the birth of children in the ghettos of Vilna, Shavli, and Kovno. This stemmed from the desire to exploit the Jewish workforce for the war effort, while also satisfying the SS authorities, which wanted to annihilate the Jews. At first the order was partially enforced, although over time, and mainly when the ghettos became concentration camps, it was enforced with greater precision.

So, the Jews lived in the world and endeavored to fulfill this *mitsve* [mitzva] and God's commandment to have children. Having children today, having children tomorrow. In short, Jews populated the world with Jewish children and their children grew up and also kept this tradition of having children.... Having children here and having children there—until there arose a modern gentleman[351] who said that so many children is not nice, and it is not fitting for such a people as the Jews to keep this tradition. And he issued a new rule, a rule which scorned and mocked God's will and commanded: "Enough," he said to European Jewry, "enough of having children and conceiving children! You shall not conceive any more children." And he threatened…and Jews were afraid and began to have children—in complete silence—so that he should not hear—and they continued having children. God's will is, however, apparently stronger than "his" evil will.

Thus, a rumor spread in the ghetto that one may now once again have children openly. The law "forbidding the bearing of children" has been revoked and now one can have children, even a dozen.[352] "He" doesn't care anymore. Could this be a sign of better things? Do they now consider us to be human? Or perhaps maybe the opposite? Perhaps "that one" thinks: having children, yes or no, it's all the same. Your fate is already signed and sealed. But let me not think about it too much. We need to use the opportunity for as long as we can to have as many children as possible.

A second rumor in the ghetto is that people will once again be able to use money openly in the ghetto. On August 26, 1942 (the beginning of the diary) the use of money in the ghetto was forbidden—Jews were not to use any money. Obviously, at first, people wanted to guard themselves against an "evil eye," God forbid someone (a stranger) should not notice that another has money on him. Gradually, people became bolder and were no longer afraid. The trade in foreign currency was increasingly accepted until they clearly understood that the rule can be revoked—because it wasn't being enforced. The Jew had children—he will [continue to] have children. The Jew was always a trader and will remain so. It's hard to battle against nature. And trade—this lies in the Jew's nature.

---

351 Hitler.

352 The rumor was false. A comprehensive prohibition was introduced against bearing children.

January 23, 1943

The Germans report in the newspapers that for security reasons they are retreating from a few points on the Russian Front. "So, for example, we had to retreat from one point a total of 25 kilometers, yet as a result of this our losses were very small." The Russians continue to attack in the Caucasus and Don arc at Voronezh, at Lake Ilme[n], at the Neva... the Germans, surrounded at Stalingrad, continue to fight.

In Africa, the Germans and the Italians are putting up resistance. Tripoli has been occupied by the English.[353]

Ghetto rumors:

A rumor spread through the ghetto this week that Russia is in turmoil. Instead of the Russian "Red Army" it has been changed to the "People's Army." The "People's Army" has also ostensibly changed its uniform. The uniform will be similar to the uniform from the time of the Tsar. And the main thing—there shall be no more political instructors in the army and the military leadership shall fight independently. I don't want to believe it! It's hard to imagine such a serious matter.[354]

Heni meets with Solya every day. Solya is increasingly "captivated" and "bewitched" by her... But he holds back...he has not yet gone under.... He fights, wins victories, and yet is continuously weakened by it...

I thought that by the end of the week (today is *Shabes*) we would already know the finale of this saga. Yet, because both sides are very strong, it is drawing out a bit. I believe that both (Heni and Solya) are already a couple. In the wider social circles people are already talking about it as if it's completely official.

Solya is a good friend to me and a loyal one. I have nothing against him. We sometimes go to Ida's home together, where the entire *khevre* is spending time together: Ida, Dora, Heni, Avremke, and Izia. Nu, people

---

353 On January 23, 1943, the British army entered Tripoli after occupying the city.

354 This rumor was partially inaccurate. The Red Army changed its name to the Soviet Army in 1946. However, the new uniform with the shoulder straps was introduced in January 1943.

such as Danke Liberman and Bebke Vidutsinsky also come to Zlata's, so it's very merry.

Avremke, who said that he had doubts about remaining in the *khevre* nevertheless "stayed" and even gave Ida a ring with her monogram in the middle of a little golden heart. The day before yesterday Izke also gave Dora a ghetto ring. Izia's name appears on it, too. There is also a little heart. Evidently everything is ok with them and the days pass in happiness and peace.

I couldn't be happier for them: they should live happily and joyfully, because I have wanted this for them for a long time, since the time when I was their close friend, so too, now, still as their friend. "Live happily, children!" This is my wish for them.

Shleyme Finkelstein is still very sick. He has pneumonia in both lungs, has a fever of 40 degrees, speaks gibberish, and keeps on screaming: I want to live! I don't want to die!

I haven't seen Bebke (Bebke Khaytovitsh) for a long time. He has distanced himself from us. He could not bear the girls and also Heni, the newcomer. This is what has become of the *khevre*: In the beginning it was comprised of: Dora, Ida, Avremke, Lyusya Maniewitz, Izia, and me as the newcomer. Later, the situation changed and there were two groups: Group one: Heni Shpitz, Riva'le, Larik Lubetzki, Izke, and Avremke. Group two: Dora, Ida, Lyusya Maniewitz (who later left the group), Solya, Bebke, Shleyme Finkelstein, and me. On January 1, 1943, the alliances changed again. Dora and Ida went back to the first group. The second was comprised of only four people. Then later, when Shleyme Finkelstein became sick, when Solya was also lying in bed with jaundice and I, too, was sick, they wanted to draw Solya into the first group. He opposed it because, as my friend, he did not want to leave me alone and this is why Heni had become a frequent visitor to him, because he visited the first group less.

So, this is what happened:

Shleyme got sick.

Bebke went off on his own way.

Solya and Heni created something of their own group and I, as Solya's friend, somehow became a member of a six-wheeler.[355]

---

355 A wagon with three axles and six wheels.

January 1943

Dora is happy with Izke, Ida with Avremke, and the four of them make up one circle.

Riva and Larik more or less make up their own circle.

Lyusya Maniewitz is lost (abandoned by the girls, nevertheless, all three of them wear loyalty rings of friendship) and is alone, without male or female friends. I really must go over to visit her: it's been a long time since I saw Lyusya.

*   *   *

My last worry while writing these lines is: where I can get a new notebook, a new diary. Ha! Tell me, maybe you know where I can get one? I will be very grateful for this…

Enough!

BASTA!

Ilya Gerber

ערשע פון דריטע העפט.

(בלאט 359).

אנגעהויבן —
שרייבן דעם - 1942-VII-26
געענדיקט - 1943-I-23

End of volume three.
(contains 359 pages).
– Started writing on August 26, 1942.
– Finished on January 23, 1943.

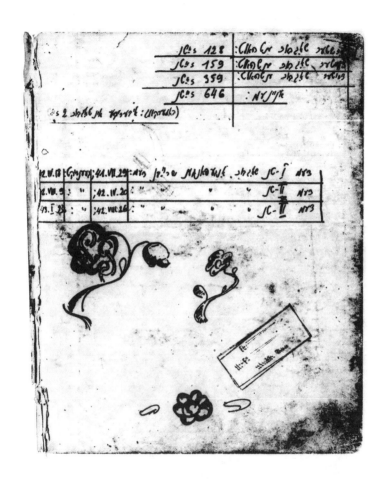

This page appears at the end of the original Yiddish diary and provides a summary of data relating to the three notebooks that Ilya Gerber kept. Only the third notebook is published here. The first notebook, dated from July 29, 1941–April 18, 1942, with 128 pages; the second notebook, from April 20, 1942–August 9, 1942, with 159 pages; and the third notebook, from August 16 [should be 26], 1942–January 23, 1943, with 359 pages. Gerber had documented a total of 646 pages.

This is the original illustration as it appears on the inner side of the diary's front cover.

This is the original illustration as it appears on the back cover of the diary's third notebook.

Index

Africa 201, 202, 210, 220, 236, 265
Akselrod, Abraham 42
Aleksotas 15, 36–37, 38, 62n44
Algeria 201n285
Algiers 201, 236
Alkanovitsh, Rissa 102
Altman 217
Amsterdam 114, 115
Antonescu, Ion 105n125
Arad, Yitzhak 12n20
Arkhangelsk 155
Arnshtam, Tanchum 205, 233
Arques River 71n62
Astrakhan 112, 155n198
Asya 76, 77
Auer, Dr. 110
Auerback, Berthold 92n97
Auschwitz concentration camp 17, 18, 204n290
Austria 74n66

Baku 112n138
Baltic Sea 154n197, 155
Balzac, Honore de 183n253
Bankier, David 21, 151n191
Bayder, Zefania 109
Bek, Boris (Berke) 121
Bełżec concentration camp 104n124
Bender, Sarah 7n1
Berezina River 116
Bergen-Belsen concentration camp 204n291
Berkman, Zvi 130–131, 182
Berlin 70, 114, 117n150, 123n158, 156n203, 183n255, 211, 234
Bernstein, Shike 80
Bessarabia 105
Białystok 103n122, 116

Bismarck, Georg von 114
Black Sea 112, 155n202
Blecher 203n288
Blum, Leon 231
Boulogne 105
Brandz, Dr. 96
Breslau 123n158
Briansk 116
Britfeld, Mrs 198
Bubtshik, Izke 118, 119, 162, 171–172
Buchenwald concentration camp 231n321

Canada 50n6
Caspi-Serebrovitz, Josef 31–33, 34, 53n19, 108–109
Caspian Sea 112n138
Caucasus 69, 112, 155, 158, 220, 236, 237, 260, 265
Channel 71n62
Chełmno 106n127
Churchill, Winston 234
Cosăuți 105n125
Cramer, Hans 31, 50–51, 140n182, 161, 228
Czechoslovakia 115n145, 123n158
Czerniaków, Adam 26

Dach *see* Trampedach, Friedrich Karl
Dachau city 50n5
Dachau concentration camp 7, 18, 63n47, 64n48, 65n49, n50, n51, 75n73, 79n84, 84n87, 85n88, 97n111, 121n156, 128n165, 130n170, 159n213, 166n220, n221, 190n266, 227n318, 231n321
Darlan, Jean Louis Xavier 236n329
Dembovitsh, Fanya 204–205

Dembovitsh, Mr. 207
Desna 116
Dessler, Salak 189n261
Dickens, Charles 183n250
Dieckmann, Christoph 12n20, 33n76
Diego Suarez 114n143, 115
Dieppe 71
Diskant, Abba 42
Dniester River 105n125, 116
Don River 154, 220, 260, 265
Don–Volga region 236, 327
Drancy concentration camp 123n158
Druskininkai 204
Dvinsk 65

Eastern Europe 123n158
Eastern Prussia 70n58, 101n117
Efremov district 116, 117
Egypt 114, 115n144, 210n306
Einstadt, Dr. 86
El-Alamein 114n142, 201n286
Elkes, Elchanan 12, 14, 18, 29–30, 34n80, 35, 65, 124n159, 210
Elnia 116
Epshtein, Lazar 20n35, 23n44
Epshtein, Yoske 111
Estonia 17, 190n264, 204n291, 220
Europe 21, 28, 150n190, 191, 211, 215, 225n316, 238n330

Feldman 206
Finkelstein, Shleyme 84–85, 98, 139, 219, 225, 228, 229, 240, 241–242, 244, 246, 249, 252, 253, 256, 257, 258, 259, 263, 266
First Fort 178n241
Flam, Gila 40–41
Flaubert, Gustave 183n254
Förenwald camp 63n47
France 72, 105, 123n158, 154, 210, 231, 235n327, 236
Frankfurt am Main 123n158

Freinkel, Lazar 65, 125, 126–128, 130, 136, 139, 145–146, 147–148

Galperin, Dmitriy 46
Gar, Yosef 12
Garfunkel, Leib 12, 14, 20, 29, 32, 33, 41–42, 53n17, 65, 206n296, 208–209, 228n319
Gat, Hani 45n106
Gens, Jacob 189n261, 190
Gens, Solomon 190
Genz, Hirsh 96
Georgia 112n138
Gerber, Boris 9–10, 37, 39, 42, 43, 62–63, 81, 82, 86, 89, 95, 96, 166, 193–194, 195, 196, 200, 206, 233, 237–238
Gerber, Chaya 9, 37, 63n47, 81, 82, 86, 89–90, 97, 156, 205, 233
Gerber, Ilya 7–9, 10, 20–22, 24–25, 30, 32, 33, 34–35, 37–38, 39–40, 41, 42–45, 46, 48n1, 49n1, n2, 63n47
Gerber, Rachel 9, 59n34, 89, 92, 166, 206, 253, 261
Gerber family 7
Germany 12, 14, 50n4, 50n6, 70n58, 87n91, 110n136, 123n157, 142, 143, 151, 196, 197, 206, 234
Getz, Edith 87n93
Girshke 225
Girzon, Yitzhak (Itshe) 168, 183, 250
Givatayim 45n106
Glagoleva, Fainna 171n230
Göcke, Wilhelm 17
Goebbels, Joseph 236
Goldberg, Amos 23, 27, 49n2, 106n127
Goldberg, Yaakov 14, 208–209
Goldin, Lyovke 255
Golub *see* Tory
Göring, Hermann 152–153
Grafman, Avraham Yizhok 192

Index

Grinberg, Yehoshua (Ike) 173, 229–230, 231
Grodno 53n19

Hamann, Joachim 50n6
Hamburg 53n20
Hameiri, Avigdor 183n252
Hamsun, Knut 244, 261
Hemfler 61, 158
Hirsh 84
Hitler, Adolf 20–22, 70n59, 112n138, 135, 140, 141, 150–152, 201, 202, 210, 234, 235
Hoch, Moshe 41
Hofmekler, Michael Leon 195, 227
Hörmann, Gustav 30, 124, 129–130, 159, 161, 170, 172, 184

India 115, 261
Irkutsk Oblast 212n308
Iserles, Nisan 231–232, 233
Israel 7, 64n48, 65n49, 84n87, 94n102, 234n325
see also Palestine

Jäger, Karl 31
Jamacco Island 210
Jerusalem 262n349
Jonava *see* Yaneve
Jordan, Fritz 14, 158
Jordan River 234

Kabak, Avraham Aharon 262
Kaczerginski, Shmerke 40, 45, 46
Kadushin, Zvi 41
Kagan, Izke 74, 75, 76, 77, 78, 81, 88, 89, 92, 94, 100, 106–107, 111, 118, 119, 120, 121, 133, 134, 135, 140, 161, 162, 163, 171, 172, 186, 195, 225, 240, 241, 244, 245, 246, 247–248, 250, 252, 253, 254, 256, 257, 260, 265, 266, 267

Kagan, Mr. 172
Kagan family 74n68, 171
Kaifler, Ernst 30, 53n17, 58n32, 66n54
Kaišiadorys labor camp 17
Kalner, Shleyme (Shlomo) 7, 9, 63, 81–82, 192, 206
Kalter 121
Kaluga region 113, 114, 154
Kalvarija 65n50
Kanzer, Mrs. 136n177
Kapelushnik, Yatl 172–173
Kapelushnik-Ayalon, Naftali 172n234
Kaplan, Leib 136
Kaplan (Verblovsky), Riva (Riva'le) 85, 250, 266, 267
Kaplan, Yisrael 12, 37n83
Karamzin, Nikolai 171
Karelia 113n140, 154n197
Karnavsky family 160
Kashira 116
Kassow, Samuel D. 12n20
Kaufering camp 11
Kaunas *see* Kovno
Kėdainiai labor camp 17, 160, 197
Keidan, Rivke 90
Khaytovitsh, Bebke 8n5, 97, 139, 219, 225, 227, 228–229, 239–240, 241–242, 244, 246, 248, 249, 250, 252, 253, 255, 256, 257–259, 266
Khaytovitsh, Mrs. 227–228
Kiełbasin 204n290
Kim 261
Kipling, Rudyard 261
Kiwioli camp 204n291
Klaipėda (Memel) 70, 77n79, 87n93, 101
Klatzkin, Yaakov 183n251
Klein, Dennis B. 12n20
Klugman, Moshe 125, 126–128
Königsberg 70, 219n313
Kopelman, Michael 212

Köppen, Heinz 30, 53n17, 58n32, 66n54, 129n167, 144–147, 148–149, 159, 169
Kozlovski, Paul 205
Kostya Riabtsev 156n203
Kot, Dov (Beke) 37, 110–111, 189
Kovner, Abba 45
Kovno city 9, 13, 14, 31, 50n5, 52n12, n13, 53n19, 54n22, 60n39, 65n49, 110, 158, 160n215, 189, 210n303, 212, 228, 233
Kovno district (Kauenland) 14, 50n7, 95n104
Kovno Ghetto 7, 8, 9–18, 19, 22–25, 27, 29–44, 46
Kowel 26
Krasnodar Krai 155n202
Kruk, Herman 19–20n32
Kuban 69
Kubiliūnas, Petras 50–51

Lake Ilmen 155, 265
Lake Ladoga 113
Lake Onega 154
Landesberg Camp 62n45
Latvia 17, 244
Laval, Pierre 234, 235, 236
Layzon, Sholemke 189
Lazarson-Rostovski, Tamar 11, 27, 54n23, 123n157, 158n210, 215n312, 234n325
Lenin, Vladimir 10
Leningrad 69, 113, 113n140, n141, 155, 244
Leningrad Oblast 113n140, 154n197
Lentzen, Arnold 50–51
Lerman, Mrs. 206
Levin, Abrashke 74, 77, 78, 79
Levin, Dov 7n4, 9, 231n322
Levin, Lazar (Alyoshke/Alois) 79–80
Levin, Moshe 17–18, 231n322
Levin, Rachel 84n87

Levin, Rochele 219, 228, 239–240
Lewandowski, Louis 195
Lewerenz 55, 72–73, 158
Liberman, Danke 76, 78, 79, 100, 119, 120, 133, 134, 135, 163, 266
Libya 115n144, 210n306
Lida Ghetto 190
Lipcer, Benjamin (Benno) 32, 33–36, 53, 68, 94, 96n110, n111, 109n134, 117, 167n222, 177, 184, 185, 205n293, 206, 209, 215
Lipcer, Maria (Malka) 96–97n111
Lipcer, Shimon (Senke/Senia) 96
Lithuania 10, 11, 13, 14n25, 16n29, 19, 31, 33, 45, 46, 50n4, n8, 65n49, 77n79, 102, 123n158, 124n159, 187, 190, 212n308, 225, 241n337, 263n350
Łódź 27, 31
Łódź Ghetto 31n66, 106n127
London 20, 156n203, 230–231
Lubetski, Larik (Leib) 80–81, 85, 95, 249, 250, 253, 266, 267
Lublin 27, 104
Lublin Ghetto 104n124, 106n127
Lurie, Wolf 59, 84, 159, 173, 185, 200

Madagascar 114–115
Majdan Tatarski Ghetto 104n124
Majdanek concentration camp 104n124
Majunga 115
Maniewitz, Esther 74n66
Maniewitz, Lyusya/Shulamit 74, 76–77, 78, 81, 91, 93, 94, 95, 97, 98, 100, 118, 119, 120, 133, 135n173, 161, 162, 163, 175, 177, 183, 186–187, 228, 242, 245–248, 251–252, 256, 266, 267
Maniewitz family 119
Margolis, Pavel 59, 173, 200
Mariampol district 160n215, 187

Index

Marwianka 97n113
Mažylis, Antanina 210n303
Mažylis, Jonas and Liuda 210n303
Mažylis, Prana 210
Meck, Nachum 16, 204–205, 206, 207–209, 211–214, 215, 216
Meck family 212
Medin 114
Melamed, Mrs. 94
Melamed, Yoske (Yosef) 94, 96–97
Memel *see* Klaipėda
Mikova 115n145
Minkovski, Levin Barukh 241n336
Minsk 116, 187
Mkovo 115
Monik 261
Montgomery, Bernard 201n286
Morocco 201n285
Moscow 20, 50n4, 69, 114, 116, 117, 154n196, 155n198, 156n203
Mozdok 112n138
Müller, Fritz 30, 129n167, 169n229, 262
Munich 123n158, 201n284
Mussolini, Benito 202

Natkin, Karl 117, 177, 178, 208
Neman River 87n92, 101n117, 140n181
Neva River 113, 155, 265
New York 28
Ninth Fort 15, 17, 27, 63n46, 86n89, 102, 103, 123, 160, 167, 168, 170, 173, 175n238, 178, 180, 192, 203, 205n294, 207, 212, 223
North Africa 210n307, 236n329
Norway 72
Novgorod Oblast 155n200
Novorossiisk 112
Nowogródek 26, 27, 106n127, 190n265
Nuremberg 191n267

Ofer, Dalia 12n20, 209n302

Ognev, Nikolai 10, 156, 165, 171n230
Oleiski, Dr. 210
Oleisky, Jacob 62n43, 64, 101n116
Oran 201n285
Orel 117
Ostland 144n185
Oszmiana (Oshmene) Ghetto 189, 190

Palemonas labor camp 17, 37, 96, 97, 103–104, 110, 111, 124, 129–130, 158–159, 160, 189
Palestine 27, 28, 201, 234n325, 235, 238n330
see also Israel
Panemunė 140, 141, 144
Paris 156n203
Peculis, Marius 123n158, 178n241
Peres, Master 65, 69, 80, 125, 128, 130, 139, 144, 146, 147
Perlmutter, Jehudah 195
Peschel, Martin 158
Pétain, Henri Philippe 154n194
Petrasun (Petrašiūnai) forced labor camp 52, 228, 232, 233
Pius XII 238
Plauen 50n6
Poland 50n5, 190, 192n269, 225
Ponar 190n264
Porat, Dina 19n31, 29
Port Moresby 114
Pravieniškės forced labor camp 123n158
Prienai 160
Prussia 117n150
Eastern 70n58, 101n117
Pskov 179, 187
Puke, Chaim 166
Puke, Yitzhak 166–167

Rabinovitz, Abba 75
Rabinovitz, Dora 48, 74, 76, 77, 78, 81, 91, 94, 95, 97, 98, 100, 119, 120, 121,

131, 133, 134, 135, 161, 162, 163,
172, 173–174, 183, 211, 219, 225,
240, 241–243, 245–248, 250, 252,
253, 256, 257, 258, 265, 266, 267
Rabinovitz, Ephraim 14
Rabinovitz, Ilik 48n1, 74, 75, 76, 77,
  78, 81, 94, 118, 119, 133, 135, 161,
  162, 172, 177, 251–252
Rabinovitz, Mrs. 133, 173
Rabinovitz, Yitzhak 124n159
Ragusa province 115
Rappaport 59
Rauca, Helmut 15, 31, 50–51, 175n238
Rehavia 262n349
Riazan 116
Riga 17, 27, 37, 86, 156n203, 161,
  168–169, 170, 172, 173, 176, 177, 179,
  184, 185, 186, 187, 191, 192
Riga Ghetto 235
Ringelblum, Emanuel 26
Riva 76
Rodniki 110n136
Rokhele 205
Rokiškis (Rokishuk) 108
Rolland, Romain 261
Rome 114, 115
Rommel, Erwin 115n144, 201n286,
  210n306
Roosevelt, Franklin D. 202, 234, 235
Rosenberg, Alfred 191, 215
Rosenzweig, Zerubavel 84, 139
Rostov 237, 260
Rozenblum, Lerke 40n90
Rumkowski, Chaim Mordechai 31n66
Russia 112n138, 113n140, 154n197,
  155n200, n202, 179n245, 265
  see also Soviet Union
Rzhev region 69, 112, 113, 114, 155

Saaremaa Island 70n58
Šakiai (Shaki) 103
Šančiai 14n24, 203

Santotski, Eta 75n73, 78, 98, 100
Santotski, Genya 76
Santotski, Ida 74, 75, 76, 77, 78, 79, 81,
  91, 94, 95–96, 97, 98, 100, 118, 119,
  120, 133, 134, 161, 162, 163–164,
  177, 183, 187, 219, 225, 239–240,
  241–243, 245–248, 249, 250, 252,
  253, 256, 257, 265, 266, 267
Santotski, Yankel 75n73, 96n110, 100,
  177
Santotski family 96, 117
Santotski, Zlata 74n65, 75–76, 100,
  119, 120, 122, 133, 134, 163, 266
Santotski-Shneerson, Nechama
  35–36n81, 76
Sapizshishok *see* Zapyškis
Schaf, J. 93n97
Schmitz, Heinrich 31, 213
Scoglitti 115
Segalovitsh, Mr. 64, 65
Segalson, Arie 31n69, 33, 74n68,
  109n134
Segalson, Moshe 31n69, 33, 157n204
Shafer, Avrom 126, 128, 192
Shaki *see* Šakiai
Shalitan, Grishke 261
Shapiro, Avraham Duber 63n46
Shapiro, Chaim Nachman 63–64
Shavli (Šiauliai) Ghetto 57, 179,
  184n256, 187, 190, 263n350
Sheynale 198–199, 204
Shifris, Vicky 75n74
Shmikat 158
Shmukler, Yaakov Moshe 14
Shneur, Z. 179
Shpitz, Heni 45, 77–78, 79, 80–81, 83,
  85, 87–88, 89, 90–92, 93, 95, 97,
  98, 99–100, 101, 121, 179–180, 187,
  195, 250, 251, 252, 253, 254, 263,
  265, 266
Shukstaliski, Solke (Solya or Solomon)
  139, 219, 225, 227, 228–229, 233,

239–241, 244–245, 246–247, 248, 249–250, 251, 252, 253, 254–255, 256, 257, 258, 259, 260, 261, 263, 265, 266
Shultz 160
Shvartsman, Dov (Bebke) 159, 160
Sicily 115n146
Slobodka *see* Viljampolė
Smetona, Antanas 50n4
Smolensk 116, 187
Snieg, Shmuel-Abba 14
South Africa 208n298
Soviet Union 10, 14, 71, 110n136, 112n138, n139, 155n198, n201, 156n203, 231n320
see also Russia
Stakhanov, Alexei 115
Stalin, Joseph 10, 141, 244
Stalingrad 112, 113, 136, 154, 170, 201, 220, 236, 265
Stockholm 20, 115
Streicher, Julius 239n332
Streletsky, Yaakov 128, 130
Stutthof concentration camp 18, 59n34, 64n48, 75n73, 76n75, 77n79, 79n84, 87n93, 96n111, 190n266, 239n334, 250n341
Stütz, Ernst 59n33
Sukenik, Pnina 183
Sutzkever, Avraham 45
Suwałki (Suvalk) 103
Svisloch River 116
Syria 234

Tabu, Madam *see* Thèbes, Madame de
Tallinn 70n58, 123n158
Tarnish, Chaim 65
Tartak, Mishke 239–240
Tauragė district 140n181
Terek River 112, 155, 220
Thèbes (Tabu), Madame de 206–207

Tiktin, Avremke (Avraham) 74, 76, 77, 78, 79, 81, 91, 94, 96, 100, 119, 120, 133, 134, 135, 161, 162, 163, 172, 173, 177, 195, 225, 240, 241, 242, 244, 245–246, 247–249, 250, 251, 252, 253, 254, 255, 256, 257, 260, 265, 266, 267
Tiktin, Chaim 172
Tiktin, Mr. 94, 96, 172, 173, 175
Tiktin, Mrs. 172, 175
Tiktin family 96n110, 173
Tilsit 101
Tobruk 115n144, 210
Tory, Avraham 11, 27, 34, 41, 42, 52n12, n16, 72n63, 86n90, 96n109, 117n149, 129n168, 136n177, 140n182, 167n222, 203n288, 208–209, 212n309, 215n312, 227n317
Toulon 210–211
Trakai district 159n212
Trampedach, Friedrich Karl 144, 145, 146, 148
Transnistria 105n125
Treblinka concentration camp 25, 26, 106n127
Tripoli 265n353
Troki 129
Tsherikover, Eliyahu 183n255
Tuapse region 155
Tula district 116, 117
Tzipkin, A. 52n13

Uglejewo 189n261
Ukraine 105n125
Unger, Michal 31n66
United Kingdom 231n320
United States 92n97, 110n136, 117n150, 231n320
USSR *see* Soviet Union

Vaivara camp 74n66, 204n291
Van der Lubbe, Marinus 214

Vayner family 173
Velikaya River 179n243
Versheves (Lampėdžiai) 52
Viazma 116
Vichy 114, 154
Vidutshinski, Bebke (Benjamin) 106–107, 163
Vienna 110n135, 123n158
Vievis labor camp 159
Vilija River 13, 34, 52n15, 67–68, 125, 138
Vilijampolė (Slobodka) 13, 17, 32, 34, 52, 79n83, 109, 131
Vilkaviškis (Vilkovishk) 160
Vilkomir (Ukmergé) 91
Vilna city 32, 34n80, 45–46, 91n96, 108, 110n136, 129, 159, 192n269
Vilna district 129n169, 189n261, 190n264
Vilna Ghetto 18–19, 23n44, 25, 40n91, 45, 57, 105, 106, 109, 111, 170, 190, 196, 215, 263n350
Vilnius *see* Vilna
Vitshun (Vičiūnai) 54, 55
Volga River 112, 201, 220
Vologda Oblast 154n197
Volpert, Jozef 100–101
Voronezh city 116, 154, 265
Voronezh River 154n195

Wallace, Lewis 179n244
Warsaw city 79n82, 125, 192n269
Warsaw Ghetto 23, 25–26, 27, 31, 49n2, 105–106
Washington D.C. 46, 230–231
White Sea 220
Wisocki, Lucian Demianus 50–51
Włocławek (Leslau) 50n5
Wolfsratshausen 7, 63n47

Yaneve (Jonava) 17, 95, 103, 160
Yashunsky-Feitelson, Sima 221–223, 224
Yatkunski, Misha 77, 95, 179
Yeivin, Yehoshua Heschel 183n249
Yelin, Meir 46
Yugoslavia 70

Zacks, Yaakov 227
Zakharin, Benjamin 59
Zapruder, Alexandra 7n4
Zapyškis (Sapizshishok) 87, 102
Zelder, Mrs. 78
Żeromski, Stefan 93
Zerubavel 207, 250
Zevakas, Mišelis 183
Zimbabwe 115n145
Zshezshmorski 84
Zupovitz, Yehudah 194n271, 231n322